CW01239932

The Great Survivor of the Tudor Age

The Great Survivor of the Tudor Age

The Life and Times of Lord William Paget

Alex Anglesey

PEN & SWORD
HISTORY

First published in Great Britain in 2023 by
Pen & Sword History
An imprint of Pen & Sword Books Limited
Yorkshire – Philadelphia

Copyright © Alex Anglesey 2023

ISBN 978 1 39903 509 5

The right of Alex Anglesey to be identified as
Author of this Work has been asserted by him in accordance
with the Copyright, Designs and Patents Act 1988.

A CIP catalogue record for this book is
available from the British Library

All rights reserved. No part of this book may be reproduced or transmitted in any form or by any means, electronic or mechanical including photocopying, recording or by any information storage and retrieval system, without permission from the Publisher in writing.

Typeset by Mac Style
Printed in the UK by CPI Group (UK) Ltd, Croydon, CR0 4YY.

Pen & Sword Books Limited incorporates the imprints of After the Battle, Atlas, Archaeology, Aviation, Discovery, Family History, Fiction, History, Maritime, Military, Military Classics, Politics, Select, Transport, True Crime, Air World, Frontline Publishing, Leo Cooper, Remember When, Seaforth Publishing, The Praetorian Press, Wharncliffe Local History, Wharncliffe Transport, Wharncliffe True Crime and White Owl.

For a complete list of Pen & Sword titles please contact

PEN & SWORD BOOKS LIMITED
47 Church Street, Barnsley, South Yorkshire, S70 2AS, England
E-mail: enquiries@pen-and-sword.co.uk
Website: www.pen-and-sword.co.uk
or
PEN AND SWORD BOOKS
1950 Lawrence Rd, Havertown, PA 19083, USA
E-mail: uspen-and-sword@casematepublishers.com
Website: www.penandswordbooks.com

To my father

Contents

Foreword ix
Introduction xv
Dramatis Personae xx

Part I: Henry VIII — 1

Chapter 1	Coming from Nowhere	3
Chapter 2	Climbing the Greasy Pole: Paget's Rise to Power	11
Chapter 3	Growing Position and Power After Cromwell's Fall	20
Chapter 4	Ambassador to France	25
Chapter 5	The Most Important and Powerful of Henry's Ministers	32
Chapter 6	Paget's Network	40
Chapter 7	Paget and Henry VIII's Foreign Policy, 1543–44	46
Chapter 8	Diplomacy and War	55
Chapter 9	Peace, Eventually	61
Chapter 10	Power Struggle: The Failed Conservative Coup	69
Chapter 11	Power Struggle: Triumph of the Reformers	75
Chapter 12	Henry VIII's Last Will and Testament: A Forgery?	80
Chapter 13	Conspiracy	87
Chapter 14	Life in William's Household	93

Part II: Edward, Mary and Elizabeth — 103

| Chapter 15 | Somerset's Right-Hand Man | 105 |
| Chapter 16 | Balancing Act – Home and Abroad | 113 |

Chapter 17	Somerset's Cassandra	119
Chapter 18	Somerset's Fall	126
Chapter 19	Peerage and Prison	132
Chapter 20	Survival	140
Chapter 21	'Long Live the Queen' (Jane or Mary?)	148
Chapter 22	Marrying Mary to Philip	154
Chapter 23	Rebellion and Repression	162
Chapter 24	Serving King and Queen	169
Chapter 25	Elder Statesman Under Elizabeth	176
Chapter 26	Retirement and Death	182
Chapter 27	Conclusion	187

Appendix: A Family Epilogue   197
Notes   209
Sources and Bibliography   222
Acknowledgements   225
Index   226

Foreword

As a small boy running around the huge house, Plas Newydd, where I grew up in the days before it was given to the National Trust, I picked up snippets of my family's history. In the damp and scary basement, there were magnificent uniforms from the Napoleonic Wars and piles of rusty swords and guns. There was also the wooden leg of my ancestor, the 1st Marquess of Anglesey, who was second in command to the Duke of Wellington at Waterloo and had his leg smashed during the battle. You moved the top part of the leg and the toe wiggled. I was told it was the first artificial leg ever that was 'articulated'; before then, it had been all Long John Silver peg legs.

Sharing one of the vast baths on the upstairs 'nursery' floor with a sibling, we would giggle at the pictures on the wall – hand-tinted photographs of the eccentric 5th Marquess, known to us as 'mad Ux', cross-dressed as Boudica, yet still sporting the drooping moustaches of an Edwardian aristocrat. In the vast blue-carpeted downstairs sitting room, called the Saloon, we'd be allowed at tea-time to play games and listen to stories read aloud or to music played on 78rpm records. (This was pre-telly. Upstairs, in the nursery we got one in the late 1950s. Dad used to come to the nursery to watch programmes like *The Lone Ranger*, but we only finally had a TV downstairs in the adult area for the World Cup in 1966.) I had pointed out to me the picture above the fireplace of Lord Alfred Paget riding with Queen Victoria in Windsor Great Park. While he smoked one of his Havana cigars, my father told the story of how Lord George Paget had apparently lit up a similar one at the start of the Charge of the Light Brigade and was still puffing away when he returned alive from the 'Valley of Death'. It proved how quickly that battle was over – and how brave and lucky the Pagets were.

We would have Christmas lunch in the Rex Whistler dining room, with magnificent centre-pieces of silver cups, horsemen and candelabra, and – of more interest to us children – silver sixpences hidden in the Christmas pudding. We saw traces of the recent generations of the family dotted around the huge and extraordinary Rex Whistler mural – my grandfather, the 6th Marquess, as an equestrian statue; my father as a small boy pictured twice, stealing apples and peeing against a wall. The presence of my glamorous and badly behaved aunt Caroline was also much in evidence, as Rex's muse and model for his paintings and in real life. She lived just over the waters of the Menai Strait at Vaynol – when she was not in Chelsea or Tangiers. She entertained in an aura of exotic perfume (Mitsouko by Guerlain), cigarette holders, Princess Margaret – in stories or sometimes actually, cocktails and decadence. The Vaynol boat house was just across the water, opposite the lawn that ran down from the house to the family flagpole and the cannons – fired only to celebrate the birth of children, in the spirit of those sexist times, more times for a boy than a girl. Caroline and my father would have shouted conversations between the island of Anglesey and the mainland.

Other glimpses of family history came on 'mystery tours' being driven around Anglesey by my father. When we passed the statue of 'One Leg', the 1st Marquess, standing on top of his column next to the Britannia Bridge, we always waved to our 'great-great-great-grandfather'. There was usually some confusion and discussion about the number of 'greats'. We visited the strange orange moon-like landscape of the Parys Mountain mines which, part-owned by the family, had in the 1780s been the largest copper mine in Europe. More recent family history was illustrated by my father slamming on the brakes as we were bowling down tiny Anglesey lanes, shouting 'Germans ahead' and reversing at breakneck speed between the hedgerows. In the Second World War, he had driven armoured cars to reconnoitre ahead of the Allied lines as they advanced up Italy and so reversing at speed, once the enemy was spotted, was one of the skills he had learnt.

How had the family history begun? In the 'Gothick Hall' at Plas Newydd, beneath horrific pictures of dead birds and hounds tearing apart a bear, were three imposing and almost identical portraits of Lord William Paget; he looked very severe and had a weird forked beard. I was told he had been an important Tudor statesman and was the founder of the family's fame and fortune.

I had been slightly curious as a boy about what was evidently an interesting family history, but I pretty much ignored it whilst my adult life took other directions. I left home physically and mentally: I did a PhD at the University of Sussex; thought I was a Maoist; worked for a publisher of illustrated books on subjects such as gardening and childbirth; with a partner founded and ran a successful small business; went to art school aged 40; and later pursued my passion for painting in a semi-professional way.

* * *

It was only after my father died, when I got involved with the National Trust's 'telling the family story' and I started to look through the amazing collections of archives, in the basement at Plas Newydd and elsewhere, that my interest was rekindled. My father had written a much-praised biography of the 1st Marquess, entitled *One Leg*, and the fascinating life of the 5th 'dancing' Marquess was becoming fashionable. Lord William Paget, however, seemed to me a mysterious figure. He does not even feature in a Hilary Mantel novel! Actually, the reason, apart from the fact that she probably had enough characters already, was that although he was a protege of Thomas Cromwell, Paget did not become influential in Tudor politics until after Cromwell's execution in 1540, which is where the Mantel trilogy of novels ends.

So I thought I would find out more about Paget. I discovered a biography had been written by an American, Samuel Rhea Gammon, in the 1970s, largely based on his PhD thesis from the 1950s. (The only other thing I was able to find out about Mr Gammon was that he was US Vice-Consul in Milan in 1961. So apparently a diplomat, or even a spy, as well as a Tudor historian?) His book proved useful as a starting point for research and writing and I am very grateful for it. But it is rather a difficult read, written in a style impenetrable to any without a specialised academic interest in Tudor history. Also specialised and very useful is a more recent PhD thesis by Andrew Johnston. Another American academic, Barrett L. Beer of Kent State University, had written a bit about Paget in the 1970s; and had edited a collection of some of his letters – jointly with Sybil M. Jack of the University of Cambridge, who had also written the *Dictionary of National Biography* entry on Paget. But that seemed to be more or less 'it'.

One reason that Paget is not better known is the lack of attention given to the middle Tudor period compared with its beginning and end. Doing a straw poll of relatively well-educated friends, I discovered that their knowledge of Tudor history seemed to jump from early Henry VIII to Elizabeth I. The end of Henry's reign and the significantly different and important reigns of Edward VI and Mary I are often unknown or forgotten about. The charismatic young Henry and his brilliant Cardinal Wolsey, Cromwell's time fictionalised by Mantel, and later, the glamour of the Elizabethan Age, feature much more in the popular imagination and in the myth of English nation-building than do the complex twenty years when William Paget was most influential. This is also true of the academic history world. It has been pointed out that the classic and influential book by the granddaddy of Tudor history, Sir Geoffrey Elton's *England Under the Tudors*, has ninety pages on Henry up till 1540 and 125 pages on Elizabeth, with only twenty-one on Edward and Mary's reigns combined.[1]

Another reason is the patchy and complicated written evidence that has come down to us about William Paget. It has been said that in general the vagaries of archival survival are what shape the writing of Tudor, and probably of all, history. Elton is of the view that, 'it may be that Cromwell appears to dominate his age so much because his papers have survived.'[2] It is not just that there are more papers, it is that they are more easily accessible. Cromwell, and others who fell out of royal favour and were executed for treason, had their archives confiscated. As a consequence, they then entered the collection of the State Papers, now housed in the National Archives at Kew. Unlucky in life; lucky in history! This did not happen to Paget's papers because he survived under four monarchs. As a result, his papers have not been preserved as comprehensively, are more scattered, and those that are in the National Archives made their way there by several complicated routes. The State Papers themselves were terribly neglected, some burnt in a major fire of 1619 and others attacked by damp and vermin. They were not properly looked after until the mid-nineteenth century. Some of William Paget's papers were plundered from the State Archive by Sir Robert Cotton in the seventeenth century and are now in the British Library, while many remained in my family's possession until recently and are housed in the Staffordshire Records Office, at Keele University or other 'local' collections.

A few letters written to William Paget, with royal signatures attached, stayed in the physical possession of my family, supposedly in the Muniment Room in the basement at Plas Newydd. There is a story attached to them. On my father's death in 2013, it was necessary, for Probate, to identify, catalogue and value any archives. In the delightful chaos of my father's study – he had fourteen desks from which he had created, in a pre-computer age, his eight-volume *History of the British Cavalry* as well as launching many other eccentric enterprises – I discovered three beautifully leather-bound books. Each contained hundreds of pages of hand-typed descriptions of family-owned documents, some going back to the time of Ethelred the Unready in AD 1004, including the founding charter of Burton Abbey, of which Lord William Paget gained possession along with the estate of Beaudesert in Staffordshire, as part of the Dissolution of the Monasteries. The Frontispiece of the first book read as follows:

Descriptive Catalogue of the Charters and Muniments of the Paget Family belonging to the Most Hon The Marquess of Anglesey
sometime preserved at Beaudesert, Co. Stafford but now at Plas Newydd Anglesey
Compiled by I H Jeayes, sometime Assistant Keeper of the MSS in the Br Museum
1934

Notes by my father from 1947 indicate that most of the documents described in these books had been lodged in the local collections of archives that were relevant to them. For example, documents to do with Anglesey and the copper mines were in Bangor University, those to do with Lord William Paget's mansion at West Drayton were in the Middlesex Record Office, those connected with another ancestor who had been ambassador to the Ottoman Empire in the seventeenth century were in the School of African and Oriental Studies in London, and so on. Paget papers could be found in at least eight different public collections in the British Isles. But there was also a list of thirty-one 'royal letters' that had been sent to William Paget and signed by the royals, from Queen Katherine Parr, King Edward VI, Queen Mary I, King Philip II of Spain and Queen Elizabeth I – the whereabouts of which was unknown. I assumed they were still at Plas Newydd.

There, the 'modern' house, built in the early nineteenth century, with its great sloping lawn that runs down to the Menai Strait, sits on top of an old Tudor house, which is now the basement. This was where documents were stored and where the 'royal letters' should have been. It was damp and chaotic down there with all kinds of stuff jumbled up with interesting historical artefacts and thousands of papers from all periods, some boxed and catalogued, many not. Cheek by jowl with every letter, invoice and bank statement kept from my parents' long lives were fascinating items such as the 1st Marquess's Waterloo letters and Lord George Paget's diaries of the Crimean War. Mixed in with piles of junk that would have remained unsold at any car boot sale were beautiful Georgian candlesticks, the odd Faberge cigarette case, a medieval torture contraption, and Napoleon's Spy Glass. On that was an inscription claiming it was a gift to an ancestor who had been an admiral in the Royal Navy, given to him when he visited Elba, from where Napoleon had escaped, only to be defeated finally at Waterloo. When the Antiques Road Show came to Plas Newydd, Fiona Bruce delivered the 'expert' opinion that the Spy Glass could be worth anything from £50 to £50,000! But the William Paget 'royal letters' were nowhere to be found.

I came to the conclusion that they had been stolen. Because in August 1968 there had been a major burglary at Plas Newydd. This was before it had been given to the National Trust and when the family still lived in the whole house. I was away from home at the time, aged 17 and hopefully having fun somewhere, not that I remember what or where. But my brother and sisters vividly recall how the household woke up to discover that overnight some very cool 'country house' burglars had 'done' the place, arriving and departing, undetected, by boat. Neat little piles of sugar and salt had been left in the butler's pantry from where their silver containers had been stolen. The main target had been a collection of beautiful and priceless miniature paintings, with the most valuable, by the Elizabethan artist Isaac Oliver, left behind because it was 'too hot to handle'. These were professional thieves. Original Tudor royal signatures were serious collectors' items, worth a lot of money. So, with the 'royal letters' unfound, I became convinced that they had also been stolen in 1968.

However, the documents expert from Sotheby's, who was dealing with the Probate valuation, was not so sure. He felt he could find them. The remarkable Gabriel Heaton, to whom I am very grateful, insisted on actually going to the various collections of archives all over the country which housed Paget papers, despite the fact that they were all supposed to be thoroughly catalogued. And, lo and behold, he duly found the missing 'royal letters', 'sitting on a shelf' at Bangor University, well looked after but being used to teach students how to decipher Tudor documents, and uncatalogued. We think that my father had probably 'temporarily' lent them to the university at some time between 1947 and his death in 2013, had then forgotten about them, and that no records were kept. Today, copies of them remain in Bangor and are in the Staffordshire archives, some of the originals are displayed to the public at Plas Newydd and some were sold to raise money to restore both the Marquess of Anglesey's Column and the Waterloo displays at the National Army Museum.

Anyhow, this complex state of the Paget archives is one of the reasons why Lord William Paget has been inadequately studied by historians.

As I was toying with the idea of writing something about him, my diary was suddenly emptied by Coronavirus and my brilliant first cousin, Louisa Lane Fox, offered to help me with research and editing. I decided to give it a go.

Introduction

Trying to enter the world of William Paget, I realised that my own very limited historical knowledge came from two completely different directions. There was the schoolboy history of England which was little more than *1066 and All That*, with a little bit of Shakespeare, and latterly Hilary Mantel, thrown in. Wars of the Roses; Henry VII, a hard man; Henry VIII, six wives, Dissolution of the Monasteries, Wolf Hall, etc.; Edward VI, the boy king; Mary, bloody and Catholic; Liz I, Gloriana, Sir Walter Raleigh – throwing his cloak over the puddle for the Queen, or Francis Drake – playing bowls and defeating the Armada, rather than trading slaves, of course.

Then, almost completely disconnected from the above, there was the European story, a lot of it in my case learnt from art history, particularly the Italian Renaissance. This art story did feed a bit into the political, religious and economic history. So, the ups and downs of Florence, Venice and Rome were, I discovered, part of the larger struggle between the France of Francis I and the Spanish-based Habsburg Empire of Charles V. Francis bought the *Mona Lisa* and the Habsburgs were the great patrons of Titian and Velasquez. The Renaissance popes of art history led to the story of Luther, the Reformation and the Counter Reformation. The art, religious and economic histories then combined with the theory of 'Religion and the Rise of Capitalism'. Patronage of the arts directly involved the emergence of banking, first with the Medicis and then with the Fuggers in Antwerp. The beginnings of global 'Western' history were also connected, with the opening up of the New World in America by the Spanish and Portuguese and the growth of trade with the East by the Venetians and Dutch. And the black African slave trade which followed.

But, although England was a bit of a backwater in relation to this sixteenth-century international story, it was of course, I now realise, not separate from it in the way it had been taught in English schools. Henry VIII and his 'new men', William Paget included, were very much part of it. William's schooling at St Paul's School and the University of Cambridge was in the spirit of the emerging European humanism which was based on the Classical world of

Greece and Rome – the inspiration for the Renaissance. Early in his career, he travelled widely in Continental Europe and learnt several languages. Throughout his days of power in Henry's reign, he was continually dealing with the France of Francis I, the Empire of Charles V and the German states of Luther's world. When negotiating with the French, he would be talking to people like Cardinal Bellay, humanist friend and patron of Rabelais, or to Mary, Queen of Hungary and Regent of the Netherlands, one of the great patrons of painting and music; when he dealt with the German Protestant states, it was often with interesting figures such as John Sturmius, known as the Cicero of Germany, philosopher and inventor of the German Gymnasium education system. It was the same Fuggers of Antwerp, with whom Paget arranged loans to finance Henry's wars, who lent the Habsburgs money to commission Titian to paint. For me, it was thrilling to discover that my ancestor arranged the marriage of Mary Tudor to, and was the chief advisor on English politics for, Philip II of Spain, the patron and subject of Velasquez's art, the man in the mirror of 'Las Meninas'.

* * *

I have tried to make this book understandable to those who are not up on their Tudor history, true of me before I started. Unfortunately, for those who are, much of the explanatory context will therefore inevitably be old hat stuff they have heard before. Similarly, on the question of style, I have tried to balance making a readable story with the more nuanced approach of academic history. I occasionally indulge in making comparisons between Tudor and modern times – considered a heinous crime by many proper academic historians. But I agree with the Tudor historian David Starkey that 'to transfer from Tudor Whitehall to the modern White House requires little more than a change of clothes!'[1] That said, it is a fine line between making justifiable comparisons and the mistake of anachronism, in other words assuming ideas and ways of living that only existed later than the period studied. An interesting example of that, of which I was quite unaware until it was pointed out to me, was the way in which I subconsciously privileged painting as central to culture. Various revisionist historians have stressed how that reflects modern rather than Tudor tastes, which gave much higher financial value to tapestries, clothes, furnishings and food. For instance, lace on a dress might cost over £1,000 or a banquet £3,000, whereas a van Dyck portrait cost £25.[2] I guess my greater interest in the painting is acceptable, because I am writing this history in the twenty-first century – quite apart from being a painter myself; just so long as I maintain an awareness of the difference between sixteenth-century values and our own.

More generally, some human motivation and behaviour in sixteenth-century England will have been very much the same as ours, but a lot of it not so much. Two areas in particular were very different from our experience in the contemporary 'West'. The much lower expectation of living long, peaceful, comfortable and healthy lives. And, not unconnected with that, the huge importance of religion – in thought and action. Both these factors were central to the personal and public lives of Tudor figures. For example, that all nine of William Paget's children survived into adulthood was exceptional. He and his wife must have considered themselves to be truly blessed. It has been calculated that for each pregnancy, the risk of death in childbirth was one in a hundred, that one in five or six children died before reaching their first birthday and that a quarter of all children failed to reach the age of 10. So a huge difference between now and then in matters of health: also in levels of, and acceptance of, violence in society – a global change detailed in Stephen Pinker's book, *The Better Angels of Our Nature*. Whereas we are deeply shocked by a rare instance perpetrated by an Islamic militant, beheading was an everyday hazard for a Tudor politician. Stocks were part of the normal punishment gear for servants in the Paget household and the hanging of a man for stealing some of his cattle went unquestioned.

As for the importance of religion, it will be constantly apparent throughout this story. As the author of the volume on the Tudors in the *Penguin History of Britain* points out, 'Christian rites and sacraments were central to people's lives. They created and validated relationships, made new affinities, and sanctioned the passages from one stage of life to another.'[3] At the trivial, but highly indicative, level, noted by the biographer of the Emperor Charles V, 'Even hard-nosed merchant bankers began their business letters with "Jesus" and the sign of the cross, peppered the contents with "God willing", and ended "Christ be with you".'[4]

William Paget was 'The Great Survivor' of the Tudor age, and was hugely influential from the later years of Henry's reign through to Elizabeth's accession. He was not, of course, the only one who bent with the changing wind: Lord St John, another of the same breed, apparently once answered the question about why he had survived by saying, 'By being a willow, not an oak.'[5] But Paget was probably the most powerful survivor. In addition, he was a Tudor bellwether, an astute reader of the wildly fluctuating political situation under Henry VIII, Edward VI and Mary I: so his story often exemplified those wider political changes. He was a 'kingmaker'. At two critical turning points in Tudor history, he had a crucial role in determining how things turned out. The first was the triumph of the reformist faction at the end of Henry's reign and the subsequent assumption of almost regal power by Hertford, the Lord Protector Somerset. The second was the victory of Mary over Lady Jane Grey. In terms of the most important issue of the times, Catholicism versus Protestantism, his influence was exactly contrary in the two cases. And, of course, in both instances, he was on the winning side. So were his actions purely self-serving?

While writing this, I was watching a TV series called *Succession*, about the ruthless power struggle for the succession in a media business empire unfolding as the old boss, obviously half modelled on Rupert Murdoch, is beginning to lose it. The parallel with the intrigues of the Tudor Court was striking. In particular, as the son launches a coup to unseat the old man, he asks one of the important investors for his support in the next day's 'vote of no confidence'. The latter replies, 'I can promise you that I am spiritually and morally and ethically 100 per cent behind whoever wins.' This does seem pretty much Paget's behaviour.

I remember my father saying that William had changed his religion opportunistically whenever necessary. He certainly switched sides frequently. Winston Churchill, speaking of himself, when he had returned to the Conservative Party after having left it for the Liberal Party at the beginning of his career, famously remarked, 'Anyone can rat, but it takes a certain amount of ingenuity to re-rat.' William Paget was a champion re-ratter. Over the course of his political career, he made five switches. In the factional infighting between conservatives and reformists at the end of Henry VIII's reign, he was initially more associated with the former but then delivered victory to the latter (switch one). In Edward VI's reign, he argued against both Somerset and then Warwick, going too far in the Evangelical direction (switch two), which led to a spell in the Tower of London ('The Tower') for his pains, from where he emerged as a dedicated Warwick/Dudley/Grey supporter so that on Edward's death he was behind the Lady Jane Grey/Protestant faction (switch three). However, when he saw the popular/political/military wind was blowing Catholic Mary's way, he, along with Lord Arundel and others, deserted the pro-Lady Jane Grey Privy Council in London and, escorted by thirty horsemen and carrying the Great Seal of State, rode out to meet Mary and her supporters at Framlingham Castle – essentially delivering the Crown to her (switch four). He was therefore well in with Mary during her reign, and particularly with Philip II of Spain, having arranged his marriage to her. But he tried to restrain Catholic extremism. You might think unsuccessfully; but it could have been a lot worse. He helped prevent the return of dissolved monastery property to the Church. He, and many others, had a strong personal interest in that. Cleverly, he also kept in with Princess Elizabeth. One of the re-found family 'royal letters' is from her in which she asked William for help and protection. As a result, he did all right when it was back to Protestantism under Elizabeth I (switch five). Olympic ratting and re-ratting!

However, his behaviour could be viewed in a less cynical and more favourable light. For instance, the way things turned out at the two pivotal moments meant continuity of government. Had the reformists not decisively won in the last years of Henry's reign and had the conservatives not decisively won at Mary's succession, there would have been the strong possibility of chaos and civil war. This is because the opposing forces would have been more evenly balanced. Judging which was going to be the winning side and helping to make its victory decisive was certainly good for the individual and his family; but it was probably good for the country as well.

* * *

One problem when trying to make sense of the intrigues of the Tudor Court, of which William Paget was a major part, is that some of the chief protagonists have a plethora of names and titles – like the characters in a Russian novel. Two of the main players, Edward Seymour and John Dudley, kept on changing their names. Seymour (brother of Jane, Henry VIII's third wife) is also Hertford (Earl of) and Somerset (Duke of – the Lord Protector in the boy king, Edward VI's reign). While Dudley goes one better. He is also Lisle (Viscount), and Warwick (Earl of), and Northumberland (Duke of). I tried the idea of calling them Seymour and Dudley throughout their lives, but soon found that does not work because contemporaries, of course, referred to them by the titles they held at any particular moment. In the end, I have done the same, sometimes adding in brackets one or more of their other names. To avoid confusion, and as a general aid to the reader, I have also included a 'Dramatis Personae' of the characters that feature in this story.

Dramatis Personae

Kings and Queens of England

Henry VIII (1491–47). On the throne 1509–47.

Katherine of Aragon (1485–36). Henry's first wife. Queen 1509–33. Mother of Mary I.

Anne Boleyn (1500–36). Henry's second wife. Queen from 1533. Beheaded 1536. Mother of Elizabeth I.

Jane Seymour (1507–37). Henry's third wife. Queen from 1536 until death following childbirth in 1537. Mother of Edward VI.

Anne of Cleves (1515–57). Henry's fourth wife. Queen for a few months in 1540.

Katherine Howard (1522–42). Henry's fifth wife. Queen 1540–42. Beheaded 1542.

Katherine Parr (1512–48). Henry's sixth wife. Queen from 1542 until Henry's death in 1547. Remarried Thomas Seymour, brother of Jane and Edward, in 1547 and died following childbirth in 1548.

Edward VI (1537–53). On the throne 1547–53. Son of Henry and Jane Seymour.

Lady Jane Grey (1537–54). Disputed claimant; on the throne for nine days in 1553. Daughter of the Duke of Suffolk and married to Guilford Dudley, son of John Dudley (Lisle/Warwick/Northumberland). Beheaded.

Mary I (1516–58). On the throne 1553–58. Daughter of Henry and Katherine of Aragon. Married to Philip II of Spain, son of the Emperor Charles V.

Elizabeth I (1533–1603). On the throne 1558–1603. Daughter of Henry and Anne Boleyn.

Kings and Queens of Scotland

James V (1512–42). Married Madeleine of Valois first and then Mary of Guise.

Mary, Queen of Scots (1542–87). Daughter of James V and Mary of Guise. Executed.

James VI (1566–1625). Son of Mary, Queen of Scots. Became James I of England in 1603.

Foreign Rulers, Ministers and Ambassadors

France
Francis I (1494–1547). On the throne 1515–47.

Henry II (1519–59). On the throne 1547–59.

French ambassadors to London: **Charles de Marillac**, 1538–43, **Odet de Selve**, 1546–50 and **Antoine de Noalles**, 1553–56.

Marguerite de Navarre (1492–1549). Sister of Francis I. Influential politically, diplomatically and as a Renaissance/Humanist patron.

Jean du Bellay (1492–1560). Cardinal and diplomat.

The Habsburgs (Netherlands and Spain)
Charles V (1500–58). Holy Roman Emperor and King of Spain and ruler of the Netherlands and much of present-day Germany and Italy. Nephew of Katherine of Aragon. Abdicated in favour of his son Philip II in 1556.

Philip II (1527–98). King of Spain and other Habsburg dominions. King of England while married to Mary I, 1554–58.

Mary of Hungary (1505–58). Sister of Charles V and Governor of the Netherlands, 1531–55.

Habsburg/Spanish ambassadors to London: **Eustace Chapuys**, 1540–45, **Francis van der Delft**, 1545–50, **Jean Scheyfve**, 1550–53, **Simon Renard**, 1553–58, **Count de Feria**, 1558–59 and **Alvaro de la Quadra**, from 1559.

De Granvelles Nicholas (1486–1550) and his son **Antoine** (1516–86), the Bishop of Arras, were both influential ministers and advisors to Charles V.

Ruy Gomez de Silva (1516–73). Influential advisor to Philip II.

Paget Family

Anne Paget, née Preston (died 1587). Married William Paget around 1535.

Henry Paget (c.1538–68). William's eldest son. 2nd Baron Paget. Knighted 1553. MP. Married Katherine Knyvet.

Thomas Paget (died 1590). William's second son. Catholic. Exiled under Elizabeth. Married Nazaret, daughter of Sir John Newton and widow of Sir Thomas Southwell.

Charles Paget (c.1546–1612). William's third son. Catholic conspirator against Elizabeth. Exile. Double agent/spy.

Daughters: **Etheldreda** (married to Sir Christopher Allen), **Eleanor** (married to Jerome Palmer and then Sir Rowland Clarke), **Grisold** (married to Sir Thomas Rivett and then Sir William Waldergrave), **Jane** (married to Sir Thomas Kitson), **Dorothey** (married to Sir Thomas Willoughby) and **Anne** (married to Sir Henry Lee).

Brother: **Robert Paget**. Catholic. Based in the West Country.

The English Court

Main Characters in Paget's Story
William Cecil (1520–98). Served under Somerset and Warwick. Became Elizabeth's chief minister.

Thomas Cranmer (1489–1556). Archbishop of Canterbury. Protestant. Burnt at the stake.

Thomas Cromwell (1485–1540). Henry's chief minister, from 1530 until he was beheaded.

John Dudley (1502–53). Created Viscount Lisle in 1542. Lord High Admiral. Created Earl of Warwick on Edward's succession and Duke of Northumberland after leading a coup against Protector Somerset in 1551. Married his son to Lady Jane Grey. Beheaded after supporting her as queen.

Stephen Gardiner (1483–1555). Paget's first patron. Bishop of Winchester. Imprisoned for much of Edward's reign. Lord Chancellor under Mary.

Henry Howard (1517–47). Earl of Surrey. Son of the Duke of Norfolk. Beheaded.

Thomas Howard, Duke of Norfolk (1473–1554). Premier Peer of England and most powerful of the established nobility. Catholic. Imprisoned during Edward's reign.

William Petre (1505–72). Co-Secretary with Paget. Retained office under Edward, Mary and Elizabeth.

Edward Seymour (1489–1552). Brother of Jane Seymour and therefore uncle of Edward VI. Made Earl of Hertford in 1537 and Duke of Somerset when he became Lord Protector on Edward's accession. Beheaded after Warwick's (Dudley's) coup.

Thomas Seymour (1508–49). Brother of Jane and Edward, of whose power he was jealous. Flirted (and possibly more) with the young Princess Elizabeth. Secretly married Queen Katherine Parr. Beheaded for treasonous conspiracy.

Thomas Wriothesley (1505–50). Paget worked with him in Henry's government during the 1530s. Made Lord Chancellor in 1544. Created Earl of Southampton 1547. Lost power soon after.

Others at the Tudor Court

Roger Ascham (1515–68). Tutor to Edward and Elizabeth and Latin secretary to Queen Mary.

Charles Brandon, Duke of Suffolk (1484–1545). Soldier and close companion of Henry.

Sir Anthony Browne (1500–48). Courtier, Privy Councillor and Master of the King's Horse.

John Cheke (1514–57). Evangelical Professor close to Edward VI, who knighted him and appointed him Secretary. Imprisoned and exiled under Mary.

William Clerk. Clerk to the Privy Seal, 1542–48.

Edward Courtenay (1527–56). Earl of Devon. Considered a possible husband for both Mary and Elizabeth because of his royal blood; he was their second cousin. Possibly involved in conspiracies. Died in exile in Italy in suspicious circumstances.

Richard Cox (1500–81). Clergyman and academic involved in Edward's education. Imprisoned and exiled under Mary. Bishop of Ely under Elizabeth.

Francis Dereham. Lover of Queen Katherine Howard. Hanged, drawn and quartered in 1541.

Anthony Denny (1501–49). Close confidant of Henry as Groom of the Stool.

Henry Fitzalan, Earl of Arundel. Lord Chamberlain 1546–50. Catholic.

John Gates (1504–53). Brother-in-law to Denny. Protestant. Close to Henry and Northumberland (Dudley/Warwick). Beheaded under Mary.

Thomas Heneage (1480–1553). Groom of the Stool to Henry. After thirty years' service, dismissed and replaced by Denny in 1546.

William Herbert (1501–70). Made one of Henry's Gentlemen of the Privy Chamber in 1546. Married Queen Katherine Parr's sister. Created Earl of Pembroke 1551. Governor of Calais under Mary and Lord Steward under Elizabeth.

Sir Philip Hoby (1505–58). Courtier and diplomat under Henry, Edward and Mary.

Sir Thomas Parry (1515–60). Served in government under Henry and Edward. Attended Princess Elizabeth when she was under house arrest. A favoured Privy Councillor and Comptroller of the Household under Elizabeth.

Richard Rich (1496–1567). Chancellor of the Court of Augmentations in charge of dissolved monastery revenues. Lord Chancellor 1548–51. Active in prosecuting Protestants under Mary.

Lord John Russel (1486–1555). Comptroller of the Household, Lord High Admiral and Lord Privy Seal at various moments between 1537 and 1553. Created Earl of Bedford in 1550.

Ralph Sadler (1507–87). Close associate of Cromwell and remained in government under Henry and Edward VI. Lost power under Mary and was briefly under house arrest. Regained office under Elizabeth.

Sir Thomas Smith (1513–77). Prominent Protestant scholar. Secretary of State under Edward. Lost offices under Mary; regained influence under Elizabeth.

Richard Southwell (1503–64). East Anglian based. Tutor to Cromwell's son. Accuser of Henry Howard. Privy Councillor from 1547. Served under Mary.

Lord St John, William Paulet (1485–1572). Privy Councillor with other high office under Henry. Keeper of the Great Seal under Somerset. Made Earl of Wiltshire 1550 and Marquess of Winchester 1551. Kept office under Mary and Elizabeth.

Thomas Wolsey (1477–1530). Cardinal. Henry's main minister 1514–29.

Nicholas Wotton (1497–1567) Dean of Canterbury and York. Diplomat at the court of Charles V and Francis I. Served under Henry, Edward, Mary and Elizabeth.

Other Characters

Anne Askew (1521–46). Evangelical martyr, tortured and burnt.

Sebastian Cabot (1474–1557). Explorer.

Sir Thomas Chamberlaine (1504–80). English Agent and later ambassador in the Netherlands. Governor of the Merchant Adventurers in Antwerp.

Ippolito II d'Este (1509–72). Cardinal. Ferrarese ambassador to the French Court when Paget was English ambassador.

Robert Dudley, Earl of Leicester (1532–88). Son of John Dudley (Lisle/Warwick/Northumberland) and brother of Guilford Dudley, who was the husband of Lady Jane Grey). Condemned and imprisoned by Mary, but pardoned. Favourite of, and suitor for the hand of, Queen Elizabeth. Married to Amy Robsart, who died suspiciously.

Sir Thomas Gresham (1519–79). Merchant and financier, served under Edward, Mary and Elizabeth. Involved in monetary policy and founded the Royal Exchange.

Sir John Mason (1503–66). Clerk and diplomat. Close associate of Paget.

Christopher Mont (1496–1572). Agent and diplomat in the Netherlands and Germany under Henry, Edward and Elizabeth. Evangelical.

Sir Nicholas Throckmorton (1516–71). Ambassador to France under Elizabeth. Involved in relationship between her and Mary, Queen of Scots.

Thomas Tusser (1524–80). Served in Paget's household, partly as musician. Author of *Five Hundred Points of Good Husbandry*.

Stephen Vaughan (1502–49). English agent who negotiated loans with Antwerp bankers, the Fuggers. Evangelical.

Nicasius Yetsweirt. Clerk of the Signet. Secretary for the French Tongue. Paget's chief assistant/clerk/fixer.

Part I
Henry VIII

Chapter 1

Coming from Nowhere

In the household of a humble artisan and in the court of the king alike the service of one man to another was the defining, dominant social relationship.

Susan Brigden, *New Worlds, Lost Worlds*

The kingdom has never been well since the king put mean creatures like thee into government.

Henry Howard, Earl of Surrey, to William Paget during the former's trial in 1547

My father read the Lesson every Sunday in the parish church in the middle of family land on Anglesey. The church was, and still is, unique, in that it was entirely candlelit and in that the words used were the old ones from the *Book of Common Prayer* of 1552. Although I am not a believer, the resonant words are lodged deep in my subconscious: 'The body of our Lord Jesus Christ which was given for thee, preserve thy body and soul into everlasting life: take and eat this, in remembrance that Christ died for thee, and feed on him in thy heart by faith, with thanksgiving.'

This is Protestant, but mildly so. It denies Transubstantiation – one of the longest words in the English language and meaning the actual physical presence of Jesus's blood and flesh in the wine and bread of Communion – but possibly slightly mollifies the more Catholic inclined as it acknowledges the centrality of this ritual of the Eucharist, or Holy Communion. It is thus typical of the moderate religious settlement that finally emerged from all the upheavals of the reigns of Henry VIII, Edward VI, 'Bloody' Mary and Elizabeth I, upheavals that were the backdrop to the story of Lord William Paget.

It is thought he was born around 1505 but nothing very certain is known about his parents. Like Wolsey and Thomas Cromwell, Paget was a self-made man who rose to honour, power and wealth through his own talent and hard work. And he would not have been too keen to reveal details of his 'low birth'. Later in his career, when, as Chief Secretary, he was investigating the snobbish Henry Howard, Earl of Surrey, for treason, the latter accused

Paget of being a 'mean creature' and a 'catchpole', or low-ranked debt-collector. Local Staffordshire histories have the Paget family down as nail-makers in Wednesbury. William's father is variously described as a sheep-shearer, or a barber, or a clothworker, or a constable, or all of the above, with origins in Staffordshire or Worcestershire but living in London. I did discover in the basement archives at Plas Newydd, in a scrapbook of family memorabilia, a brief printed account of William's life – its origins unknown, but seemingly written in the eighteenth or nineteenth century. This places William's father in a slightly higher social milieu, claiming that he was a 'Serjeant at Mace' in the (London) corporation which was described as 'an office of great respectability in those days'. The mace was both a weapon and a staff of office: it appears this job was essentially that of policeman. A sergeant at mace features in the huge retinue that accompanied the King and Cardinal Wolsey in Shakespeare's stage directions for act two, scene four of his play *Henry VIII*.

What was the England into which William was born like, economically and socially? Starting with statistics: the population doubled from 2 million to 4 million during the century. Ninety per cent lived in the countryside and half of the urban population was in London. Although the difference between years of good or bad harvest was considerable, Tudor England did on the whole manage to feed itself, avoiding the national subsistence crises of the Middle Ages. John Guy, justifiably one of the most respected of contemporary Tudor historians, reckons, 'there is much to be said for the view that England was economically healthier, more expansive and more optimistic under the Tudors than at any time since the Roman occupation of Britain.'[1]

It was, however, a massively unequal society, which became more unequal mainly as a result of increased wealth at the top but also because the standard of living of the poorest declined somewhat. There was some change from the semi-feudal ideals of good lordship and social responsibility to more 'capitalist' ways, with increased agricultural profits caused partly by enclosure of common land. This, plus the attack on the wealth of the Church, have caused some anti-capitalist historians to characterise the England of these times as 'The Age of Plunder'. Whether plunder or not, the Paget family were certainly among those who reaped the benefits.

Within the small industrial and commercial sectors of the economy, the most significant was cloth making and the most important element of that was cheap labour, since it took fifteen people a week of hard labour to produce one 12 x 1¾-yard piece of medium quality cloth. The leather and building industries came next in size. Overseas trade was less than 10 per cent of inland and coastal trade but was politically significant in that customs were an easy source of Crown revenue and because, after the rich landowners, the merchants engaged in foreign trade were the richest men in England. Cloth exports were the biggest part of this, tripling between 1470 and 1550. The trade was centred in Antwerp and was largely in exchange for imported manufactured goods. The other significant import was wine. Some coal and iron was produced in England. Much of this economic activity features in the story of William Paget.

At the top of English society, there was an extreme hierarchy from the royal apex to the layer of which William's family was a part. Below the King, in descending order, were about fifty peers who owned 10 per cent of the land, about 500 knights owning another 10 per cent, and a large but unquantifiable number of esquires and gentry owning 50 per cent. And below them were those who were not considered gentleman, such as yeomen, lesser merchants, craftsman and respectable, but non-landowning, citizens of towns, such as William's father. Within the Church there was a parallel hierarchy. Economic and social status were not equivalent, with land ownership and profession defining gentility. If you owned land, were a lawyer, university graduate, doctor, military officer or clergyman, you were a gentleman. Generally, if not, you were not, even if you were of comparable wealth. William's family probably just did not make it. But this extreme social polarisation did not preclude social mobility. Cromwell's biographer writes of his subject as being, 'classified in fifteenth-century society as yeomen: busy industrious folk who liked to see their promising boys get on in the world, and who valued schooling as the key to advancement.'[2] A major upgrade in status was possible through talent, education, entry into an urban elite, marrying above your station and, above all, gaining land. All of which applied to William Paget.

Beginning with talent and education. Because all we really know about William's early years is that, coming from humble origins, he must have been exceptionally clever as he managed to attend St Paul's School and then Trinity Hall college at the University of Cambridge – both places, then as now, of high academic standing. He may also have been very lucky or very calculating in his acquaintances. At St Paul's he made good friends with Anthony Denny and Thomas Wriothesley ('Call me Risley' in the Hilary Mantel novel). They were from backgrounds of somewhat higher status and greater influence. Denny was the son of a knight and Wriothesley's family had well-connected jobs as King's Heralds. Both were later, like Paget, to rise to great prominence in serving Henry VIII. They will feature significantly in later chapters of this story.

In addition, by going to St Paul's, Paget was entering a world not a million miles away from the royal centre of power. The school had been founded by John Colet and its first High Master was William Lily, who were both famously talented humanist scholars, part of the world of the even more famously talented Renaissance 'all rounders', Erasmus and Thomas More. All four were greatly admired by the young Henry VIII – even if he did later have More's head chopped off for not being prepared to accept him as Head of the Church.

But Paget's big break was at the University of Cambridge, where he studied civil law, because it was there he was adopted by the Master of Trinity Hall, Stephen Gardiner. There is an account of Paget, Wriothesley, who had gone to Cambridge along with Paget, and Gardiner, performing together in a play.[3] So we can assume they were close – although they were later to fall out badly. At Plas Newydd there is a portrait of Paget's first patron, Gardiner, that must have been passed down through the centuries.

Stephen Gardiner himself had become a major player when he was sent by the university on a mission to plead on its behalf to the King's then all-powerful minister, Cardinal Wolsey. Wolsey then recognised his talent and made him his Secretary.

Patronage was everything in the sixteenth century. For a young man, William Paget could hardly have done better. Paget's patron was Gardiner; Gardiner's patron was Wolsey; Wolsey's patron was the King. So William was on his way.

His early life is vividly illustrated by a poem that was addressed to him, after he had become one of the most powerful men in the land, by a schoolmate and leading antiquarian, John Leland. It opens with the sycophantic lines, 'O excellent Paget, I am eager to make your name famous, And to celebrate it with snow-white letters,' and mentions that, 'London brought you forth as a child into the kindly light,' which was where Paget studied under Lily. And continues:

> Meanwhile you arrived at a more mature age,
> Boyish days passed by.
> And so you sought a lively spring, Granta's stream,
> And frequently moistened your lips with liquor sweet as nector.

In other words, he went up to Cambridge, where the River Cam was in those days called the Granta, and got pissed a lot as a student. Plus ça change. The poem says that at Cambridge, William, 'Sought the house of sagacious Gardiner' and then went to Paris:

> You hastened there with great speed,
> Burning to enjoy the fertile knowledge of languages.
> After you took advantage of all the opportunities
> You returned to your native land and post.
> Once again you cultivated Gardiner as your patron

And Wriothesley, names dear to you,
Through whom you began to be highly recommended
To King Henry and to nobel men.⁴

* * *

When trying to understand and communicate what it must have been like to live in the sixteenth-century world of my ancestor, I have come to realise that survival, not in the political sense, with which much of this book will concern itself, but in the most basic sense, would have dominated everyone's lives. Today, Coronavirus has finally given us in the rich 'West' a taste of their reality; but only a tiny taste. In Paget's England, at least nine out of ten people were living in what would nowadays be described as extreme poverty. And even for the elite top 10 per cent, into which Paget was born, disease and death were nonetheless constant companions, with infant and child mortality utterly commonplace and life expectancy of those who survived only in the thirties or forties. In the summer of 1528, the deadly 'sweating sickness' reached London and the Royal Court. Paget, prominent enough now to be mentioned by the French ambassador, was one of many to be stricken. The ambassador's report is worth quoting:

> The King keeps moving for fear of the plague. Many of his people have died of it in three or four hours. Of those you know [mentions several names] are dead; but [mentions Paget and others], and those of the Chamber [Henry's Privy Chamber] generally, all but one, have been or are attacked. Yesterday some of them were said to be dead. The King shuts himself up quite alone. It is the same with Wolsey. After all, those who are not exposed to the air do not die. Of 40,000 attacked in London, only 2000 are dead; but if a man only put his hand out of bed during twenty-four hours, it becomes as stiff as a pane of glass.⁵

Note that a one-in-twenty survival rate, in just one of many bouts of plague that would have occurred in a person's lifetime, is considered pretty good news. The Black Death had killed a third of the population. Puts Coronavirus in perspective.

So, in this world of 'survival of the fittest', William recovered from the disease. In his early twenties, he was appointed one of the Clerks of the Signet. This was part of the royal bureaucracy under the control of the King's Secretary, who was Stephen Gardiner from 1529 and Thomas Cromwell from 1534. It was a job that was both profitable and influential. In 1529, he was also elected to Parliament and sat in every subsequent Parliament until he was made a peer.

The literature explaining how government really functioned under the Tudor monarchs is less than crystal clear. But it appears that things worked something like this. The King had enormous, essentially arbitrary, powers. His power was not completely unlimited. The nobles – ref Magna Carta, Parliament, Common Law and the Church, were all constraints. But one important way in which the King could exercise his considerable power – and raise revenue – was by granting titles, rights (for example, and importantly, to the ownership of land), pensions, monopolies and offices (basically, 'jobs' – often well paid sinecures). The actual physical, legal proof of these grants at the end of the bureaucratic process were Letters Patent on vellum, with the Great Seal attached. At Plas Newydd there is displayed a magnificent example of such from the reign of Edward VI, granting Paget the arms and crest of the Baronetcy of Beaudesert. But the process for the issuing of grants usually started in the Signet Office, which was so called because the document they produced had the small seal, or signet, attached. Our knowledge of how the Signet Office functioned is not, however, helped by the fact that its archives were largely destroyed by a fire.

We do know that the clerks received a small salary from the Crown, they were entitled to a 'bouge of court', meaning they were fed by the royal kitchens and had lodgings for two servants and stabling for three horses. Where they really cashed in was in the fees extracted from suitors for royal grants. It is calculated that they each received in the region of £84 a year from these officially.[6] But one can imagine that backhanders, under a system that took a lot of corruption for granted, increased that sum considerably. It is almost impossible to give a modern equivalent to a Tudor £84 as what you could buy then and now has changed so massively and, even for things that have not changed, some were much cheaper, some wildly more expensive. But we are talking about maybe £100,000 in modern money. William Paget remained in this lucrative post until 1542.

There were four clerks, with assistants working under them, and, as well as dealing with the relatively routine but highly profitable administration of these royal grants, they also worked as aids to the King's Secretary at the top level of government policy. As referred to in the poem above, Paget had apparently become a talented linguist, studying for a while in Paris as well as accompanying Gardiner on at least one diplomatic trip to France. He quickly emerged as a specialist in foreign policy and diplomacy.

The background to English foreign policy and diplomacy at this time was the rivalry between the Habsburg dynasty under the Emperor Charles V and the Valois under Francis I. The former was based in Spain and the latter in France but the rivalry, in war and peace, was being played out in what is now Italy, the Netherlands, Germany and the rest of Europe. The other major fault line was caused by the Protestant Reformation, the rebellion of much of Northern Europe against the Pope. These two big issues of Continental Europe were often intermixed.

From the English point of view, it was sometimes just a matter of playing off the Habsburgs against the Valois. But Anglo-French conflict by and of itself was also a factor. This was a tradition – Henry V at Agincourt, etc., which was enhanced by the fact that the English still controlled parts of what is now France – Calais and the surrounding area. Basically, when a young aggressive English or French king was looking for a punch-up to prove his machismo, his first port of call was the traditional enemy. Henry VIII and Francis I of France acted true to form. From both sides' point of view, the Scots fitted in nicely: the other traditional enemy of the English and therefore frequently the ally of France.

But, at this time, the King had got his first batch of wars against the French and the Scots out of his system. He had also run out of money: the best possible incentive for peace. This was the background at the time when the young William Paget first emerged to do diplomacy for Henry VIII.

By now, dominating the foreground of foreign policy, was the 'Great Matter'. This was Henry's attempt to get a divorce from his first wife, Katherine of Aragon, so he could marry Anne Boleyn. The policy of Cardinal Wolsey, up to then Henry's main man, was to get the Pope to agree to this. But Wolsey's policy was finally dished by the victory of the Spanish Habsburgs over the French, which gave Charles V complete control of Italy. So Charles now had the Pope under his thumb, and no way would he allow the marriage of his aunt Katherine to Henry VIII to be annulled by the pontiff. With his policy a failure, his sovereign obsessed with the divorce and many powerful people wishing his fall, Wolsey lost his power and died a broken man.

If Henry could not get agreement from the Pope to his divorce, was he bothered? A bit; but not a lot. After all, he could assert royal power over the Church; or re-assert power – historical precedents were provided. Disputes between the monarchy and the Roman Catholic Church predated the 'Great Matter'. 'Praemunire', the crime of aiding and abetting a foreign jurisdiction, had been used against supporters of the Papacy for over 100 years. Some degree of conflict between the monarchy and the Church, including the dissolution of some clerical institutions, was happening under Henry VIII before Anne Boleyn hit the scene. In addition, a break with Rome would enable him to get his hands on the wealth of the Church.

But Henry wanted some kind of legitimacy for the divorce. If he was not going to get agreement from the Pope, at least he might be able to persuade different centres of Christian learning to give it the okay. The first record of a significant foreign policy venture by William Paget is a document he managed to get out of Orleans University condemning a summons from the Pope for Henry to come to Rome. After that, Paget spent most of 1532 in Germany attempting to get support from theologians for the divorce. At the same time, he was on diplomatic missions to persuade the German princes to ally with England and France against the Habsburgs. Nothing much came of this because the Turks invaded Hungary, which united the German princes and the Habsburgs against the external enemy. Nonetheless, Paget created a reputation as a skilful diplomat.[7]

For a couple of years after Wolsey's fall, it was William Paget's patron Gardiner who had the King's ear. He was made bishop of the immensely wealthy See of Winchester and he was for a time one of Henry's chief movers in the 'Great Matter'. However, it became more and more likely that a complete break with Rome was needed and the King's conflict with the Church sharpened. Therefore, Gardiner's loyalty to the Church and his resistance to the demand for 'Submission of the Clergy' meant his influence waned. Unlike Thomas More, romanticised by the Paul Schofield/Robert Bolt film *A Man for All Seasons* and savaged in Hilary Mantel's *Wolf Hall*, Gardiner later submitted to the King and so kept his head on his shoulders and his position. But he was no longer the King's main man. That man was now Thomas Cromwell.

Chapter 2

Climbing the Greasy Pole: Paget's Rise to Power

[B]efore God ye have and shall have my heart, prayer and service next to the King's Highness above all men.

Paget to Cromwell, 1534

In 1534, either Cromwell approached Paget or Paget approached Cromwell for a transfer of patronage and loyalty. The very first letter of William's to have survived is to Cromwell and is a grovelling submission to the new boss:

> I esteem myself more bounden to your mastership than to all other, the King's Highness only excepted, for whereas indeed other men had somewhat heretofore advanced and set me forward ... being in the King's displeasure, the rest of my friends not being able to set me afoot, ye have ... regendered me.[1]

For the next seven years, during the ascendancy of Cromwell and before his fall from grace and execution in 1540, William, now in his thirties, enhanced his power, status, reputation and wealth.

He was dispatched again to find further support in northern Europe for the 'Great Matter' and to explore the possibilities of alliances against the Habsburgs. Amongst other instructions was one to deny that Henry was motivated in his divorce by lust for Anne Boleyn and to tell of her 'constant virginity, her maidenly and womanly pudicity, her soberness, her chasteness, her meekness ... [and] her aptness to the procreation of children'.[2] With the possible exception of the latter, more like the opposite of Anne's qualities! Once again, Paget returned from the Continent, having visited Poland and Prussia, without any major success but with his reputation for diplomacy further enhanced. Apparently the Duke of Prussia had a particularly high regard for him. Paget was now at the centre of Henry VIII's flirtation with German Protestants in order to advance the 'Great Matter'; as is clear from a dispatch from Chapuys, Charles V's ambassador in London, to his master which complained that Melanchthon, the intellectual leader of the Lutheran Reformation, and others of his ilk, might be invited to England:

> I know that Paget, who last year went to Melanchthon and other Lutheran doctors, has written, by the King's order, pressing them to come. Some say they are asked to come to oppose the Queen; others, for the reformation of the Church, especially in taking away temporal goods.[3]

Another letter to Cromwell, sent from Hamburg just before Paget returned home, again shows that he realised how dominant Cromwell had now become during this period of Henry VIII's reign:

> There is no news worth writing, but I write as you desired at my departure that I would in anywise do, and to thank you for that kindness towards me which, though once nearly extinguished by my negligence, your mastership has of late revived, reducing me into his favour and grace whose least displeasure towards me grieveth me more than the most cruel death. Unfeignedly, I am more bound to you than to any other but the King; for though others have heretofore somewhat advanced me, you restored me to the King's favor.[4]

At about this time, William Paget married 'well' to Anne Preston, heir to a land-owning, and rich, family. Her great-great-grandfather, Sir John Preston, had been one of Henry V's justices of the peace. The family 'seat' was Preston Patrick Hall in Cumbria. We don't know how they met but it was reputed to be a happy marriage. It is impossible to form a full picture of his private life from the scarce information available. But there is the odd clue. The poem quoted earlier has it that,

> At this time you married the Preston girl;
> She is like Cynthia borne on a heavenly chariot.
> She made you a happy parent
> With noble heirs, and she still shines forth in her faithful marriage bed.[5]

At a time when marriage was so often arranged for material benefit, it does appear that there was love here as well.

Why would Anne Preston, the only heir to a rich and distinguished family in the North of England, have agreed to marry the young William Paget, who came from a wholly undistinguished background with no inherited money or land? The likeliest answer is that they fell in love, and the happiness of their marriage, as well as the close support they gave to their children, seems to confirm this. William evidently had personal charm as well as high intelligence: he was a modest and a loving, even passionate, man in his private life; although careful and cunning in his public life. There is plenty of evidence of his good ironic sense of humour. We can assume that these qualities appealed to Anne. It turned out that they had both chosen well. William appears to have acted as a 'good husband' and his power, wealth and position improved enormously throughout their marriage.

Anne was much loved and a significant support to her husband in his private and public life. In 1545, when he received a report while abroad that she had died (it proved inaccurate, she recovered), he wrote of his heart 'well near to burst for pain and anguish'.[6] When he fell out of favour later in life, was imprisoned, with his life as well as his position under threat, she helped him regain power. Their first son, Henry, was born in 1537 and by 1555, they had nine living children, three sons and six daughters. At a time when childbirth was so often fatal for mother and/or child, Anne was evidently remarkably healthy and strong, eventually outliving her husband by twenty-four years. As William grew in power and possessions, spending a great deal of time at Court, she would have organised the households and the life of the family. The only child brought up on a large country estate, she probably built on early experience of the management of a household and its land and gardens. There are indications from the detailed records of the Pagets' West Drayton establishment, examined in Chapter 14, that she was indeed heavily involved.

From the time of his marriage, William's status and position went from strength to strength. He had become an 'esquire' with sufficient money to be considered a gentleman. In London, he leased a grand town house, Northumberland Place, from the aristocratic Percy family. And he became a country gent by leasing a manor in West Drayton. This is next to what is now Heathrow Airport. The gates to the manor house still exist, as does the magnificent Great Barn at Harmondsworth which was later added to Paget's property in Middlesex. Described by John Betjeman as 'The Cathedral of Middlesex', it is now managed by English Heritage and is open to the public on certain days.

William Paget's connection with houses and land in Middlesex, at West Drayton, Harmondsworth, Iver and Heathrow, is recorded in some detail and shows his increasing power and wealth during his thirties, in the ten years from 1537 until Henry VIII's death in 1547. The West Drayton estate was owned by the Dean and Chapter of St Paul's Cathedral, to whom it sent money and corn. The celebrated Dean, John Colet, founder of St Paul's School, is recorded as visiting it in 1506 at about the same time that William Paget was born. In 1537, William took on a lease, paying £27 a year along with an obligation to send a regular quantity of corn to the cathedral's bakehouse to be made into bread. Many commercial dealings in the sixteenth century involved barter or products rather than just money. At the end of 1540, Paget secured a new, sixty-year lease at a slightly increased annual rent. As well as the existing properties, including a manor house he was soon to rebuild, the lease consisted of 39 acres of wheat, 65 acres of barley and oats, half an acre of beans and peas, along with some furniture, two beehives and gear for brewing. Six years later, William was sufficiently powerful to 'persuade' the Dean and Chapter of St Paul's to give up West Drayton to the Crown. And from then on, he 'held it in fee' from the Crown 'in consideration of his services'.[7]

Where did the initial money come from? We've already seen how the 'profits of office' in the Signet Office – legitimate fees and bribes combined – would have been considerable. In addition, the Pagets of the Tudor world were given petty sinecure jobs by the Crown which altogether added up to a sizeable income. For example, in 1531, Paget was made keeper, bailiff and constable of Maxstoke Castle, in Warwickshire, while the owner, a minor, was a ward of the King. He received fees from various keeperships and rangerships of royal properties in Staffordshire that came to over £20 a year. In 1534, he got his hands on a licence to import 400 tonnes of French wine at reduced customs rates.[8]

Another clue as to how things worked, involving systems of 'exchange of favours', is revealed in a letter William wrote to Wriothesley. To give the context, while both Paget and Wriothesley were at the heart of government working under Cromwell, the latter was at this time more influential. The letter refers to a Mr Cofferer; the Cofferer was an official of the royal household who managed financial matters and royal resources. We can assume that Paget needed timber for rebuilding his West Drayton mansion, and oaks owned by the Crown were offered. The letter, which also reveals something of both William's wit and anti-clericism, reads, 'I had thought to have desired you to thank Mr Cofferer for his liberality. On sight of your letter, he offered me, not 10 oaks, but 30; which, knowing my little debt towards him, I declined, not as monks do abbacies, but in good faith.'[9]

* * *

Around this time, things had been moving fast in that Tudor soap opera, 'The Six Wives of Henry VIII'. Anne Boleyn's days were numbered. First, she had three miscarriages and it looked unlikely that she would provide the King with a male heir. Second, Henry had a new love interest in Jane Seymour. She had been part of the household of both of his first two wives and the Court consensus was that she was unremarkable in looks and character. Some believed she must have had hidden charms but most thought that she attracted the King because she was the opposite of Anne. Anne was fiery and feisty; Jane was quiet and pliant. Whatever the reasons, Henry was fed up with Anne and he was after plain Jane.

Third, when Katherine of Aragon died in January 1536, a reconciliation between Henry and the Emperor Charles V became possible – as long as Anne, the hated cause of the divorce from his (the Emperor's) aunt was also removed. A reconciliation was not only possible; it was desirable. The King was told by Chapuys, the ambassador from the Habsburgs, that the Emperor wanted peace to preserve the mutually profitable trading links between his people and Henry's. And, as relations between France and Charles were deteriorating, both he and Henry saw benefits in friendship.

Fourth, Anne had many enemies: the more religiously conservative, the supporters of the first Queen, Katherine, and many members of the nobility and Court who had always resented her hold on the King. Decisively, they were joined by Thomas Cromwell, who had had a few run-ins with Anne himself and whose influence she wished to end. According to Chapuys, she had told him 'she would like to see his [Cromwell's] head off his shoulders'.

It was a chop-or-be-chopped world – and Cromwell kept his head for the moment. He put together a conspiracy of Anne's enemies that culminated in the annulment of the marriage, the trial for adultery, the accusation of incest with her brother, her conviction for treason and finally her execution on 17 May 1536. Ten days later, Henry married Jane Seymour.

It is not known how much, if at all, William was involved in all of this. It is possible that his getting his hands on the Percy family's London home, Northumberland Place, may have been connected. There was an attempt to base the annulment of the Anne/Henry marriage on the claim that she was pre-contracted to one of her previous suitors, Henry Percy, Earl of Northumberland. But he, inconveniently for the royal case, consistently and strenuously denied this. As a result, the Percys were certainly well out of favour with Henry and Cromwell. Also, Henry Percy died in 1537.

But what is known is that Paget was appointed Secretary to Queen Jane, with duties that included custody of her signet and control of her correspondence. There is also mention in the literature of Ralph Sadler as the Queen's Secretary. So either they shared the duties or one replaced the other during Jane's very short – year and a half – reign. Either way, this was a significant role: the Queen's retinue numbered 200, and Paget, aged only 30 and a complete 'upstart', was now a major figure at Court.

It appears that the King was so broke at this point in his reign that Jane's coronation was delayed. But Cromwell and his men, Paget among them, now really began to divert the wealth of dissolved monasteries and other religious institutions into the royal coffers. Taking a chunk for themselves, of course. Henry, along with most English monarchs before and after him and most Continental rulers – including Charles V and Francis I – was constantly short of cash. The objective for those managing royal finances was to enable the king or queen to 'live on their own' – i.e. not to have to levy direct taxation, which needed Parliamentary approval. It might be thought that the wholesale confiscation of religious property would have added to the Crown's revenue to such an extent as to make that possible. But this was not to be, because, in order to consolidate political support, the Tudors handed over the majority of ex-religious property. By the time of Henry's death, two-thirds of ex-religious property was no longer owned by the Crown and, after Edward and Mary's reigns, the figure was three-quarters. William Paget was part of the gang that benefited.

In response to the attacks on the 'old religion', there followed a rebellion in the North of England, the Pilgrimage of Grace, which was successfully crushed. Then, in October 1537, Jane gave birth to the all-important male heir, the future Edward VI. She died soon after.

Paget, before the arrival of Henry's wife number four, Anne of Cleves, for whom he was also to act as Secretary, was involved in very varied activities in addition to the routine Signet Clerk work. Three examples in 1537–39 show him as an important deputy to Cromwell. He helped his friend and Cromwell's 'number two', Wriothesley, to get his hands on the dissolved abbey of Titchfield, writing a report for him on its development potential, which led Wriothesley to get it from the Crown. Paget was on the grand jury which dealt with the Catholic conspirators associated with Reginald Pole – the King's cousin who was the likely alternative candidate for the English throne if the Catholic powers ever acted to topple the Tudors. These were known as the 'White Rose Trials', as the conspirators were Yorkists, of the white rose, rivals to the Tudors, of the red rose. And, in November 1539, Paget was put in charge of a mission to transport 1,000 troops, with a large sum of money to pay them, to travel via Holyhead to Ireland, to hand over his command to the Lord Deputy in Dublin and then to report back to Cromwell on the state of Ireland.[10]

Meanwhile, the next episode in the soap opera is Henry's ill-fated marriage to Anne of Cleves. It is a poignant story, with fatal consequences for Thomas

Cromwell, although Anne herself does end up better off than most of the wives. Cromwell's job, after Jane's death, was to come up with a candidate for queen number four, one who worked in the game of European foreign policy and pleased his master personally. Not an easy task. But, after several candidates did not work out for one reason or another, he thought he had cracked it with Anne of Cleves. The German Protestant states, such as Cleves, were a constant threat and irritation for Charles V and the Habsburg Empire. It was hoped that an alliance between England and one of them would divert Charles from any possible plans to join with France to make war on Henry. As for the personal, Cromwell got Henry all excited by saying that everyone praised Anne's beauty, 'as well for her face as for her person' – not to mention her virtue, honesty, etc. Hans Holbein was sent off to paint her portrait. Henry liked what he saw. Cromwell was relieved. The marriage was 'on'.

But, 'Oh dear!' A bit like internet dating when the untypical and flattering photo bears little relation to the person seen sitting on their own in the corner of the coffee shop wearing a red dress, when Henry finally met Anne, he did not fancy her at all. He was furious with his advisors and blamed them, Cromwell most of all. 'Whom shall men trust?' he moaned, 'I promise you I see no such thing as hath been shown me of her, by pictures and report. I am ashamed that men have praised her as they have done – and I love her not.' He felt he had to go through with the marriage and he did. But in the marriage bed things turned out even worse. The next morning, when Cromwell asked how it went, the King replied, 'I liked her before not well, but now I like her much worse! She is nothing fair, and have very evil smells about her.' He complained about the looseness of her breasts and that he took her to be 'no maid'. He declared he was unable to have sex with her and that there was no chance of any more children 'for the comfort of the realm' from that quarter.

According to one account, Anne herself was so ignorant about sex that she thought things were going rather well, saying to one of her ladies-in-waiting, 'When he comes to bed he kisseth me, and taketh me by the hand, and biddeth me "Goodnight sweetheart" and in the morning kisseth me and biddeth "Farewell Darling".' It was claimed that the ladies had to enlighten her that this was not really quite enough. Added to this personal disaster – and the personal really was the political where Henry VIII was concerned – the geopolitical context had changed radically from when Cromwell was planning the marriage. Charles V and France had now fallen out again and both were looking to gain English friendship. So a German Protestant alliance with England became undesirable as it interfered with the possibility of allying with either of the Catholic dynasties. What finally sealed the fates of Anne (divorce) and Cromwell (beheading) were the intrigues of the still strong

Catholic faction at Court, led by the Duke of Norfolk and Bishop Gardiner. Their trump card, Norfolk's sexy 15-year-old niece, Katherine Howard, was deliberately placed as a maid of honour at Court with instructions to attract the King's attention.

So, without too much fuss, the marriage was annulled on various trumped-up grounds – Anne's possible precontract with a son of the Duke of Lorraine, Henry's lack of consent to the marriage and its non-consummation. Compared to the first divorce, no one seemed too bothered this time. Perhaps, by the time of the ending of marriage number four, everyone just accepted this was how things went in the Henry VIII marriage department? The Catholic factions, both at Court and in Europe, were of course pleased, and Anne's brother, the Duke of Cleves, was relieved that 'his sister had fared no worse'. Anne was given the status of the King of England's honorary sister and a generous financial settlement, along with Hever Castle and the manors of Bletchingly and Richmond.

She in fact stayed extremely friendly with the royals. In 1541, she was at Court for the New Year celebrations, getting on well with both Henry's daughter Mary and his new wife Katherine Howard. Fast forwarding to wife number six, Anne was one of the witnesses to the marriage of Henry to Katherine Parr. And, fast forwarding still further, she outlived not only Henry and Katherine Parr but also Edward VI. She became a close friend of Queen Mary and converted to Catholicism.[11]

William Paget had a role in the Anne of Cleves story. For the brief period that she was the queen consort, he continued in his job as Queen's Secretary. This was partly because of his experiences as a diplomat in Germany: Anne spoke only German when she arrived in England and William was likely one of very few at the English Court who also did. Probably an important reason for Paget's success in general was his knowledge of Continental Europe and its languages. Cromwell's biographer notes the importance of this knowledge for his subject, as it was shared with a very few others, such as Sir John Russell and Sir Thomas Wyatt, 'rare English cosmopolitans, exotics in the provinciality of early Tudor England'.[12]

Paget was undoubtedly another of this rare breed. There is not enough evidence to paint a detailed picture of him as a Renaissance scholar but it is pretty clear that, in addition to speaking several European languages as well as Latin and Greek, he was a man of wide learning. Scholarly tomes on Plato and rhetoric were dedicated to him and, although we have no record of his own library, there is an inventory made of the family library at West Drayton a half century after his death which is fifty-one pages long. William's second son, Thomas, was a bibliophile, but his father founded the collection.[13]

Back in 1540, another of William's duties, using his knowledge of Germany, was to arrange the return to Cleves of most of the retinue of 263 attendants who had come over with Anne. He accompanied them to Dusseldorf, bearing a letter from King Henry to Anne's mother praising her daughter's gentlewomen. When William was ambassador to France two years later, he tried, unsuccessfully, to get Francis I to suppress a French tract entitled *The Remonstrance of Anne of Cleves*, which criticised Henry for leaving her on an 'arbitrary whim'. Anne remained close to William Paget all her life: she showed her affection by leaving a diamond ring to him in her will.[14]

Chapter 3

Growing Position and Power After Cromwell's Fall

Order of the Privy Council, 10 Aug, 32 Hen VIII, that there should be a clerk attendant upon the said Council to write, enter, and register decrees, determinations, etc, in a book, and Wm. Paget, late the Queen's Secretary, was appointed and sworn in presence of the said Council.

There were many other factors, apart from the Anne of Cleves disaster, which contributed to Cromwell's fall. He was ill for a significant part of 1539. There had been years of mutual hatred and resentment between him and the powerful Duke of Norfolk. One of the reasons why Cromwell was keen for Henry's wife to be foreign was that he knew that any British bride would almost certainly be linked to one of the great noble families – which did happen with wife number five – a Howard. More pragmatically, Thomas Cranmer, Archbishop of Canterbury, believed it was important for Henry to be happy and that being able to communicate in a common language was a necessary condition. As noted, Anne only spoke German. Gardiner, Cromwell's great rival, had returned from his long stint as ambassador in France to fight for the conservative cause. Cromwell overreached himself by getting himself made Earl of Essex and Lord Great Chamberlain when the holders of those titles died in the spring of 1540. Above all, by the Anne of Cleves marriage and in general, Cromwell became too closely associated with the Evangelicals. Because Henry was naturally very conservative in religious matters when not motivated by love, issues of dynastic succession, financial gain from the Dissolution of the Monasteries or by rivalry with the Pope.

The plot against Cromwell made possible by the Anne of Cleves fiasco and led by the religious conservatives under the Duke of Norfolk and Bishop Gardiner culminated in Cromwell's execution in June 1540. Cromwell's 'right-hand men', Wriothesley, Paget and Sadler, all made peace with the successful faction and retained or enhanced their power. In Paget's case, it helped that he had kept in with Gardiner in spite of earlier leaving his service for the rising star, Cromwell. Paget and Wriothesley were both assigned by Gardiner to interrogate their old boss Cromwell, and both made statements to 'prove' his heretical and treasonable behaviour. Pretty shabby but, it has to be said, totally necessary if they were not to suffer the same fate as Cromwell. Wriothesley's biographer puts it this way: 'It required a brave or foolhardy man to support one whose career was in terminal decline; self preservation was the determining consideration and nothing was more likely to assist in that process than the betrayal, willingly or unwillingly, of a former associate.'[1]

The King's Privy Council now became a much more important source of central government decision-making. This was because power was no longer concentrated in the hands of one man, as it had been first with Wolsey and then with Cromwell. Indeed, some historians see this moment as the beginning of regularised, 'civil servant-based' government administration in Britain. This theme, which was primarily that of the granddaddy of Tudor historians, Sir Geoffrey Elton, is no longer so fashionable among academics, who now tend to stress the continuing importance of royal whim, factional infighting and 'ad hoc' government. But, to the extent that Elton's theme has any validity, it was Paget who, in Elton's words, 'was to take the lead in preserving the government created by Cromwell through the vicissitudes of the next eighteen years.'[2] August 1540 is certainly the date when a proper register of Privy Council proceedings was instituted. It has continued to modern times. Paget was appointed Clerk of the Council and the first volume of the register is partially written in his own hand. In keeping with his enhanced status, he was installed in 'double lodgings' at Hampton Court when the King was in residence. A year later, he was also appointed Clerk to Parliament. These two posts both put him at the heart of government and helped to make him very rich. The Parliamentary work was done by deputies but still brought in an extra annual salary of £40. And both posts would have provided rich pickings in fees, perks and what we would now define as bribes. In particular, he would have pocketed all the fees paid by private suitors to the Privy Council.

William, in his late thirties, was by this stage of his career well established as a close and influential advisor to the King. His future success depended on finding a way to maintain that power while keeping his head on his shoulders. Things had not, after all, gone well for Wolsey, Cromwell and others.

It might be helpful at this point to consider in general the four main issues with which anyone involved in power politics under Henry VIII had to contend.

First and foremost, in this absolute monarchy, was catering to the personal whims and desires of the King. Having grown up with a distant and dominant father and as the 'spare heir' in the shadow of his elder brother Arthur until the latter's early death, Henry had a vulnerable, if huge, ego. He desperately wanted to be, and to be seen as, a great monarch. This resulted in extravagant displays and pageants, massive building projects and rivalry with other monarchs, in particular Francis I of France and the Holy Roman Emperor, Charles V. And it caused wars. He relied on those – Wolsey and Cromwell and others like Paget – who could offer to satisfy these expensive royal needs with policies which fed the royal coffers, such as the Dissolution of the Monasteries.

Add in his appetites and insecurities in relation to women – which resulted in the six wives – and you get a dangerous mix of arrogance and paranoia that led to alternating extremities of promotion and demotion of his male advisors. Being in the King's favour was all-important; and the King's favour was extraordinarily fickle. Hundreds of heads rolled and to wield power while staying alive was no easy task.

Secondly, mixed with these personal traits, was the context of what would nowadays be called 'governance'. Nearly everyone at this time and place in history agreed that the vital element in protecting the welfare of the realm was the clear and unchallenged authority of the monarch, preferably a dominant male. Avoidance of civil war and anarchy was the number one priority. This was the culture of the times in general; expressed most famously in the political philosophy of Thomas Hobbes's *Leviathan*, written a century later. But more particularly it was the legacy of the bloody Wars of the Roses that had preceded Henry VII's reign. This and the doubtful legitimacy of the Tudors made the question of the succession and the desire for a male heir overwhelmingly important.

Thirdly was the issue of religion. Both as a personal matter and as something that legitimised – or undermined – government, this was of enormous importance in sixteenth-century Europe. The Protestant rebellion against the Catholic Church sweeping across the Continent coincided with Henry's conflict with the Pope over his desire – motivated by love and lust and the need for a male heir – to dissolve his first marriage and marry Anne Boleyn. He was also keen to usurp the power of the Catholic Church in England – in particular to get his hands on its huge wealth. However, as William Paget was to discover throughout his career, it certainly was not wise to back the new religion exclusively against the old. Henry VIII himself was in two minds – for personal and political reasons. In his speech to Parliament in 1545, he criticised the two extremes, those who were 'too stiff in their old mumpsimus' and others who were 'too busy and curious in their new sumpsimus'.[3] Throughout his reign, Henry's support swung back and forth between the religious factions. To give a particularly vivid and gruesome example of Henry's even-handedness in matters of religion: in 1540, two days after Cromwell's beheading, six priests were executed, three Evangelicals for heresy and three Papists for treason – the former burnt to death, the latter hung, drawn and quartered.

Fourthly, there was the big geopolitical issue of European power politics – the dynastic rivalry between the Habsburgs and the Valois – particularly between the Emperor Charles V and Francis I of France. And the more 'local' traditional conflicts, between the English and both the French and the Scots. These then were the issues of the times. And they interconnected with each other. The trick to thriving and surviving, as William Paget did, was to successfully balance them.

However, while he was rapidly climbing the greasy pole, Paget's status and power at this stage in his career was still limited, as shown in a letter he wrote in June 1541 to Wriothesley filling him in on the goings on in the Privy Council. Lord Dacre, a wild young aristocrat, had gone poaching with a group of mates on Sir Nicholas Pelham's land near the town of Laughton in Sussex. Their escapade had turned into a fight with Pelham's servants, one of whom was fatally wounded. When the Council met in the Star Chamber to judge the charge of murder, Paget was excluded from hearing their deliberations, as he reported,

> albeit I was excluded yet they spoke so loud, some of them, that I might hear them notwithstanding two doors shut between us. Among the rest that could not agree to wilful murder, the lord Cobham, as I took him by his voice, was vehement and stiff. Suddenly and softly they agreed, I wot not how ... His [Dacre's] judgement was to be hanged. It was pityful to see so young a man by his own folly brought to such a case...[4]

* * *

Paget's still relatively low social status might also be seen in the excuse given to the man he now replaced as ambassador to France, the higher ranking, aristocratic, Lord William Howard. The letter from the Council to the latter reads,

> The King, minding to use your service here, has sent this bearer, Mr Paget, to supply your place, being the rather induced thereto by considering what personage you are, and of how small estimation Mons. Mariliac, the French ambassador here, is. This the King proposed, and we thought it very prudently considered; so that on Mr. Paget's arrival, you may take leave. Be assured the King is your good and gracious lord.[5]

This communication is interesting because it suggests, presumably quite convincingly to its recipient, Howard, that the lower social status of the French ambassador Marillac had to be matched by the lower social status of Paget. But it may be that the real reason Henry wanted Howard back in England was to charge him with concealing the sexual indiscretions of his young niece, Katherine Howard, Henry's fifth wife. If so, the class-based excuse used to get him back was a crafty lie. Such deviousness was certainly not unusual as a modus operandi for Henry and it is the case that Howard was then convicted and imprisoned for treasonably concealing the evidence about what Katherine had got up to. But the timing for this explanation appears to be slightly wrong. The letter recalling Howard is dated 24 September and, although the accusations against Katherine were beginning to emerge about then, it was not until the beginning of November that most accounts say that Henry was told about them. Another hint as to the reasons for Howard's replacement by Paget is in Marillac's report on the question, sent to Francis I, when he arrived in London on 12 October. He mentions Paget's experience of European missions and adds that, 'the English think they need such a minister now when the times seem disposed to change and war, and Lord William [Howard] has been very slow in sending news.'[6] But, two weeks later, Chapuys reported that Marillac had told him that Paget's appointment was indeed to do with his (Paget's, not Marillac's, this time) lowly status, indicating that Henry was not serious about a marriage alliance with France – of which more later. Chapuys wrote,

> The French ambassador was very sorry to hear of [Howard's] recall, especially now that, instead of the Duke's [Norfolk's] brother, the King is sending a man of very little stuff and still smaller quality to represent him, who has never been more than a mere clerk of the Council, which is no good sign of this king intrusting to him so important a negotiation as that of a marriage.[7]

To further complicate this story, it appears that Howard did not actually return to England until the end of November, accompanying Paget at the French Court until then. Soon after his return, he was arrested. The snobbish reason might have been genuine, or it might have been merely 'sugaring the pill' for the lazy Howard when the real reason was to get the talented and experienced Paget in as ambassador, or, just possibly, it might have been a ruse to make sure Howard did not escape the treason charge by staying abroad.

Chapter 4

Ambassador to France

[The French] are neither sincere, constant nor kind longer than makes for their own profit, which they regard without respect or honor.
Paget to Henry VIII, 1543

Against this broad policy background and whatever the reason for Howard's recall, Paget was appointed in 1541 to the important job of ambassador to Francis I's court at Fontainebleau, a post he kept for the next eighteen months. On his way to the new job, with war between England and France becoming more and more likely, he sent the Privy Council a report on the state of the English fortifications at Guisnes, near Calais. This was a generally favourable report, praising 'works of the greatest magnificence and force' and stating that 'the erecting of them in so short a time is no little marvel'. But it also criticised in some detail, reporting that he 'saw many men working in the ditch, and tumbrels going to and fro into the town through the vaults, but they worked like men who are ill paid. The dike and bray about the town seem strong, but not princely works.'[1]

Interest in and knowledge about fortifications was often an attribute of well-educated Renaissance princes and their advisors. Henry VIII fancied himself as a bit of an expert in that department.

Then William had to go chasing after the French king's court on its progress around France. An expensive business and, in a message marked 'Bar in Bourgoyn (Burgundy), 12 Nov. 11am', he explains that, 'the diets [expense allowances], 20s, appointed to him are insufficient if he is to keep a table. He received, from Lord William [Howard], plate and one carriage mulet [mule].' And, a month later, mixed in with a request for information as to who was being arrested in the Katherine Howard affair, he repeated his request for increased diets, swearing that 'he will do good service'. He eventually received the message that, 'the King is content to increase [his allowance] by 10s a day.'[2]

This was the moment in the ongoing saga of Henry's wives, when wife number five, Katherine Howard, fell from grace. Archbishop Thomas Cranmer and the religious reformists managed to come up with evidence of her sexual misconduct that undermined the influence of the religious conservatives centred on the Howard family and resulted in the end in Katherine's execution. The Privy Council's letter to Paget in France about this is full of salacious detail:

> One Fras Derham had lain in bed [with her, in his doublet] and hose, between the sheets an Hundr[ed nights] ... Moreover Mannock, a servant of [Katherine, knew a] privy mark on her body ... from Mannock's confession that he used to feel the [secret parts] of her body before Dereham [was familiar] with her: and Dereham confessed he had k[nown her car]nally many times, both in his doublet and [hose between] the sheets and in naked bed ... [Now may you] see what was done before the marriage [to the King. God knoweth what] hath been done sithence, [but she had already gotten] this Dereham into her service, and trained him on occasions ... to come often into her [privy] chamber. And she had gotten also into her privy cham[ber] to be one of her chamberers, one of the women which [had] before lien in the bed with her and Dereham. What this pretended is easy to be conjectured.³

I would presume that what was 'pretended to be easily conjectured' was a threesome!

One of Paget's first jobs as ambassador was to give this news to the French king, once he had caught up with him at Fontainebleau. Francis then wrote to Henry, sympathetically, condescendingly and misogynistically to the modern mind: 'I am sorry to hear of the displeasure and trouble which has been caused by the lewd and naughty behaviour of the Queen ... The lightness of women cannot bend the honour of men.'⁴

Nice! Coming from one king to another, both of whom made a habit of trying to 'have' anyone they fancied!

Apart from conveying messages of royal empathy about their love lives, Paget's main job as ambassador was to get as much information as possible about French plans while revealing as little as possible about English plans. The French Court was split between hawks favouring renewed war with the Emperor Charles V – particularly over control of Northern Italy – and doves wanting mediation by the Pope. The war faction were the ones keen on an alliance with England. The scope for diplomatic intrigue was considerable.

An unfortunate incident occurred at this point in William's ambassadorship. His servant got into a fight with the servant of Horatio Farnese, the Pope's nephew and representative at the French Court, and badly wounded him. William had to get Henry to write to the Admiral of France: 'Hearing that a lacquey of his ambassador, Mr Wm Paget, has severely wounded one of Signor

Horatio's men, who provoked him to fight, begs the Admiral to intercede for the Lacquey's pardon.'⁵

Unfortunate; but the fact that Paget was confidently able to get such a letter out of the King speaks well of his standing by now in the royal favour.

Returning to the general question of Anglo-French relations, Henry's policy was to sell his favours to the highest bidder. However, this policy was not, as it were, played out on an even playing field on which the English were as likely to ally with France as with the Emperor. It had been before, in the days of the 'Great Matter'. Then, Henry's divorce from Charles V's aunt had provided an extra reason for hostility between England and the Habsburgs which had balanced the traditional reasons – Scotland and Calais – for hostility between England and France. But the 'Great Matter' was now history. So, if Henry was to ally himself with the French, they would have to really come up with the goods.

And, for a while, during the first months of Paget's ambassadorship, it looked like they actually might. Negotiations centred on a plan to marry Mary (Henry's eldest daughter, later queen) to the French king's second son. In the dispatch quoted above from Marillac to the French king on the subject of Paget's appointment, Mary's personal qualities were described in great detail. While she was presented as not particularly alluring, her likely childbearing capacity, which was obviously a vital ingredient in any dynastic marriage, was considered promising:

> She is of middle stature, and is in face like her father, especially about the mouth, but has a voice more manlike, for a woman, than he has for a man. To judge by portraits, her neck is like her mother's. With a fresh complexion she looks not past 18 or 20 although she is 24. Her beauty is mediocre ... The chamber woman thinks her of a disposition to have children soon, if married. Has attempted to get a portrait of her, but no painter dare attempt it without the King's command.⁶

Later in his career, William Paget was instrumental in brokering Mary's marriage to Philip II of Spain, after she had become Queen of England.

One problem with the proposed French marriage alliance at this time was that, after the conclusion of the 'Great Matter', Mary, as the daughter of Katherine of Aragon, was not considered to be legitimate by Henry. The French king, Francis, reasonably said to Paget that, if the marriage and alliance were to happen, Mary had to be declared legitimate. Paget suggested that that issue might wait until the other conditions of the match were agreed. Francis countered that that was all very well but that, if Mary were not declared legitimate, the dowry would have to be bigger – a lot bigger. The size of the dowry – which involved complex issues to do with the writing off of debts, which we don't really need to go into – continued to be a subject of much negotiation and to be a sticking point. Meanwhile, Paget was trying to persuade the hawks at the French Court that an alliance with England was a necessary condition for war against the Empire and that, unless they got Francis to moderate his demands in relation to the Mary marriage, they would lose out to the doves. As well as the dowry issue, what Henry was really after from the French, if he were to actually ally with them against the Empire, was more land on the Continent to add to Calais and/or for them to abandon their alliance with the Scots.

In the end, it was not going to happen. Henry, dealing with the Imperial ambassador to London, Chapuys, was moving towards concluding an anti-French alliance with Charles V. He probably did not keep Paget completely up to speed on this development – making it easier for the latter to avoid direct lies to the French. But William certainly knew what the game was all about, as shown by a letter he wrote to Henry saying, 'I trust I have holden the balance so upright, as your Majestie may put Your fote [foot] in which syde You will, notwithstanding anything that I have said.'[7]

There is a nice exchange at this time between William and Cardinal Bellay, one of Francis I's chief advisors, in which the latter said that there were those in the French king's council saying that

> there would be war (between France and the Empire) and England would aid the Emperor; but if so they would send the Scots, Danes and Swedes to eat up all the Englishmen in four days. Paget said Englishmen were not easy morsels to swallow, the Scots knew it and the Danes and Swedes were wise fellows and knew that those who came into England could not depart without licence.[8]

William, the skilful diplomat, here combined bantering wit with a serious threat. It is also perhaps indicative that these two could have such informal relaxed conversations although the two countries were about to go to war. Bellay was a religious reformer and a protector of free-thinkers, including his great friend Rabelais. This then was the world of European humanists rising above the ever-changing and petty alliances or wars between their countries and kings.

The deterioration in relations between England and France is shown by the dispatch Paget sent to Henry in September 1542 in which he reported that the

French king, hearing of 'bruits' (rumours) of war and that England was to join the Emperor against him, angrily spoke

> unfriendly words, detailed to the effect that Henry would make war on him ... [but that] Henry now had against him the Pope and the Scottish king and, for his sake [Francis's] the kings of Sweden and Denmark and dukes of Cleves and Prusse would also be his [Henry's] enemies, and his own people loved him [Henry] not; that he [Francis] could do more with 100,000 crs, than Henry could do with 1,000,000 crs., and that he had done much for Henry, and had refused to overrun him when the Pope, the Emperor and all the world urges him to it ... To hear which Paget's heart frobbed.[9]

You can feel the degree of intense personal rivalry between the two monarchs: almost a love/hate relationship, with the latter in the ascendant.

Any chance of a French alliance was not helped by the spectacular defeat of the Scots, France's ally, by the English at the battle at Solway Moss in December – rather bearing out what Paget had said to Bellay about the English 'not being easy morsels to swallow'. In addition, Henry could not stand the French ambassador in London, Marillac, telling the Privy Council to write to Paget that he was

> so wilful, so proud and so glorious and seems inclined rather to hinder than increase the amity, in not admitting anything but what stands with his own fantasy, that the King wishes it declared to the French King, with a request to have him replace by another of better inclination.[10]

This kind of Anglo-French animosity does seem to be almost eternal, from the sixteenth century to the Brexit negotiations!

Paget's job now was just to string along the French and delay the moment when they realised that war with England was coming. Also he was asked to get the lowdown on what help the French were giving to the Scots. A letter to Paget from the Council said that: 'His Highness' pleasure is that you shall now seek by all the ways and means to you possible to learn to know ... what shall be determined in France to send into Scotland.' And the letter went on, revealing how much an ambassador at this time must have been as much a spy and dispenser of bribes as a diplomat, 'And if for the better attainment of knowledge at this time you shall spend twenty or forty pounds it shall be repaid unto you.' (Bear in mind this meant £20,000 to £40,000 in modern money.) Paget did his job as requested because he was able to warn Henry that the French were sending three warships with 2,000 German mercenary troops and a load of arms to the Scots.[11]

With war between England and France looming, Paget was recalled – as was his loathed counterpart, the French ambassador in London, Marillac. William was keen to return to his family. Apparently he had initially been promised that his ambassadorship would not last more than a year. His report to Henry read as follows:

> After dinner presented Henry's letter to the French king, who said it was for Paget's return and asked if his successor were come. When Paget replied no, and that he would leave first, the King was so overcome with passion that he could not speak. So, to ease him, Paget said that he had been troubled with sciatica and a disease not to be named, which gave him pain in riding, and that when he came to reside as ambassador he was promised his return in a twelvemonth. 'And will you go (quoth he) before your successor come?' ... Paget said he could not tell, and showed Henry's letters, in which it was written that the dean of York should come, wereat the King seemed much relieved.

In fact, because the English were soon to go to war with the French, there was no intention to replace Paget. As an aside, it is interesting to note that, although the countries were about to be at war, Paget's dispatch went on to mention the French king, 'granting readily that Henry's sommelier in Bordeaux should be suffered to depart with the wines he had bought there for Henry.'[12] War was not to be allowed to interfere with one king providing the basic necessities for a fellow monarch!

William had not much enjoyed his time in France, personally or professionally. And it strengthened his belief, very important for his future political career, that, more often than not, the right alliance for England, politically and economically, was with the ruler of the Low Countries, currently the Habsburg Empire. He had told Henry that he had grieved, 'to have been so long here [in France] and done so little, but it is against their [the French] nature to love sincerely and against their custom to deal truly.'[13]

On the personal side, his health had not been good – the 'disease not to be named' was piles. Not a lot of fun, particularly because he had to travel hundreds of miles on horseback in Continental Europe between the courts of the Valois and the Habsburgs. If only he had had available the remedy for haemorrhoids recommended in a book of family remedies, dating from a bit later, which reads: 'Take a great silver Eel, flea him [hang him up] to rest and keep the dropping [the oil], save the first dropping by itself, and the second;

rest the Eele till it be so dry that the bones and all may be eaten, then let the patient eat … the Eel, & bones and anoint the plate with the oil of it.'[14]

For the long-suffering Paget, there was a further delay of several weeks to his return home because of mutual suspicions that the other side might hold the ambassador hostage in the event of war. Paget's dispatch to Henry from Boulogne gives a lovely example of 'you're not a prisoner; but you are really' from the French official there.

> At Boulloyn, Mons. de Bies escorted him to his lodgings and entertained him at supper. De Bies asked him when his successor was coming, and whether he would depart before his successor came. Answered as he did to the King. De Bies said he had better tarry, and that he was commanded to make him good cheer, and he should go hawking and hunting and wither he would. 'Why then', said Paget, 'I will go to Calais' 'Nay (quoth he), that you may not.' Paget said that amounted to an arrest, and de Bies begged him not to use the word.[15]

In the end, an exchange of Paget and Marillac was effected on the border between (English) Calais and France. It sounds a bit like those exchange scenes at Checkpoint Charlie in Berlin that feature in Cold War spy stories.

But, at any rate, when Paget did finally get home, as Gammon puts it, in a very rare attempt at humour, 'While his derriere and disposition had suffered from his contact with France, his reputation and fortune had been enhanced.'[16]

Chapter 5

The Most Important and Powerful of Henry's Ministers

> All power rested in the will and person of the King and was quinttessentially personal. Access was all.
>
> Susan Brigden, *New Worlds, Lost Worlds*

> Eventually Henry came to use Paget as the main intermediary not only between himself and the Council, but also between himself, the court and the kingdom.
>
> The History of Parliament

Immediately on his return to England in April 1543, Paget was appointed one of the two Secretaries of State. This was alongside his old mate Wriothesley and replaced that other Cromwell protege, Ralph Sadler, who had been sent on a long diplomatic mission to Scotland to try to arrange a marriage between the future Edward VI and the infant Mary, Queen of Scots. William, now in his mid-30s, was 'rapidly becoming the most important and powerful of Henry's ministers, speaking for the king, controlling vast patronage and being the linchpin of royal diplomacy.'[1]

In this status-obsessed hierarchical society, it is significant that at this point in his life, Paget was knighted and granted his own coat of arms. He did not much like the one issued to him – a tiger with the branch of a peach tree in its paws – and he later changed it to the distinctive black and white one which is still the coat of arms of my family – a white cross on a black background, with five small black lions on the cross and four large white eagles on the background. You could, until very recently, see it on various London pub signs – for example, the Marquess of Anglesey opposite Covent Garden Opera House and the pub that is behind the Gate Cinema in Notting Hill, the Uxbridge Arms.

(Before I inherited the Marquess of Anglesey title, I was the Earl of Uxbridge. Uxbridge is near to William Paget's West Drayton base and the Earldom was created for Henry Paget, a descendant of William Paget's who was a royal courtier in the eighteenth century. When his son was created Marquess of Anglesey for his achievement on the battlefield of Waterloo, the Earldom then became a 'courtesy title' for the eldest son. Male primogeniture being the rule, the eldest son of the eldest son then became Baron de Beaudesert, a title which had been given to William Paget – as we shall see later in this story. For the first time – as a result of increased modern lifespans – from 1986 when my son was born until 2013 when my father died, these titles were all in use across three generations: my father was Marquess of Anglesey, I was Earl of Uxbridge and my son Ben was Baron de Beaudesert. Such are the arcane complexities of English aristocratic systems. During the writing of this book, my son Ben and his wife Katherine have had a baby boy: so the Marquessate, Earldom and Barony exist again. If anyone still cares, one would hope that soon male primogeniture in the British aristocracy might be replaced by absolute primogeniture, i.e. without sex discrimination.)

Paget was initially the junior Secretary of State. But soon after his appointment, Wriothesley was ill and, when he recovered, was made Lord Chancellor. His replacement, William Petre, was definitely junior to Paget, who was often addressed as 'Chief Secretary'. Tracey Borman writes in *Henry VIII and the Men Who Made Him*, 'Although no man had been able to fill Cromwell's shoes, Paget perhaps came closest.'[2] In the four years from 1543 to Henry's death in early 1547, Paget's power grew and grew. In the collected *Letters and Papers of the Reign of Henry VIII*, for 1545 and 1546, only Henry's name crops up more often than Paget's.

As the biographer of Archbishop Cranmer points out, 'the political significance of [Paget's] appointment was ambiguous'.[3] In relation to the swings between the conservative and reformist factions that characterised the last ten years of Henry's reign, what was Paget's position? On the one, Catholic, hand, both before and after the Cromwell era he had been closely associated with the conservative Bishop Gardiner. Gardiner still thought of him as reliable and his appointment as a political triumph. On the other, Protestant, hand, Paget was also friends with the Evangelical Cranmer. For instance, when in 1539, the conservatives were in the ascendant and Evangelicals were being forced to agree to Henry's relatively 'old religion' Six Articles, Cranmer used Paget as the intermediary to warn a prominent Evangelical theologian, Alesius, to flee the country.

Where did Paget stand? In the middle. As did his Sovereign. Judged by modern humanist ethical standards, this can be seen as essentially reasonable, but as somewhat hypocritical in practice. The definitive history of the English Reformation sums it up excellently:

Henry's was an age that instinctively identified the best path as a middle way between extremes, Aristotles' 'Golden Mean.' Yet throughout a decade punctuated by brutal parallel executions, England had painfully learnt that the King's 'middle way' was not a mild theological ecumenism, but an assertion of his right to discipline anything he chose to define as dissent.[4]

However, judging by the ethical standards of their times, the behaviour of the King and his chief minister, would, I imagine, have been either more completely condemned as evil or more largely praised as good, depending on your religious views. Because, if you believed passionately in a particular brand of religion, then the pursuit of the middle way could only be seen as evil and whether the motive of those who pursued it was one of conviction or of convenience would be unimportant. For the true believers, whether on the Catholic or Protestant side, the martyrs were the heroes. On the other hand, for those who were less interested in the rights or wrongs of whether, for example, the wine actually turned into Jesus's blood during Communion or only did so metaphorically (the latter view known as 'sacramentarianism'), to avoid a civil war over such issues was paramount. To the modern mind, distinctions could be made between those like Sir Thomas More, who happily burned Evangelical martyrs despite his own martyrdom, and those, like Cranmer, who never encouraged Henry in his brutality. But one suspects that, at the time, most supporters of the middle way would have accepted that a fairly ruthless suppression of the religious extremists was the only method to stop them tearing each other apart in a bloodbath that might have made Henry's brutal parallel executions seem like a vicar's tea party. It is an example of the eternal ethical debate of the merits of the pure position – absolute, universal human rights, 'not in my name', versus the impure, relativist, 'world as it is', 'lesser of evils', moral stance.

So what was the nature of Paget's power? Although the parallel is inexact for a multitude of obvious reasons, one aspect of the Chief Secretary's role was similar to the Chief of Staff of the modern US President. Paget's prime source of power was his direct access to the King. During this period, the Royal Court moved between Whitehall, Greenwich, Windsor and Hampton Court. Henry might also go on a 'progress' about the country, as he did in the summer of 1543, or on shorter military expeditions viewing coastal fortifications in 1543 and 1545, as well as the major adventure to fight the French in 1544. Between April 1543 and Henry's death, William was with the King all the time apart from the seven months when he was abroad on important diplomatic missions. Henry wanted him to be on hand. For example, it was reported to Chapuys,

Charles V's ambassador to England, that, before sitting down to dinner, when encamped outside Boulogne in July 1544, Henry made sure that Paget joined him. By the end of the King's life, it is clear that the bond between Henry and William had become really close. van der Delft, Chapuys's replacement, reported three weeks after Henry's death that, 'the late king three or four days before his death insisted on having him [Paget] with him alone, they passing entire nights in conversation together'.[5]

Paget was very much Henry's private secretary as well as his Secretary of State. So whether correspondence was private or political, addressed to Henry, the Privy Council or Paget, everything was channelled through his office, where it was opened and sorted. William read aloud letters to Henry which he had decided needed the royal ear. And often it would be parts of a letter, or a precis of one, giving him enormous power over how an issue was presented to the king. Letters written to other royals actually in the King's own hand (known by archivists as 'holograph' letters) were often drafted by William before Henry 'copied them out'. When Henry was acting as Commander-in-Chief during his war against France and sent orders to his military commanders that were too secret for discussion by the Privy Council, these were mostly written by Paget. For instance, in September 1546, there's an order to carry out a night raid on French fortifications near Boulogne which is annotated as 'draft in Paget's hand written as though from the Council'. (This curious incident, which happened after England and France had signed a peace treaty, is explored in more detail at the end of Chapter 9.)

As with Wolsey and Cromwell before him, Paget's skill had to be as much that of a courtier as that of an administrator, cooperating with the Gentlemen of the Privy Chamber to read Henry's mood, choosing when and how to get Henry's involvement in government decisions. His working environment at Court varied enormously, depending on where the boss was, physically, day by day, hour by hour. He had access to Henry's study which was next to the royal bedchamber. But he also had his own office, employing more than ten staff, near to, but not part of, the royal 'Privy Chambers'. He very seldom got home to his family at West Drayton. Because he was hardly ever 'off duty' at this time in his life, with letters often written after midnight, he acquired a house in Canon Row which was very close walking distance from Whitehall and Westminster. His workload must have been immense but he seemed to have happily accepted that this was the price he had to pay: although, on one occasion he did complain about having been left at Court working while others had gone off hunting.

* * *

Head of Paget's staff was Nicasius Yetsweirt. It is not known how he found him but it is probably not coincidental that this talented assistant was from Continental Europe, an educated and sophisticated Fleming. Just as William was Henry's main man at this time, it was Nicasius who was William's chief fixer. How the relationship worked is shown by an episode in the autumn of 1546, which is documented in detail because the two were apart at that moment and had to write to each other. As usual, the issues dealt with were a mixture of royal/State business and personal matters, Paget and Yetsweirt's. The main government matter was to do with money that Henry claimed Francis I owed him, which the French king had agreed to, in writing, seven years earlier. The French swore they knew nothing of this and wanted to see the original letters. So Nicasius was delegated to find them and show them to the French ambassador in London, who was to have them copied and to verify them. Yetsweirt was then to take the verified copies over to Calais to show to the French. Before leaving, he called in to see the Earl of Hertford and Thomas Wriothesley, the Lord Chancellor. Acting as mouthpiece for Paget, he gave them important information about the King's health, which had temporarily improved. He passed on some instructions to Hertford about his job – he was about to depart for Calais to be military commander – and he brought various warrants which needed Wriothesley's authority to release money. Although the payments were duly authorised, Wriothesley joked that cash was 'very drye'.

Once in Calais, and having handed over the letters to the French, Nicasius pursued his personal business, which was obviously for him a large part of the reason for his being there. He hoped to marry the daughter of a prominent figure in Calais, Sir James Bourchier. That William made this favourable match possible for his assistant is shown by Nicasius's letter to him thanking him for his help in his 'sute which it pleased your mastership not like a master but as a most loving father to comend I do not doubt but that your commendations have wrought with mr bourchier [sic] and others here as I trust before my departure hence to see such succes therof as shall be my full contentacon.'

He was indeed successful, and Paget's servant therefore married the granddaughter – though only by his mistress – of John Bourchier, 2nd Baron Berners, a powerful noble who had been very influential in the earlier years of Henry's reign. Yetsweirt next continued his official mission, travelling into Flanders to report on the political situation there. Then, on his way back through Calais, he dealt with another personal matter, this time on behalf of his boss. For unknown reasons, the Paget family had living with them at this time the daughter-in-law of Lord Cobham, who was the deputy in charge of Calais. She, it appears, was considered 'trouble', having fallen out badly with both her husband and her mother-in-law. William's family may have been about to move to their estates in Staffordshire, so Nicasius's job was to persuade Lord Cobham to get his daughter-in-law to move out – to friends' or her sister's. It is unclear whether Yetswiert succeeded in this. Probably not, as he signs off a letter to Paget, 'your wisdom doth perceive what is like to follow in this matter whose novissima (I fear me) will be pejora pricribus'. In other words, 'the last will be worst than the first'. This whole episode reveals how closely Nicasius worked as William's main political and personal assistant, as well as demonstrating, once again, how intertwined private and public matters were in Tudor times.[6]

William's other protege and assistant was John Mason, who acted as clerk of the Privy Council. Again, as with Wolsey and Cromwell, Paget's huge power arose from his dual role as the courtier who was the closest advisor to Henry with the most regular contact, at the same time as being the bureaucrat who was Secretary to the Privy Council, controlling its staff who drafted the letters and documents that transformed the Privy Council's decisions into action. He was also the messenger between the Privy Council and the King. And he controlled the Privy Council agenda. He regularly had a Sunday night session with Henry to discuss with him the Privy Council's schedule for the following week.

Because the Privy Council was, second only to the monarchy, the most powerful institution in the land, it is worth digressing to examine the sorts of thing it actually did during these years. From the perspective of modern central government, with its pyramidal structure of prime minister, cabinet, cabinet subcommittees, government departments, etc., and its fairly clear organisation of roles down from broad policy to detailed action, Tudor government seems extraordinarily random.

If you look at the records of the Privy Council, it becomes clear that there was very little rational prioritising of important issues over trivial ones. As Geoffrey Elton says, 'nothing that happened within the realm appeared to fall outside its competence.'[7]

Wriothesley's biographer lists some of the very random things it dealt with while Paget was its Secretary and Wriothesley its President as Lord Chancellor. There were major issues, such as organising the sea defences of England and of Calais/Boulogne, communicating with foreign powers, and instructions about religion and the punishing of heretics. Then 'middle-level' matters, such as dealing with the complaints of those oppressed by the powerful and wealthy, posting ambassadors or the negotiation of prisoner exchanges. But also plenty of trivial things such as the payment of couriers or the issuing of passports. Right down to dealing with the servants of the Earl of Bath for putting on 'lewde plays in the suburbs of London' or resolving a dispute as to the course of a drain near Glynde in Sussex.[8] While there may have been some movement in the direction of the Privy Council acting as a 'modern', 'rational' organ of government from the Cromwell years of the 1530s to the Cecil years of the 1560s to 1590s, its involvement in trivial and random issues clearly persisted. To give one Paget family example from 1570, two pages of the Acts of the Privy Council in October of that year are spent dealing with a Staffordshire neighbours' dispute between Lord Paget (William's son) and a Sir William Griseley over rights of way concerning a bridge and road and water rights.[9]

Not surprisingly given its unrestricted remit, the Privy Council in the 1540s seems to have met nearly every day and often for many long hours. There is a letter from Paget to Petre in November 1545 mentioning how incredibly busy they were. The somewhat 'academic' dispute among Tudor historians as to how much the Privy Council was a modern bureaucratic organ of government separate from the Royal Court (Elton) and how much it was 'culturally and politically subsumed within the court' (Starkey) might be partly answered by where, physically, it met. The evidence for this is not definitive, it was not in a fixed location, and there is confusion in the records because of variable use of the words 'Westminster' and 'Whitehall'. It appears the Council did usually meet 'at Court' but probably not in the more private areas of Henry's palaces, so not involving the close personal access to the monarch enjoyed by the Gentlemen of the Privy Chamber. So a bit of a boring draw in this minor battle of the Cambridge history dons.[10]

But back to Paget, who was as much at home in the Privy Chamber as the Privy Council. As his power grew and, equally important, as knowledge of his power grew, letters to Henry were often accompanied by letters to Paget seeking his support or advice. This meant that Paget was crucially involved in the creation of policy. In the matter of religious practices, the hottest political hot potato of the day, Paget had the King's ear. So, when an Evangelical, such as Cranmer, was trying to advance his reformist agenda, he would consult Paget as to how far he could push the King. For example, in 1546, when Henry refused Cranmer's petition for him to authorise the removal of all the statues from churches, Paget persuaded Cranmer to pursue an alternative Evangelical reform – for services to be conducted in English. And he had read the royal mind correctly because Henry did agree to that.[11] We will examine in subsequent chapters Paget's central role in Henry's foreign policy – particularly the war, and then peace, with France. But in this area of policy his access to and influence on the King was also regarded as vital. When, in August 1545, the three grandees who were essentially running the war with France – the Lords of Suffolk, Lisle and St John – wrote a collective letter to him giving their opinions on important matters of strategy and tactics, they significantly add, 'to be shown to the King if Paget thinks good'.¹²

Paget was increasingly the King's mouthpiece. In June 1545, he wrote to Norfolk, England's premier peer, 'the King has seen your letters, to me and to the whole Council, and takes their contents in good part', and Paget continued throughout this letter with similar phrases that speak on behalf of the King: 'the King means to…' etc. You wanted to know what the King was thinking? Ask Paget. Thus Charles Brandon, Duke of Suffolk, while campaigning, so away from the Court, on 18 July 1545, wrote to Paget, 'Marvels that, lying here so long from the Court, he has heard nothing from Paget; and having an inkling that Candishe, comptroller at Bulloyn [Boulogne], has not acted to the King's contention, would hear what Paget knows therein.'¹³

You wanted a royal favour in the patronage food chain on which society was organised? Ask William. He undoubtedly became the top broker at this time. Suffolk again, a few days later, sent a begging letter to Paget to intercede on behalf of one of his retainers, who has himself been begged by one of his retainers – lower down the food chain – about the payment of wages by the Crown, in relation to a farm near Portsmouth. In another example, Paget made sure that Nicholas Wotton, then the English ambassador to the Emperor Charles V, acquired the remunerative position of Dean of York.¹⁴

Because the two most important figures to emerge in Edward VI's reign were Somerset (Edward Seymour/Hertford) and Warwick (John Dudley/Lord Lisle/Northumberland), it is not surprising to see the wily and prescient Paget already building good relations with both of these powerful men by using his influence with Henry to help them. In 1544 and 1545, Hertford incurred heavy expenses soldiering with the English armies in Scotland and France and was desperately in need of royal financial aid. In several letters to Paget, he 'is compelled to make a suit to the King, being so far in debt', begged him 'to see the relief of the writer's necessity' and 'desires Paget to set forth this suit', to let him off money owed to the Crown from monastic property in Devon and to try to get a financially beneficial land exchange with the Bishop of Salisbury. Paget brokered a complicated commercial deal for Hertford which gave him royal licences allowing trade between England and France, despite war between the two countries. This involved English woollens being exchanged for French goods such as wine, via Jersey, which Hertford controlled, with him taking a juicy cut. And, in the winter of 1545/46, Lisle was helped by Paget in various suits to the King. He also sold him a house in Kew, which might well have been partially a reward.¹⁵

Chapter 6

Paget's Network

> By emphasising personal relationships and informal power networks, historiography shifted from focusing on the formal institutions and conventions of politics ... to recognising the importance of informal politics at the royal court.
>
> Humanist-trained scholars at the royal court tied the new intellectual current closely to practical politics.
>
> Both from *Politics and Religion in the Reign of Henry VIII: A Historiographical Review*, by Nadine Lewycky, an account of the history of Tudor histories

In these last five years of Henry's reign, Paget was able to really consolidate his personal power base and wealth. Alison Weir, in *Henry VIII, King and Court*, speaks of how he was able to use his influence with the King 'to exercise extensive patronage, dabble in a little blackmail and grow rich'.[1] He built a grand mansion at West Drayton. In 1546, he bought eleven former episcopal manors in Derbyshire, Worcestershire and principally Staffordshire, centred on Beaudesert. He had become a serious landowner and was exploiting commercial opportunities to develop his woodlands and establish ironworks. By modern 'Western' standards, he was corrupt, as his power and wealth flowed directly from the King's patronage and his government activities. One suspects it was all a bit like how it is now in Putin's Russia, or in Saudi Arabia or China. But, by the standards of Tudor times, Paget was apparently regarded as rather an honest chap. Weir again: 'Paget screened most of the documents and information intended for the King, as well as those sent out by Henry, but there is little evidence that he ever tampered with them; either he was honest or he covered his traces well.'[2]

Henry VIII, although constrained by other centres of power such as the great noble families, Parliament and the Church, was essentially, institutionally, an absolute monarch. And, in absolute monarchies, simply because so much authority flows from one individual – think Louis XIV's famous statement, 'L'Etat, c'est Moi' – their personality and involvement determined the real extent of their power. Henry was an exceptionally dominant personality; what, in the more old-fashioned histories of England, used to be called a 'strong' king, and he was that throughout his reign. However, the degree to which he personally determined State policy did vary considerably throughout the thirty-eight years he was on the throne. Initially, when he was a young blood having fun jousting, hunting and womanising, he left most policy up to Wolsey. That is, until policy interfered with his personal life – his desire to divorce Katherine and marry Anne. Later, for a while, he was happy to leave a lot up to Cromwell. Until, once again, with the Anne of Cleves marriage, public policy again interfered with his personal life. (In both cases, his personal life was inseparable, as in all absolute hereditary monarchies, from the most important aspect of public life – the succession.) With the fall of Cromwell, and the waning of the jousting/hunting/womanising years, came the period of Henry's most active involvement in public policy – roughly from 1530 to 1544. However, in the last three years of his life, as he grew older and more ill, he once more relaxed his hold on affairs of State. Thus Paget, like Wolsey and Cromwell before him, was able to wield huge power, although he did so with greater modesty and restraint than they had done. And so, unlike those predecessors, he survived.

* * *

Before turning to the big policy issues with which Paget had to deal as Henry VIII's chief minister, it is worth taking a closer look at the circle of friends, work colleagues and political associates that he had built up by the last years of the reign. These all seemed to share the same classically based humanist world view, mixed in, in some cases and to varying degrees, with an inclination towards Evangelical religious positions. In addition to Yetsweirt and Mason, he was very close in his work and personal life to his co-Secretary, Petre, who had similarly emerged from academic success, the 'Great Matter' campaign, Cromwell and the dissolution. Petre was close to the Paget family and the two were often dinner guests in each other's houses. We will see how he was the man to whom William turned when he was abroad and believed that his wife had died. Evidence for how often Petre dined with Paget survives in the meticulous accounts kept by the former showing 'tips' given to the latter's cook and other servants.[3] William also seems to have been pretty close to the main English representatives abroad with whom he dealt on diplomatic matters – Christopher Mont, Thomas Chamberlain and particularly Stephen Vaughan. Details of their relationships will be shown in the next chapter on foreign affairs. Of significance for his political power, Paget was good friends with both of the King's doctors, William Butts and Thomas Wendy, and the hugely influential gentleman of the Privy Chamber, Anthony Denny. Denny was a schoolfriend who William could rely on to maintain his personal contact with Henry when he (Paget) was away on diplomatic missions. The close connection between the two of them becomes evident and is of great political significance in the weeks just before and after Henry's death and in particular in relation to his will. Until they eventually fell out politically, William's other schoolfriend Wriothesley also remained personally close to Paget: he was one of the godfathers to Paget's second son, Thomas, born in 1543. The other godfather was Thomas Cranmer, who had been Archbishop of Canterbury for ten years by then.

Many of William's personal circle do seem to have been very well connected and very useful for his political career. Other examples were his friendships within the household of the heir apparent, Prince Edward. Edward's tutors, in particular Roger Ascham and Richard Cox, were close to Paget. Letters from Ascham show that Paget was his patron and that he got him a pension. Apart from being a tutor to Princess Elizabeth as well as Prince Edward, Ascham was famous as the author of the first book on archery, which was published in 1545. It was dedicated to Henry VIII but also gave fulsome thanks to William Paget in its preface. Cox was godfather to William's eldest son, Henry, and there are letters showing that they were good friends, including one in which Cox said, 'it delighteth me as much to babble with you as to talke sadly with many others.' There was discussion between them of the possibility of Henry Paget being educated alongside Prince Edward because they were the same age – though this did not seem to have actually happened. The seven-year-old prince wrote to Cox asking him to thank William Paget for the gift of a sandbox.

Most of these people in Paget's circle were Evangelical, but not all. And they shared an interest in humanist scholarship, which was often non-doctrinal. What happened to them when Catholicism returned under Queen Mary is indicative. For example, Cox felt the need to flee; but Ascham did not, and worked under her regime as her Latin secretary, continuing in the same job under Elizabeth. Although the religious martyrs, Protestant and Catholic, achieved fame in history books that were frequently written with a religious bias, there were rather more individuals involved in Tudor government who were as 'flexible' as William Paget, whose probable Evangelical tendencies were trumped by his desire to deliver stable government, which dovetailed neatly with his personal and family interests. There is an interesting letter from Cox to Paget in which he says that measures such as the Dissolution of the Monasteries should be in the service of 'godly' religious reform. 'Godly' was the word most often used by Evangelicals to signal to each other. Cox goes on to say that unfortunately such measures were being exploited by 'wolves' for their own gain and that the King should act like a 'godly lyon' (lion) to defeat the wolves. Frankly, it is difficult to see how such sentiments could be squared with the fact that Henry VIII, Paget and others close to the King were massively benefitting materially from the dissolutions. Could the Coxes of this world have really been unaware of this? It's unlikely. Presumably they did not really care too much so long as it was the 'godly' wolves that won out.[4]

* * *

Henry VIII's last years were dominated by three big questions. The wars with France and Scotland; the problems those wars caused for government finance and the factional infighting between the religious conservatives and reformists at Court. These three things were closely intertwined. Henry's pendular swings in religious policy were usually in sync with the oscillations of his foreign policy. And there was a very specific connection between the reform of religion, where it involved the confiscation of Church assets, and the need to raise money.

Paget was at the centre of all three issues. For the sake of clarity, despite the interconnection, we will look at these topics and his role in them separately, starting with finance.

In December 1543, Henry had agreed by a treaty with the Emperor Charles V to attack France with 42,000 troops, including many foreign mercenaries, by June of the following year. Henry himself commanded the armies in France for three months in the summer of 1544. The subsequent war, accompanied by another with Scotland, lasted for two years. The military and financial situation deteriorated when the Emperor made a separate peace with France at the Treaty of Crepy – which indeed it was from the English point of view! The initial budget for these wars was about £250,000. But the final cost was far higher, more than £650,000. Various innovations in European warfare which were happening at exactly this period, including the development of the artillery fortress on land and improvements to the galley fleets at sea, created an arms race that hugely increased the cost of war. It has been calculated that the cost of Charles V's campaigns grew from an annual average of 430,000 ducats in the 1530s to 900,000 in the 1540s – more than double.[5] Similarly, the financial situation for Henry grew worse and worse during the wars of his later years. England was effectively bankrupted, only saved from complete disaster by the arrival of peace – just in time. Towards the end of the period, it was a serious worry as to whether the troops could be paid and the English State had almost lost its creditworthiness – with Continental bankers looking at 15 per cent interest and full repayment of loan and interest in nine months. In addition to these massive loans, mainly arranged in Antwerp through the King's permanent representative there, Stephen Vaughan, more and more desperate measures were considered or enacted to shore up the finances. These included the sale of Crown lands, forced loans from wealthy nobles and bishops, the sale of the benefits arising from royal wardships, converting Crown plate into currency, debasing the coinage, and selling the lead stripped from the roofs of dissolved monasteries and the plate from churches. To the modern mind, much of royal finance would seem to be essentially plunder and banditry. Of course, justifying it by linking it with religious reform was an essential part of the sophistry of the English Reformation. Thus, in July 1545, Hertford (Edward Seymour/Somerset) wrote to Paget:

> where you desire my opinion secretly of your intention 'to borrow some of the plate in the churches' I think it is the readiest way of relief and the least chargeable to the King's subjects because God's service consisteth not in jewels, plate and ornaments ... and those things better employed for the weal and defence of the realm; which being well persuaded to the people shall satisfy them.

Hertford is a bit worried that this reveals that the King 'is driven to shift for money', but, then again, he thinks that is 'suspected and spoken of already'. Significantly he adds, 'I refer my opinion to you [Paget] and others who can more deeply weigh things.'[6]

Between the second half of 1544 until Henry's death in 1547, Paget operated with Wriothesley as the ad hoc committee on wartime finance. Between them they arranged and authorised the sale of Crown lands. Paget arranged loans from Antwerp bankers such as the Foggers, mainly through Stephen Vaughan. Paget was directly involved in organising and paying the mercenaries who were the backbone of Henry's army. For example, in August 1545 Vaughan reported to Paget that, 'Certain captains have this day asked for money,' saying that they were warned by Paget's letters to 'make themselves ready, and that money should be sent by commissioners'.[7] Paget and Wriothesley were in almost daily contact by letter. Paget's role was mainly telling Wriothesley what money was needed; with the latter trying to provide it. So, not surprisingly, as the situation became more dire, tension between the two men grew, with the Chancellor letting rip to the Secretary that, if he had been as careful in saving money as others had been in gathering it, there would have been a surplus available. But they had 'swept the house here clean'. In September, he wrote to Paget of the terrible state of the finances and 'yet you write to me still pay, pay, prepare for this and that'. He asked him 'to remind the King touching Parliament' (for money) as 'I see not how we shall live without some present help.' And he warned Paget that if debasement of the coinage was taken any further it would become worthless because 'touching the Mint we be now so ferr out with it, that, and you take any peny more from it this three monethes … you shall utterly destroy the trade of it, and men shall clearly withdraw their resort thither.'

The relationship between the two men reached breaking point, with an angry letter from Wriothesley on 7 November complaining that, 'You [bid me] runne as thoughe I could make money [I would] I had that gift…' And, at the Privy Council meeting the next day, further 'words were spoken'. But it is worth remembering that these two had been close friends from way back in their school and university days. So they patched things up, with Wriothesley writing apologetically later in the day that 'weighty occupations' had engendered in him 'melancholy humours' and protesting to 'not take the matter seriously and is sure that my lady [Paget] would take his part.'[8] That the English State managed to avoid total bankruptcy, just, was because Paget's tireless efforts for peace were eventually crowned with success. That quest for peace is a large part of the story of his role in Henry's foreign policy. To which we now turn.

Chapter 7

Paget and Henry VIII's Foreign Policy, 1543–44

The best waie is bothe to kepe them from agreeing and from being either of them any greater.
>Paget's view on handling Francis I of France and the Emperor Charles V in his 1546 'Consultacion' document on foreign policy

Given his previous diplomatic experience, it is hardly surprising that Paget's first focus as Principal Secretary of State was in the field of foreign policy. The policy was Henry's – in all its narcissistic glory and shame. Much of its enactment was Paget's. Sometimes he was able to shift it in a more rational direction. In terms of modern British government, Paget seems to have combined the roles of Foreign Secretary and of the Principal Private Secretary at the FO.

In the latter role, he administered the actual mechanics of communication with foreign powers. At the most basic level, that meant overseeing a government postal and courier system – for example arranging relays of post horses to Dover, and financing royal couriers with advances to make their own way to foreign cities, and giving ambassadors allowances to pay for the couriers' return journeys. It meant constant correspondence with ambassadors, or with other important agents of the Crown based abroad, such as Stephen Vaughan in the Low Countries. This exchange of news was the basic information that informed policy decisions. Most important, in this age of absolute monarchs, was the Court gossip relayed by the ambassadors, particularly from the courts of the big two, Francis I and Charles V. But these sixteenth-century communications were slow and variable. Charles V's biographer quotes a fascinating analysis of 10,000 letters received by the government of Venice from ten different locations between 1497 and 1532. The average, or 'normal' time for a letter to arrive from Rome was four days, from Paris twelve days and from London twenty-four days. And, at least as significant as the slow average speed was the unreliability of the timing. Only 38 per cent of the letters from Rome arrived in 'normal' time, with some taking up to nine days.

The equivalent figures for Paris were 13 per cent and thirty-four days; for London 12 per cent and fifty-two days.[1]

As was normal for government in this age, the personal was intertwined seamlessly with the official. So Paget looked after the personal interests of the ambassadors and agents. In February 1544, the ambassador to Charles V complained to Paget that his expenses had greatly increased by having to follow the travelling court of the Emperor and 'begs Paget to remind the King'. In May, the ambassador to Brussels asked for licences to export beer and horses from England. While Stephen Vaughan requested, in view of his many services, to be granted 'the fee simple [absolute ownership] of a few houses that his Majesty gave to me and mine male heirs in London'. And three months later he thanked Paget and the King for so doing.

Just as Paget looked after his ambassadors and agents' personal interests, they looked after his. So, we have the royal courier collecting for Paget from the Low Countries some plumes enhanced with gold, made by the same craftsman who made similar ones for the King; Chamberlain, another royal agent in the Low Countries, arranging the delivery of sable furs for Lady Paget and reporting that, 'Your coffer, barrel of sturgeon and bits, I have laden in a hoy [type of ship] which departs within two days'; Vaughan wrote to Paget that he had sent him, 'in the ship that carries the King's gunpowder', all sorts of gear, including 'ells of the best crimson velvet to be had in Antwerp'; and the ambassador to Charles V worried about Paget's wine delivery. The details of these personal benefits were openly recorded in the same messages as the official reports, without any embarrassment, as this was completely normal for the time. Along with information about Italian and Papal goings on, Edmund Harvel, representative of England in Venice, added, 'the drugs which Paget required [are] to be delivered' and, mixed in with news of what the Emperor was up to in Germany, Chamberlain wrote, 'Would be glad to hear that you like the crimson velvet and white damask. Your chimney tiles shall be made within these 14 days.' As many examples show, the Paget family must have been living a life of great grandeur and luxury by this time. Coming from Antwerp for the Chief Secretary, in addition to all the above items, was not only silver plate stamped with his arms, but also four or five musicians/minstrels for the household. And a royal grant of May 1545 licences him, 'to retain, over and above his daily attendants and those under him in offices, 40 persons, gentleman or yeomen, in his livery'. Not bad for the son of a shearsman.[2]

In this 'you scratch my back, I'll scratch yours' relationship between the Chief Secretary and the representatives of his country abroad, there's a particularly close tie between Stephen Vaughan and Paget. Probably dating from the days when they both worked for Thomas Cromwell (the Vaughan/Cromwell relationship features in the Hilary Mantel books), the Paget and Vaughan families were obviously close. Vaughan's wife had died recently and he wrote touchingly to Paget that the cloth, 'for your night gown and my lady's [Lady Paget] murrey velvet will I send with all diligence, but I shall be very curious in choosing the colour, because my lady would have it like to the colour of a damask that my late wife ware.' And the letter continues, describing how his maid,

> named Anne Kydney, who has been in his house three or four years, is by evil enticement fallen into great lightness, drawing to her a great rout of lewd fellows who use his house as their own and threaten his servants. To be so shamefully abused while serving his Prince in a strange country almost drives him out of his mind and is worse than twenty fevers. Begs Paget to send one or two 'honest and sad men' to the house to examine the servants, and, making as little bruit as possible, warn the maid that her conduct has come to the King's ears, and rid her out of the house, in which she has shown so evil an example to his young children and other servants, speaking to her, however, in such a way as rather to win her from evil than drive her to it by despair, and get the names of such as haunt the house, that Paget may punish them.[3]

One imagines that 'honest and sad' might mean 'honest and severe'! This quote not only reveals the 'exchange of favours' culture, the close relationship between Paget and Vaughan but also the extraordinary level of detailed involvement that the Chief Secretary had in affairs. In addition, the fact that Vaughan, a very important and effective player in the world of Tudor government and finance, seemed so hopeless when managing his domestic affairs because his wife had died hints at the underrated importance of women in sixteenth-century history: an aspect we shall later return to in relation to William Paget's wife, Anne.

Paget's main role in Henry's foreign policy was to handle the triangular diplomacy between England, France and the Empire in the face of the war with France. For three years he was to spend a lot of time on diplomatic missions to the Continent. Although this was his forte, he suffered for it because it meant a great many Channel crossings and he was not a good sailor. Before the nineteenth century, crossing the Channel was quite a business, wind dependent and often delayed. Because of the direction of the prevailing wind, it was quicker from Dover to Calais than the other way round, but crossing times varied from three to twenty hours and ships often had to wait outside the harbour for high tide or to row passengers to the beach in a small rowing boat. After one bad crossing, William wrote to his co-Secretary Petre, 'I need not tell you I was sick, but indeed I was so sick I would have given one thousand pounds [if I had been a rich man] to have been on land.'[4]

The background was that, at the end of 1543, Henry and the Emperor had agreed to invade France in person by the end of June in the following year. Their strategy was a pincer movement, Henry from Calais, Charles from Luxembourg. Charles's motivation was fairly clear. It was to safeguard his dominions, which were continually harassed by the French. The English motivation was less obvious. In so far as English foreign policy in relation to France and the Habsburg Empire was 'rationally' motivated, it had to do with maintaining the European 'balance of power' – a motive which has continued to be very important down the centuries.

It may seem strange that this would result in an alliance with Charles: because, at first sight, he appeared to be infinitely more powerful than Francis. His empire was huge, ruling the Netherlands, Spain, Germany and most of Italy, with the goldmine of Central and South America thrown in. France was just France, though intermittently triumphing in constantly wartorn Italy. But that Charles's dominions were vast and widespread was precisely his problem. In addition to confronting the French, he had to simultaneously deal with the Turks and the Lutherans. In an age when the physical presence of a charismatic absolute ruler often made the difference between success and failure, his situation is vividly illustrated by an analysis of the location and movements of his life. Ten thousand days spent in the Netherlands, 6,500 in Spain, 3,000 in Germany, and 1,000 in Italy. He visited France four times (195 days), North Africa and England twice each (99 and 44 days respectively) and spent 260 days at sea travelling between different parts of his empire.[5] Back in 1520, when the rivalry between Francis and Charles was just beginning, the former smugly remarked of the latter, 'Because his dominions are scattered in various places far from one another, and are as disobedient and difficult … he will be forced to hold and keep them without trying to acquired anything more.'[6] Whereas Francis felt no such inhibitions in respect of his own actions. In April 1542, Paget passed on to Henry VIII a canny opinion given him by a French minister:

> England is a kingdom perpetuel, and so is Ffraunce. Our masters, their children, their succession may royne [reign] forever; we be under one clyme and one complexion, we be at one hande one to another. Th' empereur is but one, and when he is dead sum Almayn [some German] may be empereur, I wote [know] not who. Truth it is that Spayne is a

kingdome, but what is that alone? ... And as for Italy, when th'empereur is dead who shalbe master?[7]

So one can understand why Henry and Paget could, perfectly rationally, regard France as at least just as much a threat to the European 'balance of power' as the Empire.

However, Henry's motivation also seemed quixotic and narcissistic. He had a personal rivalry with Francis I and a grievance that he had failed to receive the 'pension' agreed at the end of the previous war in exchange for renouncing English claims to French territory. And there was the perennial issue of French help to Scotland. But one has to conclude that Henry just fancied a bit of military glory as well. Anyhow, in the succinct words of the Preface to the *Letters and Papers of the Reign of Henry VIII* for these months, 'There was always enough national prejudice against France and the Scots; and the King was only proceeding on old lines of policy to cripple the power of the latter first and the former afterwards.'[8] In the spring of 1544, the English, under Lisle (John Dudley/Warwick/Northumberland) in charge of the fleet and Hertford (Edward Seymour/Somerset) commanding the army, attacked Edinburgh and defeated the Scots. With Scotland dealt with for the moment, Henry could turn his full attention to the war with France.

* * *

Henry dispatched Paget on a mission to integrate his war plans with those of the Empire. Before leaving, Paget called in on Chapuys and he immediately wrote to the Imperial authorities to confirm that 'the said secretary is a discreet personage and in credit with his master' and 'has always shown inclination to the Emperor's service'.[9] Charles was in Speyer in the Rhineland. But Paget first went to Brussels to coordinate the war plans with the Emperor's Regent, his sister, Mary, Queen of Hungary.

She was an interesting character, whose life illustrates the complexities of the Europe-wide Habsburg Empire. So it is worth digressing for a moment to explain who she was. Born in Brussels, daughter of King Philip I of Spain and granddaughter of the Holy Roman Emperor Maximilian I, she was married aged 10 to Louis King of Hungary – although they did not live together for a few more years. In Hungary, she met Luther and she continued to have some sympathy for Protestantism. She was madly in love with her husband and was devastated when he was killed at the battle of Mohacs, the decisive victory of the Turkish Ottoman Empire of Suleiman the Magnificent. That death marked the end of the Hungarian dynasty, the dynastic claims passing to the Habsburgs. So Mary initially stayed on as queen of the part of Hungary not annexed by the Turks. Despite attempts to marry her a second time, to James V of Scotland and Frederick of Bavaria, she vowed never to remarry and always wore the gold heart-shaped medallion that her husband had been wearing when killed in battle. (When she died many years later in Spain, she left instructions for the medallion to be melted down and the gold given to the poor.)

But her brother the Emperor Charles V did persuade her to take the job of Governor, or Regent, of the Netherlands. He respected her talents as a ruler. However, brother and sister had a sometimes stormy relationship. For example, she was the guardian of one of their sister's children after their mother died. When Charles arranged, for the usual dynastic reasons, to marry one of them, Christina, aged 10, to the Duke of Milan and for the marriage to be consummated immediately, Mary resisted and managed to delay the moment for two years. She succeeded in this because the convention was that, although children could be married, they were not supposed to share a bed until they were 12. Also, relevant to our story, she was always a moderating influence on Charles, promoting peace, whether with France or between the Habsburgs and their Protestant subjects. Although she was obliged to suppress Evangelicalism in the Netherlands, she tried to enforce her brother's religion as little as possible. Not known as a great looker – she suffered from the notorious Habsburg thick under lip – she was renowned for being passionate about hunting. She was also a great patron of music and a collector of art. Her collection included the astonishingly beautiful Roger van de Weyden Deposition of Christ which is in the Prado and the famous *Arnolfini Marriage* painting in the National Gallery.

So William's first stop was to meet this formidable woman, effectively ruler of the Netherlands, in her Brussels palace. As he reported back to the King, he first told her of 'the progress of Henry's affairs in Scotland, at which she rejoiced'. She then asked how English preparations for the invasion of France were coming along and he replied that 'the King's folks would shortly begin to pass the seas'. She promised to 'send forth her navy' and prepare supply wagons to help. Paget reassured her that, once the English had invaded, she need not worry about French attacks, 'as they would more look to defend themselves than invade others'. They also discussed the attempts by the French to break up their alliance. She said she had heard of 'letters between the King and the French king, who had similarly gone about to allure her'. And Paget answered that 'he had heard of the French king's sending her hawks [knowing of her love of hunting] to insinuate a practice [an intrigue/negotiation] and trusted that she had and would answer as honourably as Henry had done.' She, in turn, was suspicious and asked to see what Henry had actually replied to the French and the well-prepared Paget whipped out the appropriate letter to show her.[10] Of course, throughout this period, both the Empire and the English were constantly talking to the French about a separate peace in breach of their alliance, despite, at the same time, offering reassurance that such a thing was out of the question.

When Paget arrived to meet the Emperor himself in Speyers after a few days' journey, it was a similar conversation. The Emperor's response to Paget's report of the English success in Scotland was a bit of blatant ego massage from one monarch to another, saying, 'although Henry had beaten them so often in Scotland, it was a novelty to spoil and ruinate the principle city of a realm with so many towns and villages and come home so far by land with so little loss.' Charles declared that, 'he's specially pleased that they sent him a Councillor to visit him … that the world might see the love between them [Henry and himself].' Paget showed him the correspondence between the French and Henry to reassure him that a separate peace would not happen. Then they both had a go at the French. Paget pointed out that the French wrote in, 'such a fine French sort as to imply that more had been done than was done', although he was sure that the Emperor 'was not inexpert of the French practices'. And Charles replied that he did indeed know very well, 'the French king's finesse and his fashion to charge other men with things which himself deviseth'.

According to their agreement, Henry and Charles were both supposed to lead their armies in person. But, despite their pride and machismo egos, they were both of a certain age and not very healthy. So there was a bit of sparring about that. Chapuys had written before Paget's mission about Henry's imprudent obstinacy in wanting the military glory of leading the army, 'for, beside his age and weight, he has the worst legs in the world, such as those who have seen them are astonished that he does not stay continually in bed' and yet how he 'would hold it a point of honour to go' if the Emperor did. And so, in this conversation between Paget and Charles, the Emperor urged Henry to be prudent, whereas, 'for himself, he is well and lusty, and ten years younger than Henry.' Paget, knowing that Charles suffered from gout, replied by pointing out the inconvenience that would arise, 'if the Emperor's invasion of France should be checked by falling sick of gout or other disease' and he threw in another subtle argument to dissuade the monarchs from leading their armies. He said that it was 'more convenable for a lieutenant to spoil and waste a country', pointing to the example of how 'this late journey into Scotland is much to Henry's reputation [whereas] if he had gone in person, and returned without taking and keeping some strengths, men would have thought he had done little.'

This sparring about rulers leading their armies, the machismo of monarchs, then segued into the more substantial detail of what was to be the agreed nature of the English and Imperial campaigns. Paget established, and the Emperor did not disagree, that Henry could lead his army personally or not, as he wished; that the English invasion force could be more like 30,000 rather than 42,000 men; and that the English campaign need not necessarily push deep into France. The account of this important meeting then reads, 'Was proceeding thus when the Emperor [perhaps weary of standing, for they had been together and hour and a half] said he would think more of it and was ready to give them leave to depart.' But, so far as I can see, Charles never did get back to Paget on this. So, while Paget's limit on the English contribution to the war was implicitly accepted by Charles, it was not explicitly agreed. Which was something that became relevant when the Empire later made a separate peace with the French. But Paget's mission had been fairly successful and the Emperor's letter to Henry on the day of his departure, 'thanks him for sending a person of such quality'.[11]

On the return journey, Paget called in at Antwerp to try to sort out what was a typical problem to do with the hiring of mercenaries for Henry's army. The commissioners for the Crown had been trying to get hold of 4,000 infantry and 100 cavalry commanded by one Chrisoff von Landsberg. But it was reported to Paget that these mercenaries, knowing they had got the English over a barrel, were demanding 'double pays'. Worse, it was claimed that Landsberg told Stephen Vaughan that, 'he had been bold in his days to displease an Emperor and a king of Rome, and so he durst a king of England.' And, when Vaughan, in reply, 'spake somewhat roundly to him', he threatened to cut him to pieces. Not surprisingly, Paget's advice, backed up by a Privy Council order, recommended Vaughan to get shot of von Landsberg. However, two days later, Vaughan got a message to Paget that the mercenaries' 'folly towards him they now seem to repent' and, furthermore, he feared that 'the sending of them back might give an ill will to the King's service and an excuse to serve France.'[12] It seems the final result was a compromise involving employing the cavalry but not the infantry.

Employing mercenaries meant dealing with very dubious characters. For instance, there was a certain Ludovico dalle Armi, a thug who was involved in several violent incidents in Italy while employed by Henry to recruit mercenaries. Paget had to smooth things over with the Venetian authorities. He also continued to be involved in the vexed issue of soldiers' wages. In April 1546, he wrote to Petre, that it, 'would be well if the King would give like wages to his own men as to strangers', because, when an English soldier sees a mercenary better paid, 'his heart is killed'.[13] But, with the mercenaries able to offer their services elsewhere – including to the enemy French – and the English finances at breaking point, this situation was never likely to be remedied.

After Antwerp, Paget went through Brussels again, where he missed a return meeting with Mary Queen of Hungary because she had 'gone hunting'. She reported that, 'after waiting for Paget's coming two days she went to the fields.' As he did not have anything important to tell her, 'he would not have her leave the chase'. 'In that', she said, 'he was courteous, but she would rather have spoken with him than taken her pastime, were it only to make her affectionate recommendations to the King.'[14] William was probably keen to get home after his no doubt very exhausting, if productive, mission. Indeed, after recounting all to the Privy Council, he went off to his newly built mansion at West Drayton for a rare and well-earned rest of four days, sending a message that is the Tudor equivalent of an 'out of office' email, 'I depart tomorrow in the morning to my house and will not be here again until Saturday.'[15]

For the next month, Paget was involved in setting up the regency of Queen Katherine Parr and the stay-at-home Privy Councillors to cover the absence of the King and his accompanying councillors while they were away at war. And, to consolidate the peace with Scotland, he helped negotiate the marriage of Henry's niece, Lady Margaret Douglas, to the Earl of Lennox.

Chapter 8

Diplomacy and War

> [We] have cause to be at the point of despair to find any friendship in either of them longer than they maye not chose.
> Paget on France and the Empire, from his 1546 'Consultacon'

In June 1544, Henry, along with Paget, went off to France to play at soldiers. There is a magnificent picture from the Royal Collection displayed at Hampton Court of *The Embarkation of Henry VIII at Dover*. This actually shows another time Henry left the country, to meet Francis I on the 'Field of the Cloth of Gold' in 1520. But one imagines the scene twenty-four years later would have been similar. The royal party arrived in Calais on 14 July and were keen to get into the action, not least because there was plague in town. They reported to the Duke of Suffolk, Henry's military commander besieging Boulogne, 'for they begin to die here of the sickness'.[1] Not so keen, however, as to arrive before Suffolk could reassure them that their headquarters would be out of range of the French artillery!

Paget, along with other rich landowners, had contributed his own band of 100 retainers, soldiers to the cause. These were men gathered from his West Drayton estate and, indicative of the nature of sixteenth-century warfare, there is a list of how the 100 were armed. Only fifteen had firearms, which were hagbuts (long barrelled guns), fifteen were archers and the remaining seventy had either pikes (a long spear) or bills (curved and hooked blades mounted on a staff). It appears William had little to do with them. They would have simply been part of the force under Suffolk's command outside Boulogne. Henry stayed in France for three months, and achieved his much trumpeted – though really rather minor – military victory by capturing Boulogne. At the end of September, he and Paget returned to England.[2]

Despite the war, there continued to be diplomatic negotiations between France and both her adversaries. As ever, William was heavily involved. The instructions to Cardinal Bellay and the other French negotiators in early September were to offer some, though not all, of the 'pension' that Henry claimed that Francis owed him if the English gave up Boulogne. Interestingly those instructions ended with the authorisation to, 'make promises of money to such as seem to have influence in this business, especially to secretary Paget'. We do not know whether bribes were actually offered but the French and English delegations met at Hardelot, south of Boulogne, where they talked for several days and 'supped together' while their armies were still fighting a few miles away.[3] This was often the way in sixteenth-century wars between monarchs. But meanwhile two important events made these negotiations largely irrelevant. Boulogne fell, and more significantly, the Emperor made a separate peace with France at the Treaty of Crepy.

The Emperor sent assurances that he 'would not forsake his old approved friend for a new reconciled friend' and Henry did not have strong grounds for complaint in that he had been looking at the possibility of a separate peace himself and because he failed to help his ally by carrying the war into the heart of France. But essentially Henry was now left high and dry. The only sensible option was to make peace with France. But this was not to be for another twenty months. The problem was Boulogne: not terribly important in itself, but taking on 'symbolic importance'. Neither side was prepared to give it up. This was Henry's 'magnificent' military victory, his tinpot Agincourt. While for Francis it was a part of France and its loss a humiliating defeat.[4]

However, the tireless Paget had to go to meet the French for further peace talks. These happened in Calais under the neutral chairmanship of the Bishop of Arras, the Emperor's representative; Cardinal Bellay again leading the French delegation. Everyone said how much they wanted peace. But Bellay made it clear that 'their master would, for the weal of Christendom, continue the pension and pay the arrearages at reasonable terms, but would not renounce the amity of Scotland or forgo Bullogne [Boulogne].'[5] In the account sent to Henry, the English made it equally clear that they would not give up Boulogne. At this point, the discussions 'began to wax warm' with the English claim that there was not a man in the realm 'but would spend all he had in its [Boulogne's] defence' and the French bragging, equally unconvincingly, 'of their army of 30,000 men that should come yet to besiege Boulloyn'. Incidentally, a little aside, being a dyslexic who finds spelling difficult, I find it very gratifying that the great and the good in Tudor times did not give a fig for correct spelling. There was no standard spelling. If it sounded right, it was right. Paget had three different spellings for Boulogne in this one dispatch to his King: Bullogne, Boulloyn and Bullen!

The real worry for Paget and the King at this point might have been that the Emperor and the French, possibly aided by the Pope, would gang up on England. Cardinal Bellay tried to play on this fear. Paget's account read, 'the Cardinal took me, the Secretary, by the hand apart' and warned that few of the French king's council were sympathetic to Henry and that 'the bishop of Rome had ... offered to spend in this quarrel all jewels he hath and his triplicem coronam.' Paget pooh-poohed this and reported to Henry, slipping in a nice bit of flattery, 'as your Majesty warned me ... to beware of their [the French] subtlety, I said yea and nay, and that, as for your being left alone, you mistrusted not the amity of the Emperor.' A few days later, Paget and Bellay had another go at coming up with a peace treaty, throwing in to the mix the possibility of marrying Henry's younger daughter Elizabeth to 'some prince of France' and swapping Boulogne for some other bit of territory. But once again nothing came of it as both sides wanted Boulogne, and the war continued in a fairly desultory fashion.[6]

Despite Paget's denial to Bellay of any worry among the English about the Emperor's continued friendship, there was in fact real concern on that front. A backup strategy, if the worst happened, was alliance with the German Protestants. Using a classic bit of diplomatese, that would do for any era in the FO, he suggested, 'it seems not amiss to entertain them with practice.' Christopher Mont, his agent with the German states, wrote to him that various German Protestants, 'hearing of the peace between the Emperor and the French king ... feared some danger ... and also some injury to Henry, through the wiles of the Roman pontiff' and that they therefore wanted to explore the possibility of alliance. There was further communication, but nothing concrete emerged.[7]

More importantly, this worry – that conflict with the Empire would occur at the same time as war with France – increased when problems arose from practical issues to do with the exercise of neutrality by the Empire in the Netherlands. The English expected Charles to both allow English employed mercenaries to cross their territories and to deny the transport of supplies to the French army. The Emperor, reasonably, saw this as a rather one-sided interpretation of neutrality. When the English impounded ships that were transporting herrings for the French army, Charles V did his nut, or, in the words of Wotton, the English ambassador at the Imperial court, writing to Paget, 'taketh a little pepper in the nose'. Charles retaliated by arresting Stephen Vaughan and other Englishmen in Antwerp and impounding their goods. For a few months, trade between England and the Netherlands was seriously disrupted. There was a moment in January 1545 when Paget and Henry panicked that Charles might be actually contemplating war with England. Paget wrote to Lord Cobham, governor of Calais, 'The King, having last week dispatched a post to his ambassadors with the Emperor and hearing nothing again ... requires you to learn the truth ... with all possible diligence,' and adds, 'Hast [Haste] post, hast, hast for thy life, for thy life, for thy life.' In other words, EXTREMELY URGENT. This addition was marked 'from Westminster, 21 Jan at 10pm'. Is it too fanciful to see this as equivalent of the slightly hysterical late evening email, maybe after a drink or two?[8]

Anyhow, William had to set off yet again to smooth things down with Charles, after first having to endure a particularly horrible Channel crossing. When he arrived in Brussels, the Emperor was in a distinctly unfriendly mood. Paget had never seen him 'so round and quick'. When taxed about the separate peace with the French, he snaps back, 'it was your not going forward according to your treaty that drave me to do as I did.' (Charles seemed to have forgotten that, in their previous meeting before the attack on France was launched, described above, he had failed to dissent from Paget's suggestion that Henry might well not push deep into French territory. Charles had not explicitly agreed to it either, and Paget felt that his silence implied consent.) They then bickered over the value of the seized goods. It was a hostile atmosphere and Brussels was awash with rumours of a deep rift between Charles and Henry. The isolated and weak English position was not helped by the arrival of news that the Scots, who had been increasingly united in opposition to English domination since the sacking of Edinburgh a year before, had inflicted a significant defeat on the English army of the north at the battle of Ancrum Moor. Paget nonetheless rejected what he saw as an inadequate offer from the Empire to resolve their disputes.[9]

And, as things were not going too well, even while in mid-negotiation with the Empire, William dispatched an envoy to talk to the French, specifically to Francis I's sister, Marguerite, Queen of Navarre. The choice was not coincidental. She was another fascinating strong woman whom Paget encountered while doing diplomacy for Henry. Like Cardinal Bellay, like Paget, like Henry himself when he was not being a brutal tyrant, she was a creature of the Renaissance and the Reformation, a cultured humanist, admired by many such as Erasmus. She was a patron of the arts and literature, a supporter of Leonardo and Rabelais and she was sympathetic to Protestantism – or was at any rate a force for religious toleration. Anne Boleyn had known and admired her when she had been at the French Court. Interestingly, a year before Paget's mission, Anne's daughter Elizabeth (later Elizabeth I) had translated a poem, 'Mirror of the Sinful Soul', written by Marguerite, when Elizabeth was only 11. She then presented it to her stepmother, Queen Katherine Parr. Of more direct relevance to Paget, the Queen of Navarre had been very friendly when he had been ambassador in 1542, when she had told him of her regard for Henry and her dislike of Charles. Now Paget's envoy told her that Henry, 'wanted to abandon the Emperor, who had made peace without him and was seeking to ruin them both'. And he made the offer of marriage between one of the English princesses and the French heir, the Duke of Orleans, throwing in the additional tasty little incentive, that since Edward, Henry's son, was a weakling and liable to die, then 'Orleans should be king [of England]'. Maybe the French were tempted, but in the end they answered 'non', unless Boulogne, always the stumbling block, was first returned.

The French did not only reject this peace offer, they also leaked it to the Imperial side in order to embarrass Paget. And he certainly was embarrassed. As he told it to Henry, one of the Imperial negotiators, a certain Mr Scory, paused in the midst of the talks and, 'after three or four turns, walking in the chamber, said suddenly, smiling, "What, Monsr. le Secretary, you are waxen of late a great Practitioner with the Queen of Navarre."' 'The words so amazed me,' Paget continued, 'that he might have seen my blushing had it been day.'[10] Nevertheless, despite the embarrassment, and quite possibly partly because of pressure resulting from this double dealing, Paget did eventually get a reasonable agreement with the Empire. This was that all grievances be referred to an arbitration commission appointed by the two sides. In this commission, which then sat for a few months, inevitably the two sides did not often agree on practical matters. But at least trade between England and the Netherlands could resume and the possibility of a dangerous break with the Empire had been avoided. The fundamental reason for this (as all good Marxist historians would tell you!) was the vital commercial interest – mainly over wool and cloth – between England and the Netherlands, Charles's richest province. But Paget's skilful, if devious, diplomacy certainly helped. In fact, when Paget got back to London, it was reported that his negotiations, 'much pleased the King and Council, who … told the mayor, sheriffs and burgesses of London that relations with the Emperor were never better and they might trade freely.'[11]

But for William the success of his mission will have been completely overshadowed in its last weeks by the news that his wife Anne was dangerously ill. He begged his co-Secretary Petre to look after his children if she were to die and 'if she be alive to go to her and comfort her in the King's name,' adding, 'I trust, though his Majesty knew it, he will not be displeased withal.' He then hears that she has died. This is a moment, when researching my ancestor's life while in Coronavirus lockdown, I felt the chill of real history, as T. S. Eliot puts it in the *Four Quartets*:

> That the past experience revived in the meaning
> Is not the experience of one life only
> But of many generations – not forgetting
> Something that is probably quite ineffable:
> The backward look behind the assurance

> Of recorded history, the backward half-look
> Over the shoulder, towards the primitive terror.

On 6 April 1545, William Paget wrote again to Petre that he was leaving tomorrow to return to his

> sorrowful house where I shall not find what I left behind me at my parting, but a sort of poor miserable infants weeping and lamenting their inestimable loss of their mother, my most obedient, wise, gentle and chaste wife, the remembrance of whom sitteth so deep in my heart that ... the same well near to burst from pain and anguish. I thought to have had a fortunate journey (and touching the common affairs it is so), but, to me, it is the most grievous that ever I had, and, were it not for the goodness of my master and my desire to serve him and my country, I would desire no longer to live.[12]

It must have been an incredibly sad journey home. But, miracle of miracles, he arrived to find her alive! We can assume she was suffering from one of the very frequent plagues of Tudor times, probably the sweating sickness that had nearly killed the young Paget and had carried off Thomas Cromwell's wife, and that, in the words of Boris Johnson, British Prime Minister contemporary to this writing and another survivor of a serious illness, 'it could have gone either way.' By 20 April, several ambassadors were writing to Paget to say how glad they were to hear that 'my lady your bedfellow' had fully recovered.

Chapter 9

Peace, Eventually

[Paget] had told the King [Henry VIII] that unless the situation was untangled with the King of France, then [there] would be war which would damage not only each Kingdom but the whole of Christianity.
de Selve (French ambassador) to Connetable (French minister), August 1547

Meanwhile, the war with France was hotting up. Reports of a likely French invasion came flooding in to Paget and others. He was closely involved in detailed preparations. To take one example, he was in communication with one of the royal agents in Antwerp about the purchase and delivery of 1,200 Italian-made 'hacquebute' guns, powder and 4,000 Norwegian spars to form shafts for lances.[1] There is correspondence with the Duke of Suffolk, the King's military commander in the South of England, on building up the defences around Portsmouth. They had enough spades and shovels, sent from London, but were short of mattocks (similar to a pickaxe). The King himself had noted this deficiency, so you can imagine that they got to work pretty sharpish to get more of those mattocks made in nearby Winchester and Southampton and promised to get them delivered 'by Monday'.[2]

For a brief moment, it did look as if the English would be needing all the arms they could get and all the defences they could build, because a French fleet arrived in the Solent and the *Mary Rose* calamity occurred. This infamous event, involving the loss of an important ship, its treasure and 500 men, was not caused by enemy action but by the ship capsizing because water rushed in through the open gun ports when a sudden breeze sprang up.[3] However, luckily in view of this disaster, the French invasion never really materialised. There was an ineffective attack on the English fleet and a couple of very minor and short-lived landings – one recorded in a plaque at Seaview on the Isle of Wight.

The threat to the south coast receded, but the danger of losing Boulogne, or even Calais, in battle, persisted. Still more worrying to Paget and others was the appalling damage to the national finances caused by the continued war. But they had to tread very carefully because Henry was still determined to keep Boulogne, which he referred to as 'his daughter'. And he was being encouraged in his obstinacy by the Duke of Surrey, his hothead commander on the Continent. Paget, and Surrey's father, the redoubtable Duke of Norfolk, were risking Henry's anger (and we all know what that could lead to) when Norfolk wrote to his son, 'Mr Paget desired me to write to you in nowise to animate the King to keep Boleyne.'[4]

Despite Henry's determination to keep Boulogne, William had to cross the Channel yet again to meet the French for peace talks. After another terrible crossing, on which he reported he was 'as sea sick as ever man was', he met with the French delegation, while the German Protestants acted as mediators this time.[5] The policy Henry and Paget were pursuing was a complicated double game. If we just consider bilateral Anglo-French relations, it was fairly straightforward. Both sides wanted peace. They offered each other various combinations of financial incentives, proposals to do with Scotland, and marriage alliances: but repeatedly stumbled on the issue of Boulogne. Where things got complicated was when the five-way relationships, mainly over religion, between the Emperor, the German Protestant princes, England, France and the Pope, were added into the mix. The German Protestants were mediating because they saw the war between England and France as bringing the latter closer to their enemies, or potential enemies, the Emperor and the Pope. While the Emperor was also mediating because he saw the war as preventing the help of France, and maybe even England, in his desire to crush, or at any rate control, the German Protestants. So Henry's policy was aimed at encouraging both, the Protestants and the Empire, in their hopes, even though these were in direct contradiction with each other. The objective being that both the Protestants and the Empire would then put pressure on France to agree to a peace on Henry's terms.

So, while Paget led the negotiations with the French mediated by the Protestants, Bishop Gardiner was at the court of Charles V to negotiate with the French under the auspices of Imperial mediation. This fitted with the natural inclinations of both English envoys, in that Gardiner inclined to Catholicism and Paget to Evangelism. But there was a difference. Gardiner really was a 'true believer', seeing the German Protestants as having 'detestable opinions', whereas Paget, as we see throughout his life, was much less of a religious fanatic. And he was well in with Henry's double game. When the Protestants were suspicious of and complained about Gardiner's mission, Paget reassured them that it was much better to have him abroad at Charles V's court than back home influencing Henry in a conservative/Catholic direction. And he reported to Henry that he had kept the Protestants happy by telling them, 'that he [Paget] is Evangelic' and, 'has promised [for the advancement of this matter] much more than he will abide by' (as Will Somers – Henry's jester – says). This devious diplomacy did not bear immediate fruit – in that peace with France was still several months off. But it probably did succeed in putting pressure on the French. And, notwithstanding their contradictory aims, both the Protestants and the emperor remained adequately satisfied with English policy for the time being. So, with peace not yet achieved but looking a bit closer as a result of his efforts, Paget got back to Dover on 6 January 1546, with, poor man, as he reports to Petre, yet another 'seasick head and stomach'.[6]

The year 1546 opened with some rather half-hearted diplomatic activity. Gardiner agreed a treaty with Charles V, further patching up the frayed relationship following the separate peace with France of a year earlier. And Paget was involved in talks about the possibility of Prince Edward marrying either the infant Mary, Queen of Scots or one of Charles's daughters. But, as the spring campaigning season arrived, the focus was again on the war with France around Boulogne. The Earl of Surrey launched an attack on a French fortress that went badly wrong. Although Paget reassured him that 'His Majesty, like a prince of wisdom, knows that who plays at a game of chance must sometimes lose,' Surrey, in a move that is significant in the domestic political intrigues to which we will turn in the next chapter, was replaced as commander by the Earl of Hertford (Seymour/Somerset).[7]

With Boulogne now more vulnerable than ever and the Crown nearing bankruptcy as a result of war, Paget, accompanied this time by Lisle (Dudley/Warwick/Northumberland), embarked on his sixth mission in search of peace with France.

It was yet another bad crossing. 'I savour still the ship and am very ill of being therein all this night,' he reported to Petre.[8] Ten days later, he wrote again, urging him to use his influence on Henry in the direction of peace. Peace, he said, is the 'present remedy' needed and he was hopeful that 'we will bring [it] from hence if you will send it first from thence.'[9] After further delays, the English and French delegations finally met. Negotiations did not, however, get off to a good start. They could not even agree whether to meet at the English fort of Guisnes or the French one facing it at Ardres: both were near Calais. So they ended up having to meet in a damp tent in a field between the two, in foul wet weather. Throughout the ensuing negotiations, it is curious to note that both the French and the English alternated offers involving one side keeping Boulogne and the other getting a big cash payoff. Initially it was the English who kicked off with the suggestion that they might give up Boulogne if the French came up with 8 million crowns in gold. The latter replied, 'You speak merrily. All Christendom have not so much money.' After a lot of sparring – this opening meeting lasted from 11.00 am to 6.00 pm – the English lowered the figure, first to 6 million and then to 3 million. But neither this nor any other basis for peace was agreed and the envoys decided to refer back to London and Paris. Paget reported despairingly that the French invited them to go hare hunting together the next day and saying acidly that he wished they would 'give less of their courtesy and more of their money'. He adds, 'If we agree not now (and I doubt it much) I will never open my lips for peace again, for, with prayer to God and with mind, heart and body, I have travailed for it in vain, for the quiet of my master and country.' All those fruitless hours of talk and those terrible Channel crossings were finally getting to him.[10]

On top of it all, Lisle, who admittedly was the English Admiral, left the negotiations to do a bit of fighting the French at sea. About which Paget was not at all happy, telling him he had better return 'to accomplish his commission (from which he was not revoked)' and 'pointing out in friendly sort that this departing from his charge seems neither honourable to the King nor him'. The French could hardly be expected to take the peace negotiations seriously when one of the chief envoys broke off mid-talks to fight them. And when it was suggested to them that Lisle might be replaced, they answered that, as they had begun with him, they 'will make an end [with him] or else let all alone.' (i.e. end the talks.) In view of the intense rivalry between Lisle (Dudley/Warwick/Northumberland) and Hertford (Seymour/Somerset) that is one of the central issues to emerge in Edward VI's reign, it is interesting that Lisle's threatened replacement at the talks was indeed Hertford. Anyhow, having been annoyed, Lisle did return to the negotiations sharpish, although he also complained to Petre that Paget 'does me a little wrong'.[11]

At this point, the French finally came up with a proposal that Paget felt he could recommend to Henry. England was to keep Boulogne for eight years, after which it was to be handed over to France, so long as the French paid 2 million crowns and returned to paying the pension that was agreed many years ago in exchange for the English renouncing their claims to other French lands. The disputed arrears were to be arbitrated. The treaty was to include peace with Scotland. Paget strongly recommended the deal because in reality it meant full possession of Boulogne, plus some cash. To make the point, when selling it to Henry, he retold an anecdote about a man condemned to death by a king. The king has a favourite donkey and the man, to save his life, promises to make it talk within a year. When he is told that is impossible, he answers, 'either the king will die, or the ass will die, or the ass will speak, or I shall die.'[12] In other words, by the time the eight years was up, the French might forfeit Boulogne through non-payment, or the French king might die, or there would be some other excuse not to give it up. 'Possession is nine tenths of the law.'

This was the breakthrough. But a treaty was not yet done and dusted. With spectacularly bad timing, on the very day that he wrote to London recommending the deal, William became ill – probably because of the damp and draughty tent where they had been meeting. Lisle reported, 'Sir William Paget goes this day to Callys [Calais], either to let blood or to purge, fearing a fever and unless he keeps himself very well I fear he will have it.' Meanwhile, Henry, while not disagreeing with the outline of the deal, quibbled about certain details, for example demanding that Paget ride with his French counterpart along the border between English and French 'France' to delineate the exact boundary. A few days later, Paget, having partly recovered, was obliged to do exactly that and because of an unresolved dispute about which tributary of a river determined the border, lost patience with the French, describing them as 'a false proud nation' and threatening, when writing to Petre, to ignore the safe conduct given to the envoys and to take them hostage if the talks collapsed.[13]

As often in the end game of a fraught negotiation between traditional enemies, war and peace hung in the balance until the very last moment. Paget and Lisle did eventually agree the details of an actual draft treaty with the French. But Henry, for no good reason, took his time getting back to them. The French threatened to leave and Paget had difficulty in persuading them to stay. Until the treaty was actually signed, both sides feared that the other was stringing them along without really wanting peace. So it is probable that Henry's eventual instruction to Paget and Lisle, 'to proceed in the name of God to the conclusion of the Treaty', and the signing of the Treaty of Camp the next day, came just in time – and to everyone's immense relief. It appears the treaty was so named because it was signed near a village called Camp – not, as I had assumed, because it was negotiated in a tent. Let alone because they all wore tights! Two days later, Paget was back in Dover writing to the King, 'The peace is signed and sealed and he has it with him but, with lying all day on the sea, he is too sick to ride. Signifies the good news and trusts to be with the King tomorrow.'[14]

Not surprisingly, Paget thought his advice was key in getting Henry to agree. Speaking to the French ambassador two years later, he claimed that

> he alone was the cause of the peace … and of the promise made by the late King to return Boulogne … And he dared to say that even the Cardinal of York [Wolsey] or Cromwell had not had the freedom to speak so frankly to the said King of the restitution of Boulogne, who was sometimes enraged when Paget explained his reasons.[15]

Although Paget was obviously 'bigging himself up', he had reason to be proud of having persuaded Henry to renounce the fruits of his only 'personal' military victory, the capture of Boulogne – even if the return was to be delayed. To have given Henry that advice must have taken courage; to have succeeded, great skill.

Given how important the relationship between Hertford (Seymour/Somerset) and William Paget was to prove in Henry's last days and then during the reign of Edward VI, it is worth illustrating how they had become very close at this time. While Hertford was away fighting the Scots, William had written regularly to keep him up to date on Court gossip and politics. After the Treaty of Camp was signed, Hertford supervised the building up of Boulogne's defences and was again in frequent communication with Paget. Their intimacy is shown by an ironic reference to William's notoriously bad 'sea legs', when Hertford refers to his own very calm Channel crossing, adding that it would have been a pleasant one for Paget, 'because ye are so good a seaman'. Employing troops who were keen to return home to build a breakwater to create an artificial harbour, Hertford devised an incentive scheme to speed up the work. He divided the men into competitive teams, offering financial rewards for fast work and the promise of returning home early to those who finished their section first. He successfully begged Paget to arrange for extra money to be sent and wrote to him bragging that 'such a piece of work was never done with such a number in so short a time'.[16]

Before leaving this account of foreign policy, it is worth telling a story about Anglo-French relations that occurred in the autumn of 1546. It is interesting for what it reveals of both the skill and the deviousness that characterised the diplomacy of Henry and Paget. The French were building a fortress near Boulogne that Lord Grey, governor of the town, felt threatened English security. The peace treaty had left it somewhat ambiguous as to whether this kind of thing was allowed by either side. An attempt was made to get the French to stop work. If that failed, as it did, Henry and Paget believed it was necessary to destroy the new French fortifications. But the Privy Council were unanimous in their view that any officially sanctioned attack would seriously endanger the newly made peace. So Paget drew up a letter, to which he attached the royal signature, forbidding Lord Grey to take action. But, at the same time, the messenger who was to deliver this letter was told to directly contradict it verbally and, indeed, order Grey, with the King's authority, to go ahead and raid the French fort. A night raid to destroy the fortifications duly occurred. And a secret letter (the one written in Paget's hand 'as though from the Council' referred to at the beginning of the last chapter) is sent, confirming the verbal order to Grey to 'overthrow in the night what they [the French] have wrought'. This arrived after the raid had happened but would have covered Grey's arse if the Privy Council had challenged his action – which was, after all, in direct conflict with their official order. The English raid meant that the new peace seemed to be shattered and many people feared that war would be renewed. That it was not was due to this devious fiction, concocted by Henry and Paget – that Grey had been told not to take any action, as per the official order from the Council. Therefore, Paget could tell the French ambassador, de Selve, that Grey had acted rashly and without orders. And de Selve could report to the French king that 'Paget asserts that his King said on hearing of it [the raid] that he thought that Lord Grey was too wise a man to act so rashly.' This was, in the language of the Preface to the *Letters and Papers*, a 'dish of diplomatic mendacity'. In other words, a barefaced lie. But it worked, the French were satisfied and the peace held.[17]

How can we sum up Paget's role in English foreign policy in the last three years of Henry VIII's reign? In August 1546, he penned a 'consultacion' for the king and council, an overview of English foreign policy. His 'care', or worry, centred on Francis's desire to get Boulogne back, the Pope's objective of regaining his 'tyranny over this realm' and the fact that neither Charles nor Francis could be trusted, of whom he said, 'little faith to given to any of their promises (when the breche of the same may serve their purpose)'. He stressed that England needed to build its strength, home and abroad, establishing as much unity as possible, 'gathering of riches as muche as may be convenient', spending as little resources as possible on dealing with Scotland, and seeking friends wherever she could. He advised seeking the friendship of the Venetians because they 'be very ryche and strong both by sea and land'. (Nothing much seems to have ever developed in that direction. Perhaps Henry was not keen. Or, more to the point, one wonders what could really have been in it for the Venetians?) He also considered an alliance with the German Protestants, but was aware of the dangers of alienating the Catholic powers. Indeed, the great fear remained either that the Valois and Habsburgs might unite against England or that one or other of them might achieve European hegemony, allowing the victor to turn its ambitions against England. He stressed the advantage of brokering peace between the Empire and its Protestant 'subjects'.[18]

In fact, peace and stability were Paget's priorities, at home and abroad. But in foreign affairs it had to be peace with honour in relation to France and a peace that did not allow the Pope to return as a rival authority to the English monarchy. William had to deal with the ego-driven and inconsistent whims of his monarch, as well as the irrational advice of warmongers such as the Earl of Surrey and the religiously motivated influence of the likes of Bishop Gardiner. He had to fit in with the deviousness of the double game that Henry so loved to play in European politics. Though this last was no great stretch for him; it was not for nothing that he was known as the 'Master of Practices'. It took seven trips and innumerable hours of negotiations to finally achieve peace with France. But that peace treaty, despite a weak English position, was pretty favourable when compared with what the French had offered at the beginning. Paget was a force for moderation and rationality, both by limiting the scope of English involvement in the war in the first place and by securing the final peace treaty. The Crown was saved from bankruptcy, just. And good relations with the Emperor and the German Protestants had been maintained at the same time.

The endless uncomfortable travel and repeated missions in search of peace took their toll. William complained that 'no man travels with more pain than he', and he left his wife 'in despair of life', 'and nine young children and his house out of order'; but, he added in a letter to Petre of March 1545, 'he was glad to take this journey for the sake of his Sovereign's affairs'.[19] The horrible Channel crossings and hours of negotiations paid off in the end.

Chapter 10

Power Struggle:
The Failed Conservative Coup

The artist, the magician that conjured the wind, was William Paget, the royal Secretary and the shrewdest politician on the Council.
David Starkey on the 'wind' that blew away
the conservative faction in 1546

Intrigue flourished throughout Henry VIII's reign. The scope for individuals and factions to fight each other for power followed from Henry's character and style of government. Whereas his father, Henry VII, had headed an organised and consistent managerial system, Henry VIII was wildly inconsistent about people and policies. Yet everything centred on him: which way he was facing at any moment pretty much determined the result. For individuals after power, from Wolsey to Paget, having the King's ear and pleasing him was the be all and end all. But no one man could keep in with Henry and control the agenda for long, as Wolsey, Cromwell and others discovered to their cost. Henry's huge ego simply would not allow it. The adage from classic Westerns that, 'this town ain't big enough for the two of us' applied, and there was never any doubt as to who was leaving town – or biting the dust. Paget had learnt the lesson that, however much power he gained personally in a quiet way, he must never give Henry the impression that he thought that he was the King's equal. We will never know whether, had Henry lived longer, Paget's preeminent influence would have gone on growing to the point at which he would have suffered the same fate as Wolsey and Cromwell. But his character was less domineering than theirs and, in as far as he had a policy agenda, it was the moderate, possibly the mediocre, 'middle way', favoured by English civil servants throughout the centuries. And that favours survival.

If no one man could hope to keep power, it was necessary to join others to form alliances. In addition to the motive of personal advancement, these factions formed around certain institutions and issues. Institutionally, there was the Privy Council versus the Privy Chamber. Even in Wolsey's day, the so called 'minions', Henry's playmates in the Privy Chamber, men such as Nicholas

Carew, Henry Norris and Francis Bryan, had emerged as rivals both to the Cardinal and the Privy Council. Later Cromwell had packed the Chamber with his men, generally reformers such as Ralph Sadler and Anthony Denny. The composition of the Privy Council also varied considerably throughout the reign and, though its members and those of the Privy Chamber were of course both appointed by the monarch, it is not unreasonable to see the two bodies as rivals. Another fault line was based on that favourite distinction of the English, social class. On the one hand you had the old established nobility, with the Howard family top of the tree; on the other, Henry's out-and-out 'new men' who came from nowhere, Wolsey, Cromwell and Paget the most prominent among them. And in between were the recently risen minor aristocracy and gentry such as the Boleyns, Seymours, Dudleys and Wriothesleys. The other issue was the immensely important business of religion. There were the clear conservatives like Gardiner and the Howards and the definite reformers such as Cranmer, Hertford and Lisle. In between were those like Wriothesley, leaning to the Catholic, or Paget, leaning to the Protestant. Quite often these three divisions lined up: Privy Council, old aristocracy and religious conservatism on one side; Privy Chamber, new men and Evangelicalism on the other. But not always. A rigidly factional interpretation of events, chiefly based on religious differences between conservatives and reformers, would be wrong. The actions of someone like Paget, or indeed of Wriothesley, do not always fit into such an interpretation. Disagreements about foreign policy did not always line up neatly. For instance, Gardiner and Norfolk, although broadly in agreement over religion, disagreed violently about international alliances, with the former supporting Charles V and the latter favouring Francis I. More generally, there was a common desire to maintain stability and order among Henry's ministers which has to be balanced against their religiously based differences.

Therefore, factionalism does not explain everything. But it was a major influence which grew in the last years of the reign. The war with France and the problems with the Empire had temporarily restrained it. And initially three of the cheerleaders for religious factionalism, Gardiner for the conservatives and Hertford and Lisle for the reformers, were away, campaigning or on diplomatic missions. But, in the second half of 1546, once these three were home and there was a relaxation in foreign policy tensions, the infighting could really begin. Henry's poor health and the prospect of his demise gave it extra urgency.

The failed 'coup' of the conservatives came first. Their method was to attack out-and-out Evangelical heretics and through them to try to discredit more moderate reformers who were powerful because they were close to the King. The Queen, Katherine Parr, her gentlewomen and the gentlemen of Henry's

Privy Chamber were their target. Wriothesley and Norfolk began with a reasonably successful move against an Evangelical, Edward Crome, who was a favoured preacher of the Queen. When threatened, he recanted his reformist views and agreed to 'the disclosing and opening of all things' – i.e. naming names. He fingered twenty 'heretics' who were arrested and his evidence pointed towards the Queen and some of her ladies and to reformists in the Privy Chamber. But his evidence in itself was not enough to really nail them. Next they had a go at George Blagge, a favourite courtier of the King, who affectionately called him 'his pig'. Blagge had apparently agreed with a sermon of Crome's and had mocked the Catholic view that, during the Mass, the bread literally became the body of Christ, by asking, 'What if a mouse should eat the bread?' Wriothesley ordered his arrest and arranged a guilty verdict. The 'pig was well on his way to roasting' when Sir John Russell, a civilised fellow courtier, got wind of it and told the King. Henry was furious and forced Wriothesley to ignore the guilty verdict and draw up a pardon.[1]

The conservatives' next move was to arrest Anne Askew, a prominent Evangelical who had links to the reformers at Court. With an extreme brutality even by Tudor standards – and with illegality in so far as the rule of law ever applied – Wriothesley, the Lord Chancellor and the equally ruthless Richard Rich, another prominent government legal figure, personally operated the rack to torture her. Racking consists of gradually stretching the body, causing excruciating pain by increasing strain on the shoulders, hips, knees and elbows. By her own account, told before her broken body was later burned alive, 'they did put me on the rack because I confessed no ladies or gentlemen to be of my opinion and therefore they kept me on a long time.' I was relieved to discover that my ancestor had a rather less shameful part in this story. He had interviewed her earlier but he had no desire to get her to implicate others or to torture her. More than that, he wanted to give her a way out of suffering and the horrible fate of burning at the stake, actually suggesting that she recant her religious views temporarily but then deny her confession later, on the grounds that she was forced into it. She did not take his advice, of course, being a true fanatic seeking martyrdom.[2]

Overlapping the Anne Askew affair was a more direct attack on the Queen by the conservatives. There had been rumours earlier in the year, referred to in a letter from Stephen Vaughan to Paget, that Henry was getting fed up with Katherine Parr. But the major incident involving the Queen happened in August; admittedly the story comes from one uncorroborated and biased source, the Protestant *Acts and Monuments of the English Martyrs* by Foxe. His story is that Katherine was nagging Henry to be more Evangelical in the presence of Bishop Gardiner. Henry complained about how it had 'come in mine old age to be taught by my wife'. Gardiner, seizing the opportunity, agreed that women should never be allowed to have any religious opinions and suggested that he find evidence of the Queen's heresy and have her arrested. A bit later, Henry moaned further about being lectured to by his wife when speaking to his physician, Mr Wendy. Wendy, who was sympathetic to Katherine and reform, warned her of the threat. She went to Henry, said no way was she trying to tell him what to do, and that she only talked religion to distract him from the pain of his ailments – as you do. Who knows, with her life on the line, maybe she also made him happy in other ways? For whatever reason, her apology was fully accepted and when the hapless Wriothesley, not having heard of Henry's change of heart, arrived with armed men to arrest the Queen, a furious Henry told him to get lost, dismissing him as, 'Knave, Arrant knave! beast! fool!'[3]

Whether this story is true or not and whether Gardiner, Norfolk and Wriothesley were really involved in a planned conspiracy or 'coup' remains disputed by historians. But what is not in doubt is that, by the end of the summer of 1546, their bid for power had failed. Next it was the turn of the reformist faction. Helped by Paget's support, they had much more success. David Starkey describes the events and Paget's central role in them in dramatic terms:

> The events of July and August meant the wind was blowing favourably for the 'new'. But that the wind turned into a gale which blew away the 'old' and uprooted the great house of Howard was a work of political art. The artist, the magician that conjured the wind, was William Paget, the royal Secretary and the shrewdest politician on the Council. Known as the 'master of practices', he was a natural 'politique'. Or, as Bishop Ponet put it less kindly, he 'will have one part in every pageant, if he may by praying or paying put in his foot.'[4]

As with the conservative 'coup', there is some disagreement among historians as to how much the success of the reformist faction resulted from a planned conspiracy and how much 'events just happened', to deliver them victory. The supporters of the latter view even contend that Hertford, who was after all the next king, Edward's, closest male relative, did not so much seize power as inherit it. As believers in conspiracy theories of history are at pains to remind us, successful conspiracies, by their very nature, usually leave few traces. Participants are careful not to write much down in case the coup fails. And there indeed is not much direct evidence of conspiracy in the events of August to the beginning of December 1546. Direct evidence, maybe not; but plenty of indirect evidence in the triumph of the reformist faction.

At the beginning of August, their triumph had not seemed inevitable, because Henry was still keeping his options open. One Gurone Bertano, an Italian who came to London under French auspices and with Henry's blessing, was on a strange mission to explore whether a reconciliation between England and the Papacy might still be possible. This was secret, hidden from all in the Privy Council except Paget. After a long meeting with Paget on 2 August, Bertano reported to the French ambassador, who reported to Francis I, that he 'had good hopes of success'. And, on 16 August, the conservatives in the Privy Council still seemed powerful, with van der Delft reporting to Charles V that the leaders there were Gardiner and Wriothesley, along with Paget.[5]

But it does seem that a major shift in the balance of power had occurred by a few weeks later. By 3 September, van der Delft reported of his dinner with the three conservatives, Gardiner, Wriothesley and St John. He told them how much he regretted 'the advance of certain persons whom he wished as far away as they were last year'. He meant Hertford and Lisle. The three conservative Councillors 'made no answer but expressed their usual devotion to the Emperor's interests'[6] – the Tudor equivalent to the 'You might say that; I couldn't possibly comment' of *House of Cards* fame. In addition, the Bertano mission failed. As Cranmer's biographer puts it, 'It was a crucial moment for the future of the Reformation in England, and ... the secret dynamic of it is locked forever in King Henry's mind, as he meditated whether to overthrow all that he had done in the previous decade and a half.'[7] Why didn't he? Most fundamentally, he probably did not want to surrender his exclusive authority as Head of the Church. Also, in international politics, reconciliation with the Papacy was currently unnecessary as there was peace with France and the Habsburgs were too busy elsewhere, fighting German Protestants, to bother with English heresy.

At the end of August, the composition of the regular and active Privy Council changed significantly in the reformist direction, gaining Cranmer, Arundel, Hertford and Lisle and losing Gardiner, Tunstal and Rich. When Henry left on what was to prove his last royal progress out of London in early September, he was accompanied only by reformist Councillors, with the conservatives left behind. Another possible indicator of the way the wind was blowing was when Lisle was only banned very briefly when he punched Gardiner in the face in a full Privy Council meeting. Admittedly Gardiner's biographer thinks that the fact that he was not banned after the incident indicated that he, Gardiner, still had clout. But I am less convinced by this argument because it was, after all, Lisle who 'reportedly' threw the punch. The whole incident is anyway a bit uncertain, as with much in this story of factional fighting, because it is only told in a dispatch of the French ambassador, and he is not explicit about the date or the cause of the fight.[8]

Within Henry's Privy Chamber, there was also change favouring the reformers. Sir Anthony Denny, who was a definite reformer, replaced Sir Thomas Heneage as first Chief Gentleman and Groom of the Stool (yes, a big job much sought after!), who was not so partisan. Denny's previous post, as second Chief Gentleman, was taken by another reformer, Sir William Herbert, Katherine Parr's brother-in-law. Heneage had served Henry for twenty years and the justification for his dismissal is unknown; he apparently left Court under a cloud. But the emerging faction, Hertford, Lisle and Denny, with Paget's help, were suspected of being responsible. Paget's precise role, in this and other manoeuvres around this time, cannot be proved. But most contemporary commentators seemed to think that he was hugely influential with Henry, who, though growing sicker by the day, remained the sole arbiter of personal and factional power. Writing later, Paget certainly claimed that the King 'opened his pleasure to me alone in many things'.[9]

The next major incident was the definitive fall of Gardiner. The bare bones of this episode are simple enough. In November, Gardiner, who was bishop of the very wealthy See of Winchester, incurred Henry's displeasure by refusing to exchange some episcopal lands with him and, from then on, he was excluded from all power. What is unclear, and remains a matter of historical controversy, is how much this event, along with others before and after, should be seen as part of a plot by the reformist faction. Gardiner's biographer sees it as not a plot, but simply caused by his subject's mistaken confidence in his relationship with Henry leading him to think he could get away with a refusal. The fact that Paget, along with others, had recommended to Gardiner in the first place that he agree to the King's proposal might suggest that Paget was not deliberately engineering the bishop's fall. Unless, however, he was being devious. Somewhat supporting the plot theory is Gardiner's letter to Paget, in which he said that he had not heard the detail of Henry's discontent over the 'matier of landes, but confusely, that my doinges shuld not be wel taken'. This could suggest that at any rate Gardiner himself suspected that his position was being presented to Henry in as negative a way as possible. Gardiner also prayed Paget to deliver his separate apologetic letter to Henry – perhaps suggesting he feared he might not show it to the King. Certainly Paget did not actively intervene on Gardiner's behalf in this matter, despite being begged to do so. Because, two days later, Gardiner received a crushing reply from Henry, very probably drafted by Paget, decisively excluding him from Court.[10]

Chapter 11

Power Struggle: Triumph of the Reformers

These were the years of ruthless jockeying by ruthless men.

The sudden assault on the great dynasty (the Howards) which had given so much to the king and whose history had been so entwined in the story of Henry's reign resists a definitive explanation.

J. J. Scarisbrick, Henry VIII

The events of November 1546 to February 1547 and Paget's central role in them consist of two main narratives. The first is the continued success of the reformist faction and the demise of the conservatives. The second is the 'coup', centring on Henry's will, that made Hertford Lord Protector – effectively sole ruler – on Henry's death. These two stories overlap both in content and chronologically. But, for the sake of clarity, I have dealt with them separately: the first told here and the second kept for the next chapter.

The significant event to complete the triumph of the reformist faction was the fall of the Howard family. As with the previous episodes in this story, there is controversy as to whether this resulted from conspiracy or not. Some argue that there is no need to look for a plot to explain the fate of the Howards. It was all their own stupid fault, particularly where the actions of Henry Howard, Earl of Surrey, were concerned. In the wry words of the preface to the *Letters and Papers*, 'It was easy enough to stir up trouble in the family of the Duke of Norfolk. Never was there less domestic love anywhere. Father and son, brother and sister, disliked each other.'[1] The Duke and Duchess were alienated and the Duke's mistress, Elizabeth Holland, presided over the family seat at Kenninghall. Henry Howard was evidently wild, foolish and arrogant, considering himself above the law, having earlier been imprisoned and forced to join the navy for crazy disorderly conduct. He was a romantic figure, a poet/soldier who has been characterised as a gifted juvenile delinquent. He snobbishly loathed and despised inferior nobles and the gentry, let alone complete upstarts like Cromwell and Paget. And he had 'form' for possibly treasonous behaviour. He had been questioned previously about allegedly claiming that his father, and thereafter himself, would be king if Henry died. Unlike Hertford and Lisle, who had been fairly successful as military commanders, Surrey had not been. He had been responsible for a defeat by the French in January 1546, described in a previous chapter. So he was already out of favour with Henry.

Against this background, Surrey was accused of treason at the beginning of December, by Sir Richard Southwell, a committed Catholic and former companion in arms. Surrey denied the accusation and, apparently, true to form, suggested the issue be resolved by a 'man to man' fight in their shirts. Initially both were arrested while the accusations were investigated and there is no clear evidence that Southwell's allegation was part of a plot. But it might well have been. Because the follow-on gives every indication of a wish to nail the Howards rather than any attempt to unearth the truth. Surrey's associates were interviewed in 'tell us what we want to hear, son, and we'll go easy on you' mode. Surrey's father, the Duke, was arrested and, perhaps most telling of all, Southwell was not only rapidly released but was actually part of the team sent by the Privy Council to Norfolk to gain more evidence. When they arrived at Kenninghall, the main Howard seat, this team, which included Gates and Carew from Henry's Privy Chamber as well as Southwell, proceeded to intimidate the Duchess of Richmond, Surrey's sister, and Elizabeth Holland, Norfolk's mistress. The former needed little encouragement to shop her brother and father, stating that 'although constrained by nature to love her father, whom she ever thought a true subject, and her brother, whom she noteth to be a rash man, she would conceal nothing but declare in writing all she could remember.' Interestingly enough, the Gates/Carew/Southwell report to Henry is as much about what they could find to plunder, for his, and no doubt their own, benefit, as it is about extracting confessions. They were disappointed by what they found of the Duchess's possessions, but were hopeful of the rest, reporting,

> Examined her [the Duchess's] coffers and closets, but find nothing worth sending, all being very bare and her jewels sold to pay her debts ... Then searched Elizabeth Holland, and found girdles, beads, buttons of gold, pearl and rings set with diverse stones ... Meanwhile sent trusty servants to all the Duke's other houses in Norfolk and Suffolk to prevent embezzlement [!], not forgetting Elizabeth Holland's house, newly made, in Suffolk, which is thought to be well furnished.

They signed off, 'By next letters will report further of these matters, and also of the Duke's jewels and lands.'[2] Reading this, quite typical of the Tudor way of government of which Paget was now so prominent a part, I found, at the risk of indulging in anachronism, the word 'kleptocracy' popping into my head. It is defined in Wikipedia as 'A government ruled by corrupt politicians who use their political power to receive kickbacks, bribes and special favours at the expense of the populace, or simply direct state resources to themselves, relatives or associates.'

The actual charges against the Howards were scattergun, with pretty much anything and everything that their accusers could think of thrown at them. The French ambassador reckoned that there were two main crimes of which Surrey was thought guilty: he failed to attack a castle in France when he could have done so while commanding English troops, and he threatened to destroy his political opponents, of whom he 'said there were some who made no great account of him but he trusted one day to make them very small'. Charles V's ambassador thought it was all about 'a secret discourse between them [Surrey and Norfolk] concerning the King's illness six weeks ago, the object being to obtain the government of the Prince [Edward]'.[3]

William Paget was the main investigator. He questioned the imprisoned Norfolk at length, asking about secret cipher communications and possibly treacherous dealings with the Bishop of Rome. Norfolk denied everything, complained about how everyone had had it in for him and his family from way back in the days of Wolsey and Cromwell and, showing how desperate he now considered his position to be, begged that the King be shown his letter in his defence, 'and remit out of his noble gentle heart the displeasure conceived against me. By his Highness' poure prisoner, T. Norfolk'. Although denying these charges, Norfolk, realising the game was up, subsequently confessed to concealing his son's guilt.[4] Paget was meanwhile very successful in getting evidence that Surrey had, without authorisation, taken on a coat of arms that implied a claim to the throne, an action considered treacherous. He got two Depositions out of Sir Edmund Warner. The first one reads:

> Being commanded by Sir William Paget, chief secretary, to write what had passed between the Earl of Surre[y] and me concerning his pedigree, arms and other matters which may appertain to the King or his posterity, I say that the Earl, among other coats, showed me that he might bear the arms of King Edward the Saint; and I did not agree that he might do so.

The second, while involving what would nowadays be considered inadmissible and hypothetical 'hearsay' evidence, was potentially even more damning for Surrey. Warner's Deposition again starts by saying, 'Being commanded by Sir William Paget, knight, chief secretary to write such words as have been between me and the Earl of Surre[y] that might touch the King and his posterity…' but then adds 'or that I have heard from others to that effect'. He says that he had heard from a certain Master Deveroux that an example of Surrey's 'pride and vain glory' was that he may have said, 'if God should call the King to his mercy, who was so meet to govern the Prince as my lord his father' (i.e. the Duke of Norfolk).[5] This evidence was very dubious but just the kind of thing Paget and the other accusers were after, because it was treasonous to suggest that the Howards would 'rule' Edward and also to speak of the King's death. In the list of charges against Surrey, another salacious one was that he had tried to get his sister to seduce the King to enhance Howard power. She was not actually up for this, it appeared. But, given what the Norfolks had managed with poor beheaded royal wife number five, Katherine Howard, the accusation had some credibility.

When Surrey came to trial on 13 January 1547, Paget was one of the judges. In a dramatic moment, the two had an explosive exchange over the central accusation about Surrey's traitorous use of the royal coat of arms. Paget lays into him, 'your idea was to commit treason, and as the King is old, you thought to become King.' Surrey spits back, 'Catchpoll! What hast thou to do with it? Thou hadst better hold thy tongue, for the kingdom has never been well since the King put mean creatures like thee into government.' Perhaps because of Surrey's vigorous defence, including this appeal to snobbism, or maybe, more prosaically and honourably, because of the lack of solid evidence, the jury were initially – in fact for six hours – unable to reach a verdict. Paget had to go back to consult Henry and spend an hour with them during which he managed to 'persuade' them to come up with the required 'guilty'. Then, as the record reads, 'Sentence, to be taken back to the Tower and thence led through the City of London to the gallows at Tiborne, hanged, disembowelled, etc (as usual).'[6] As he was, luckily for him, an earl, Surrey was in fact beheaded. Rank usually determined method of execution in Tudor times. Norfolk was also condemned to death but he managed to escape the sentence owing to the King's death. He remained in the Tower until he was released in Mary's reign and died in his bed aged 80, extraordinarily old by the standards of the time.

So, was there a conspiracy? While there is not much direct evidence for one and while I would generally favour the accident over the conspiracy theory of history, it does in this instance seem just too much of a coincidence that one event after another 'just happened' to favour the reformist over the conservative faction, and with the result that they had power when Henry died. Also, much as I hate referrals to higher authority, it cannot be ignored that three of the big daddies of Tudor history, Geoffrey Elton, J. J. Scarisbrick and David Starkey, all vote for conspiracy. Which is not to say that the conspiracy, if there was one, would necessarily have succeeded if things had fallen out slightly differently. Katherine Parr might not have kept Henry's affection; his mood, no doubt largely determined by his health and in particular the pain caused by his horribly gammy leg, had only to have been different at certain critical moments; Gardiner might not have fatally overestimated his clout; Surrey might not have acted like such a complete idiot; Hertford and Lisle might not have had the success they did on the field of battle. And what if Paget, so heavily involved but leaving few traces, had jumped the other way? There is a memo that surfaced at Surrey's trial written by him in the spring of 1546 which shows him considering forming an alliance with Paget to achieve power for his faction. 'That Mr P should be Chancellor of England,' it reads. David Starkey is of the opinion that, 'To have detached Paget from Hertford six months earlier would have changed everything.' And adds, referring to the drawing up of Henry's Last Will and Testament, 'Now, however, Paget was to achieve his master-stroke for the other side.'[7] The next chapter examines that 'master-stroke'.

Chapter 12

Henry VIII's Last Will and Testament: A Forgery?

> Our chief labour and study in this world is to establish him [Edward] in the Crown Imperial of this realm after our decease in such sort as may be pleasing to God, and to the wealth of this realm, and to his own honour and quiet.
>
> Henry's will, folio 19

Henry's will was an important document which significantly influenced the direction of English history. But how much of it was really his will is debatable. It was the subject of controversy in Tudor and Elizabethan times, and still is today. Trying to make sense of the evidence involves complex detective work. Paget's role in the will's production and in how it was used is central. Before examining that and the will's authenticity, it is worth explaining just why it was so important. It determined the succession. Back in 1536, after wife number two, Anne Boleyn, had been beheaded and before wife number three, Jane Seymour, had given birth, Henry forced Parliament to pass an Act of Succession. This declared Mary and Elizabeth, children of the first two wives, as illegitimate and determined that any children by Jane, or any subsequent wife, should succeed. The Act also gave the King the right to appoint his successors in his will and therein to appoint a Regency Council should his heir be a minor at the time of his death.

Seven years later, with a male heir alive in the person of the boy Edward, another Act of Succession was passed. This confirmed the crucial role of the will which had been established in the first Act, and returned Mary and Elizabeth back into the line of succession after Edward and his heirs, and after any children Henry might have by his current wife number six, Katherine Parr. However, it did not actually make Mary and Elizabeth legitimate. This Act, which was accompanied by a will that has not survived, states that the reason for its creation was that the King was going to fight 'against his ancient enemy the French king' and needed to determine 'how this realm standeth at the present time in the case of succession.'[1]

In the Last Will and Testament which has survived, drawn up just before Henry's death, the line of succession is spelt out in great detail. The first in line were obvious: Edward and his heirs. Second in line, if Edward were to die without heirs, were any children Henry might yet have with wife number six, Katherine Parr. Only a month before his death, Henry not only considered that possibility but even added in the heirs from 'any other our lawful wife that we shall hereafter marry'. Wow! The rhyme, 'divorced, beheaded, died, divorced, beheaded, survived', might have been even longer. Third and fourth in line were Mary and her heirs and Elizabeth and hers. Though in both cases only if their choice of bridegroom were approved by the Privy Council. And strangely, once again, as in the Act of Succession, although they are named in the line of succession, their legitimacy was not restored. At one point in the will, the words 'lawfully begotten' after their names have been carefully and clearly crossed out. Fifth, 'the heirs of the body of Lady Frances, our niece, eldest daughter of our late sister'. This meant Lady Jane Grey. This provision interfered with the normal line of succession in two ways. For some reason, Lady Frances herself was excluded. No one knows quite why: though there is speculation that Henry did not think much of her husband, who might have ruled as king. Secondly, the descendants of Henry's elder sister were excluded. That meant Mary, Queen of Scots. The reason for this, keeping the Scots out of the succession, was clear. And there was one final very remote relative in this line of succession, Margaret, daughter of Eleanor, second daughter of Henry's sister Mary. This business of the line of succession as specified in Henry VIII's will was to be a really important issue for years to come: on the death of Edward VI – with Lady Jane Grey's very brief 'reign' and Mary's triumph, in Elizabeth I's reign when those who supported Mary, Queen of Scots's claim to the throne considered the will invalid, and finally on Elizabeth's death, when James VI of Scotland became James I of England.

This question of the succession is the first reason why the will is so important. The second is to do with its role in determining the government of England during the minority reign of Edward VI from 1547 to 1553. The will appoints sixteen men, of whom ten were Privy Councillors and six were not, to be executors and to rule while Edward was a minor. (He was 9 in 1547.) It names a further twelve, of whom nine were Privy Councillors and three were not, to be their assistants. We will return to the question of who was included, who excluded. The central thing to realise, however, is that these people were authorised by the will to rule as a collective, with decisions to be made by all, or 'the most part' of them. There was a 'carte-blanche' clause in the will that allows them to 'order what things so ever they or the more part of them ... think necessary or convenient for the benefit honour or surety' of the country.[2]

And this clause was indeed used as justification for setting up the Protectorate under Hertford. But there can be no doubt that, if Henry had wanted a Protectorate under one man as the government during his son's minority, he would and could have said so in his will. Given the level of factional infighting that had occurred and was likely to continue within a government of many equal councillors, it is surprising that this is what he favoured. But perhaps, like so many autocrats throughout history, he just could not bear the idea of someone else ruling. That would certainly fit with his character and behaviour throughout the reign. Or, maybe, like de Gaulle, he even rather liked the idea, subconsciously at least, of 'apres moi, le deluge'. So rule by a council is what Henry wanted. But it was not what he got. The will itself, as per the 'carte-blanche' clause, and more importantly various interpretations/glosses added to it, mainly by Paget, was used to justify the Protectorate of Hertford. And then, later in Edward's reign, in October 1549, to justify its dissolution.

That is why the will is so important. Now for the story of how it was written and interpreted. At the end of December 1546, Henry had a bad fever and he weakened, to the extent that van der Delft reported that 'the King is so unwell that, considering his age and corpulence, he may not survive another attack'.[3] The King gathered together his closest advisors, including Hertford and Lisle as well as Denny and Herbert, his Chief Gentleman of the Privy Chamber and, of course, Paget. Most of the evidence for what happens from here on comes from what Paget says happened, in his statement made to the Privy Council soon after Henry's death and in letters he was to write to Somerset (Hertford) later on. With the addition of further stories from the ever detailed but ever unreliable Foxe in his *Book of Martyrs*.[4] Henry ordered Paget to draft a new will and they discussed who to include and exclude as executors and as members of the Regency Council. Most of the names were predictable, including those particularly close to Henry, such as Denny, Herbert and Paget or those with high office such Cranmer, Archbishop of Canterbury, or the Lord Chancellor, Wriothesley. The big exclusion was Bishop Gardiner, and, along with him, Thomas Thirlby, Bishop of Westminster, because, according to Foxe, he was 'schooled by Gardiner'. It seems likely that this was very much Henry's personal decision, with the possibility that Paget and Hertford actually argued for Gardiner's inclusion. We have seen how Henry was already angry with Gardiner for his refusal to do a land swap and, according to one account, Henry said of him that he was 'a wilful man, not meet to be about his son' and that, although he (Henry) could control him, others could not; 'I myself could use him and rule him to all manner of purposes, as seems good to me; but so shall you never do.' Probably behind this was Henry's concern to protect the Royal Supremacy from beyond the grave because he feared, correctly, that

Gardiner would try to mend the breach with Rome. At the other end of the political spectrum, as it were, there was the slightly surprising inclusion of two not very prominent non-Privy Council members to the list of assistants, Sir Richard Southwell and Hertford's younger brother, Sir Thomas Seymour. Was Southwell being rewarded for his important part in the destruction of the house of Howard? Was the inclusion of Hertford's younger brother an indication of conspiracy, or even clear evidence that the will was forged? It has been claimed that because Sir Thomas Seymour was not made a Privy Councillor until 23 January and was nonetheless included in the will as one, the will must have been tampered with. This is not correct. He is not listed in the will as a Privy Councillor. So it is not incontrovertible proof that the will was fake. However, his inclusion might still be considered suspicious.

Further changes were made from the pre-existing will. But, as this earlier will has not survived, we do not know what these were. Paget was then instructed to draw up the final document. Historians agree that it was Paget who drafted it, with the actual writing in the hand of Mr Honnyngs, a clerk of the signet and Privy Council who worked for him. The twenty-eight pages were, if we are to believe the official account, seen and signed by Henry, and witnessed, four days later on 30 December. The signatures at the beginning and end of the document are not in Henry's own hand but are in the form of the 'dry stamp'. This is not in itself an indication of dodgy dealings. To save Henry the slog of endlessly signing documents, the 'dry stamp' system had been set up, whereby an impression of the royal signature was stamped on the paper and then carefully inked in by one of three authorised people, Denny, Gates, or, more often the appropriately named clerk, Mr Clerk. So use of the 'dry stamp' was an established procedure. Having said that, its use to sign the will is, prima facie, suspicious. With a document as mega-important as this, on quite another level from all the other documents and known to be such by all the participants in its production, might it not have been sensible to get him to actually sign it? If, of course, he had been still able to do so. We will return later to the question of Henry's physical and mental health, which is relevant to the authenticity of the will.

The witnessing of the will does seem fairly believable, as it was signed by the people one imagines were hanging about the King: the gentlemen and grooms of the Privy Chamber, such as Gates, Henry's doctors, including Mr Wendy, and the clerk, Clerk. And there were a lot of witnesses, ten in all. Though, as with much of the evidence, you could, at a stretch, read this fact the other way – i.e. that to have so many witnesses indicates a desperate desire to make a document that was in fact dodgy seem credible. Another detail about the will, used to support the forgery case, is the claim that the spacing of the lines on the last, signed and witnessed, page is different from that on the other pages. If true, this might suggest that witnesses signed a blank page that was later added to the will. However, it appears this claim is mistaken and the spacing is in fact the same as on the other pages.

Before leaving the physical document, it is necessary to delve further into the complexities surrounding Henry's signature and the use of the 'dry stamp'. As mentioned, the latter was considered a perfectly proper and legal procedure. It was used on hundreds of official documents in the last eighteen months of the reign. What happened was, at the end of each month, a 'hold-all' register that listed all the items signed by stamp was then submitted to the King for confirmation. According to the introduction to the volume containing these monthly registers, held in the National Archives at Kew, this confirmation was executed by the King's own hand. But not, significantly, with a freehand signature; rather by him inking in another 'dry stamp'. As one imagines it is impossible to distinguish between a 'dry stamp' inked in by the royal hand and one inked in by others, this does seem to be a very strange procedure which would hardly serve to authenticate with any great credibility. But apparently that is how it was. And its relevance to the legitimacy of the will becomes clear when considered alongside the fact that the will was not included in the 'hold-all' register of all documents for December, dated the 31st, although it could have been if it was signed, as claimed, on the 30th. But it was then included, as the second to last item, in the January list of documents signed by the 'dry stamp'. This register is undated. And perhaps that is significant, in so far as for all the other months, the registers are dated – and they are all dated on the last day of the month. If it was drawn up on the last day of January, as per the usual procedure, it could not have been approved by Henry. Because he had died early in the morning of 28 January. The items in this register nonetheless refer to the King as if he were alive and able to give his consent. The one referring to the will, number 85, is worth quoting in full:

Your Majesty's last will and testament bearing date at Westminster the thirty day of December last past, written in a book of paper, signed above in the beginning and beneath in the end, and sealed with the signet in the presence of the earl of Hertford, Mr Secretary Pagett [sic], Mr Denny and Mr Harbert [sic], and also in the presence of certain other persons whose names are subscribed with their own hands as witnesses to the same. Which testament your Majesty delivered then in our sights with your own hand to the said Earl of Hertford as your own deed, last will and testament, revoking and annulling all other your Highness' former wills and testaments. W Clerk.

And, while on the subject of this January register, note that item 80 is as follows:

> A bill to pass by Act of Parliament for the better assurance of your majesty's grant in fee simple to Sir William Pagett, knight, chief of your Majesty's two principal secretaries, of certain lordships, manors and parks, etc, which the bishops of Coven[try], and Lich[field] and Chester lately gave and rendered to your Highness.

Well, well! Rather too convenient, perhaps?[5]

There are a few other bits of circumstantial evidence that have been used to bolster the case for a full-blown Paget/Hertford conspiracy in relation to the will that are *not* so convincing. The first is the belief that the Privy Council met from 8 December to the 4 January in Hertford's house. Apparently this was not the case; it was Wriothesley's house. As he was not seen as a prime conspirator in the sense that Hertford was, the location of the Council meetings cannot therefore be used as evidence to support the conspiracy theory. But, equally, as Wriothesley had by this stage ceased to be heavily allied to the 'conservative' faction, neither can it be used to completely rule out conspiracy. Next is the idea that Henry could not bear to consider his own death – and therefore is unlikely to have been as involved in creating the will as claimed, making forgery more likely. On this issue, there are two unreliable narrators on opposite sides; Foxe supporting the idea, while Paget's statement to the Privy Council soon after the death contradicts it, when he says that Henry 'felt himself sickelie and that if ought shuld comme to him but good, as he thought (he sayde), that he could not long endure, he mynded to place us all about his sonne as men whom he trusted and loved above all other specially.'[6]

Paget's testimony here, to which we will return, is unreliable because it leads to the justification for replacing Henry's desired government of equal councillors with Hertford's Protectorate. On the other hand, it does sound reasonably credible in itself. The final piece of not-wholly-convincing circumstantial evidence used by 'the prosecution on behalf of forgery and conspiracy' is the idea that Henry was too far gone to have made the will in the way it was presented. Once again, the evidence for this is less than decisive. Patently he was very ill and getting worse. But he was quite 'up and down' and there were plenty of instances of him being in control until right at the end. For example, the French ambassador saw him on 13 January and remarked that, 'he seems now fairly well'. And Henry gave firm detailed instruction to Paget on a matter of foreign policy on 23 January, only five days before his death.[7]

There is a famous painting in the National Portrait Gallery of Henry on his deathbed, handing over to his son and the Protestant elite. He points to the enthroned Edward as his successor; the Pope and his monks are shown being banished; and a 'picture within the picture' approves of iconoclasm, the smashing of idols. As with so much about the transfer of power at the end of Henry's reign, there is a lively academic debate about the date, purpose and meaning of the painting and about the identity of some of those depicted. But there seems to be agreement that the man standing prominently next to Edward, as his chief minister, is Hertford/Somerset and that the figure at the end of a row of sitting councillors, sporting his distinctive forked beard, is Paget. He is occupying his habitual position of modest, but powerful, 'eminence grise'.

Chapter 13

Conspiracy

[The] Earl [Hertford] well perceiving the crown ready to fall upon Prince Edward his nephew's head ... took a walk with Paget in the gallery; where he held some serious conference with him concerning the government.

John Strype's *Chronicle*

Whatever the truth about the authenticity of the will and however much Paget and Hertford (Somerset) did or did not deviously collude in the weeks before Henry's death, it is crystal clear that they did conspire together, against the King's wishes, while he lay dying and in the days that followed. The conspiracy delivered the government of the realm into Hertford's hands as the king-like Lord Protector and their actions can reasonably be characterised as a 'coup d'etat'. The early nineteenth-century chronicler John Strype describes what happened:

While King Henry lay on his deathbed in his palace at Westminster, Sir Edward Seymour, Earl of Hertford and Sir William Paget, among others, were at Court; and Paget, being Secretary of State, was much about his person: whom being a man wise and learned, and well versed in the affairs of state, both by reason of his office and his several embassies abroad, the Earl prudently made choice of for his inward friend and counsellor. By the King's desperate condition, the Earl well perceiving the crown ready to fall upon Prince Edward his nephew's head, before the breath was out of his body, took a walk with Paget in the gallery; where he held some serious conference with him concerning the government. And immediately after the King was departed they met again, the Earl devising with him concerning the high place he was to hold, being the next of kin to the young King. Paget at both meetings freely and at large gave him advice, for the safe managery of himself, and of the mighty trust likely to be reposed in him.[1]

This account is confirmed by Paget himself in a letter written to Somerset in July 1549, which refers to the discussion they had had in the gallery at

Westminster 'before the breath was out of the body of the King that dead is' and immediately after 'devising with me concerning the place which you now occupy' – meaning his place as the ruler of the country, the Lord Protector.[2]

When Henry died early in the morning of 28 January 1547, Paget, Hertford and a very few others in the know kept the fact secret for nearly three days. This was not that unusual when a king died, or indeed with the demise of a modern autocrat, but it was crucial in that it gave Paget and Hertford the chance to get their ducks in a row, before Parliament, the Privy Council and the wider world had to know. They sprang into action. Leaving Paget in charge at Westminster, in physical possession of the will, Hertford dashed off to collect the 9-year-old Prince Edward, now King, making sure he had control of him from the start. Edward VI's first biographer gives a rather touching account of the tearful response of Edward and his sister Elizabeth when told of their father's death: 'Never was sorrow more sweetly set forth, their faces seeming rather to beautify their sorrow, than sorrow to cloud the beauty of their faces.'[3]

How exactly Paget and Hertford cooked things up at this point, and in their meetings in the gallery outside the Henry's deathbed, is uncertain. They left few traces. But that cooking occurred is virtually certain, not only because of the result and as shown in the letter from Paget of July 1549, but also by a very revealing letter that Hertford sent to Paget the day after Henry's death. It sounds as if it was pretty frantic late-night cooking:

> This morning, between one and two, I received your letter. The first part thereof I like very well; marry, that the Will should [not] be opened till a further consultation, and that it might be well considered how much thereof were necessary to be published; for divers respects I think it not convenient to satisfy the world.

He goes on to say that, although Paget will have to reveal the existence of the will and how it names executors and councillors when he first tells of the King's death and although he will then later have to show the will to Parliament, 'in the mean time we to meet and agree therin, as there may be no controversy hereafter'. He signs off, 'From Hertford, the 29th Jan. between three and four in the morning' and with a 'ps', 'I have sent you the key to the Will.' He must have mistakenly rushed off with the key to the box containing the will. The letter is marked, 'To my Right loving Friend, Sir William Paget ... Haste, Post haste, haste with all diligence, For thy life, For thy life.' Another example of the Tudor equivalent of 'UNBELIEVABLY URGENT' – which we have encountered before.[4]

There is evidence that Hertford, on his way back to London, won over one of the Regency/Privy Councillors to the idea of his rule as Lord Protector. This was Sir Anthony Browne, Master of the King's Horse, who had accompanied Hertford on his mission to collect the boy king, Edward. Getting him on board was important as he was associated with the conservative Catholic faction. But, beyond that instance, how, or how much, Paget and Hertford persuaded, threatened or bribed their co-executors we will never know. There was probably a lot of that going on. Circumstantial evidence is there: most of the named councillors were well rewarded and the most reluctant, Wriothesley, soon lost power under the Protectorate. But it may also be that Paget and Hertford succeeded mainly by simply being in control of the way in which Henry's will was presented, by the argument that a Protectorate was a necessity and by convincing any doubters that this was what was going to happen, so they had better accept it, or they could kiss goodbye to their power, wealth and status. In the first meeting of the Privy Council, on 31 January, the will was presented in a very slanted way, it being stated that, although

> a greate nombre appoyncted to be executors with like and eaqual charge, it shuld be more than necessarie aswel for t honour, surety and gouvernement of the most royal persone of the King … that somme special man of the nombre and company aforesaide shuld be preferred in name and place before others … otherwise … within shorte tyme but growe into mucho disordre and confusion.

Avoiding 'mucho disordre and confusion' was indeed the overwhelming priority of most people involved in government in the aftermath of the bloody Wars of the Roses. And that 'special man' was of course Edward's uncle, Hertford, who was to be given, 'the furste and chief place amonges us, and also the name and title of the Protectour of all the realms and dominions of the Kinges Majestie that now is, and the Governor of his moste royal persone.' For doubters, the pill was sugared by the condition that the Protector 'shall nat do any Acte but with th advise and consent of the coexecutors'. But this was rapidly forgotten as Hertford consolidated his power. The way in which the will is presented at this first Council meeting of the reign is clearly contrary to Henry's intention. The 'carte-blanche' clause, that allowed anything 'necessary or convenient for the benefit, honour and surety' of the realm, could be pointed to and indeed was, in that the statement at the Council reflects its language. But that is pretty thin stuff. Nonetheless, despite the fact that a Protectorate under Hertford was clearly not what Henry wanted as indicated by his will, all the councillors went along with the interpretation that Paget and Hertford had cooked up. The 'coup' had succeeded.⁵

With power assured came the division of the spoils. In the will itself, Henry specified many legacies, including one for Paget, who received the not negligible sum of £300. However, the big distribution of goodies, in the form of money, land and titles came a bit later and by means of a questionable reference to the royal authority. There is a clause in the will which reads that any grants, gifts, etc. that have been promised but not yet accomplished should be fulfilled. It has been argued that this 'unfulfilled gifts' clause was not unusual. But to use it to justify a massive handout of titles, land and money does seem very fishy. And Hertford got the biggest wedge, made Duke of Somerset with major land grants and given the position of Earl Marshall of England. In addition, a marquess, two earls and four barons were created and plenty of land and money was handed out. Lisle became Earl of Warwick, Wriothesley Earl of Southhampton and Sir Thomas Seymour became a baron. Denny, Herbert and Paget did pretty well too. We have detailed above how William received 'certain lordships manors and parks' under the authority of the dubiously authorised January 'dry stamp' register. Given that Henry's will was very long, consisting of over 6,000 words, and very detailed, including legacies to sixty-six named individuals, why on earth would he not have included these huge hand-outs of titles land and money in it, if that had been his wish?

All this bounty was justified by combining the 'unfulfilled gifts' clause with Paget's very detailed account of how Henry had earlier 'promised grete things to divers men'. Paget's account of Henry's wishes was presented to the Privy Council on 6 February. He claimed that at the time of the arrest of Norfolk and Surrey, when there was discussion about the distribution of the Howard lands, Henry had expressed concern that 'the nobilitie of this realme was greatly decayed' and had instructed Paget to draw up a list of names for advancement. This list was contained in a book that Henry put away in his nightshirt. Sadly, William explained, the book had gone missing and, before the decisions would be acted upon, God had taken the King from them. However, in the rightly cynical words of one writer on the last days of Henry VIII, 'all was not lost. Mirabile dictu! [wonderful to report] Paget, like any efficient civil servant, was of course blessed with a photographic memory and his vivid, detailed and wholly convenient recollections' could form the basis for all the extra creations and grants. His story was backed up by Denny and Herbert. And in what Starkey calls the 'shameless back-scratching' of their alliance, they furthered each other's interests. Paget claimed he said to Henry:

considring what paynefull service Master Denye [sic] did take daylie with him [remember Denny's job as groom of the Stool], and also moved of honestie for that Mr Deny had divers tymes ben a suter for me and I never for him, I besched his Majeste to be good Lorde unto him, and to give him Bungaye [Bungay in Suffolk, where Denny came from; the castle there being a Howard property], which I had heard he much desired. His majesty moche commended my sute…

Denny and Herbert repaid the compliment and gift. They claimed that they pointed out to Henry that Paget

> had well remembered all men saving one. And his Majestie aunswering therewithall, you meane him self, we, the said Sir Antony Denny and Sir William Herbert, aunswered, Yea Sir, and soo praysed the sayd Mr Secretary and soo did also his Majestie, saying that he remembered him well ynough, and that he must nedes be helped.[6]

Whether Paget's story and Denny and Herbert's supporting statements are true or false remains uncertain, like so many of the events in this saga. When you read the full account of the justification for their distribution of the spoils as they presented it to the Privy Council, it does smell fishy. The tone throughout is that of those 'who do protest too much'. But, on the other hand, there is a document in the State Papers, with convincing-looking amendments in Paget's own handwriting, which fits with his story, with his description of what he presented to Henry following the King's request for a list of names to swell the ranks of the aristocracy. Most likely the story was not a complete invention but was adjusted to fit how Paget and Hertford wanted to reward those who had supported their actions.

Reviewing the overall picture – the last months of Henry VIII's reign, his will, its interpretation, the assumption of king-like power by Hertford, and Paget's role in all that – what conclusions can be drawn? First, Paget and the reformist faction consciously manoeuvred to gain power, even though luck and the foolish actions of the conservative faction helped them. Second, the evidence surrounding the will itself is inconclusive. It seems likely that it was mainly Henry's will. But it is 50/50 whether the document that survives was actually seen, approved and signed by Henry on 30 December. It is pretty certain that Paget drafted that document and it seems likely that he was responsible for two clauses in particular, the 'carte-blanche' and the 'unfulfilled gifts' – the ones that he and Hertford used to interpret the will in a very slanted, if not downright dodgy, way. There is an argument that, if the will was an outright forgery, why on earth did the forgers not simply get it to appoint Hertford as the Lord Protector. But this can be countered by saying that that would have been too blatant and unconvincing. If Paget, the 'Master of Practices', was going to cook something up, it would be much more subtle than that, subtle enough indeed for it to still be a matter of controversy over five hundred years later. Third, Paget was definitely a major part of a successful action to deliver the government of the country into the hands of the Lord Protector, Edward Seymour, Earl of Hertford and newly created Duke of Somerset. Some historians have thought it necessary to see Paget's actions as either ensuring the victory of one faction over another for his own benefit, or as securing order and stability with as broad a base of support as possible from the elite, at a moment when a boy king and the international situation threatened chaos. I think they can reasonably be seen as both.

Chapter 14

Life in William's Household

> The household, consisting of the family, its servants, dependants and possessions, was the centre of all social, economic and artistic life, and the focus of political allegiance.
>
> Susan Brigden, in *New Worlds, Lost Worlds*

With Henry VIII dead and Somerset firmly installed as Lord Protector, a new chapter opened, in Tudor history and in the life of Lord William Paget. In the next section, we will continue the story of William's turbulent political career during the reign of Edward VI. But first I want to paint a picture of the kind of life that he and his family were living at this time. Although by now in possession of much land and properties in Staffordshire and of a large London house, they were mainly based at West Drayton, and luckily there are extensive records concerning that house and estate.[1] Although no illustrations of the red-brick mansion have survived, the details of the Gatehouse, which still stands, resemble Hampton Court. It is therefore reasonable to assume it was a mini-Hampton Court in its architectural style. Not so mini, though, as shown by an inventory of 1556 which lists over fifty rooms, and records that show forty-seven fireplaces – the only form of heating. This was a big household. In addition to William and Anne's suites, the elder children, sons Henry and Thomas and daughters Anne and Jane, along with their servants, had their own rooms.

As did Paget's two wards, and in due course sons-in-law, Thomas Willoughby and Sir Christopher Allen. Their relationship to the family is an interesting indication of how a powerful man such as Paget would further enhance the family's wealth through arranged marriages. The Crown controlled the wardships of orphan children, of which, given the life expectancy, there were many. When an orphan was made a ward, the Crown, or those designated by the Crown, gained control of his or her money. Thus those with influence at Court tried to secure profitable wardships: Willoughby was the heir to a considerable estate and Allen to a rich London alderman. After being brought up in the Paget household, Thomas and Christopher were married to William and Anne's daughters, Dorothy and Etheldreda. This was a similar use of marriage, though at a lower level, to that employed by monarchs and dynasties in the sixteenth century, from the Habsburgs down. It has been dubbed 'matrimonial imperialism'.

Returning to the large West Drayton household. There were at least twenty retainers or servants living on the premises who had their own rooms; among many others, a chaplain, a steward, an estate manager, a 'clerke of the kitchen', the cook 'George of ye kitchen', ' the boyes of the kitchen', a butcher, a candlemaker, a 'horse keeper' and a carter and wagoner. The 1556 inventory describes exactly how most of the rooms were decorated and furnished. The level of luxury naturally differed enormously between the rooms occupied by the family and their guests, and the servants' quarters. Some rooms had internal porches, wood panelling and were extensively hung with wall hangings, often tapestries; others did not. This was not just a matter of aesthetics but crucially of comfort, as these additions excluded draughts. The quantity and quality of the furniture also varied greatly; that described as 'joined' was beautifully made by craftsmen using mortice and tenon joints, that as 'playne' was nailed together by less skilful carpenters. 'Joined' tables were luxury items, whereas boards on trestles were used in the servants' rooms and also in the large hall of the house where the staff ate their meals. 'Joined' beds, some being magnificent four-posters with curtains and valances in stunning fabrics, were in the family and guest bedrooms; plain bedsteads in the others. Chairs were relatively rare items in Tudor times, often reserved for the head of the household, with others sitting on stools or benches; which is where the modern use of the word 'chairman', of a meeting or company, comes from. The nature of the furnishings in a bedroom gave a pretty precise reading of the status of the occupant. So the estate manager had a plain bedstead and a table made from a board and trestles. But, although he only had a stool, it was 'joined' and his windows were hung with two silk curtains. This was much better than the furnishings of the lower servants. But the household steward was definitely one up from the estate manager, in that he had some panelling, 'halfe a portall of waynscot', and a 'joined' bed hung about with red and yellow silk. His two tables were only trestle tables but he had a chair as well as a 'joined' stool and he enjoyed wall hangings of red and yellow buckram in addition to two red and green silk curtains on the windows.

The family and guest rooms were seriously luxurious. William's bedchamber had two inner portals and all the walls were oak panelled. His fourposter was surmounted and curtained by hangings of blue silk, velvet and taffeta interwoven with real gold and silver thread. Along with a lot of other sophisticated furnishings, there were three major paintings, one of Christ and Mary and two of himself. Were these to maintain his presence for the sake of Lady Anne or others when he was away? Seems a tad egotistical to the modern mind, but probably not unusual for a sixteenth-century grandee. The two portraits are likely to be the one now in the National Portrait Gallery and one of those at Plas Newydd. The first is thought to have been painted by a Flemish court painter in 1549, when Paget was 44. His look is calm and serious, maybe a little worried. He holds a white rod of office which shows he was Comptroller of the (Royal) Household, a post he held from 1547 to 1550. The second was probably painted a few years later in Brussels. Both display insignia of the Order of the Garter.

Another curious entry in the inventory is of two weapons, a halberd and a 'holy water sprynkle', which was a spiked iron ball hanging from a chain, given a delightfully ironic and anti-clerical name. The existence of these in his bedroom indicate how close were basic issues of survival and violence, of life and death, despite William's exalted position and the veneer of civilisation and culture. In a small room adjoining the bedchamber there was a cupboard, covered in a carpet imported from Tournai, in which he kept 'certain evidences', his important papers such as title deeds.

The five guest rooms were magnificent, each designed around a colour; the Purple, Red, Yellow, Orange and Green Chambers. To take the Purple example. There was a portal of oak panelling. Over the fourposter was a canopy of purple velvet on which 'my Lord and Ladies armes [were] imbrodered'. A bell-pull of plaited 'sylver' rope for summoning servants hung next to the bed, which was piled with comfortable bedding and topped with a purple satin quilt bearing the Paget coat of arms and surrounded by purple damask curtains. There were two Turkish carpets – one of which covered a cupboard, two chairs upholstered in purple velvet, cushions also embroidered with the family arms and window curtains made of blue Bruges satin. On the walls were six tapestries depicting the Virtues. The other guest rooms were similarly appointed and with appropriate variations. The Yellow Chamber had sub-colour themes of blue and black and tapestries woven with 'verders of flowers'; the Orange Chamber had sub-themes of blue and gold and tapestries of the biblical story of David. One gets the feeling of some pretty serious interior decorating going on here and suspects the hand of Lady Anne. Indeed there is evidence that she was 'hands on' because in the inventory for 'the gret wardrobe' is a list of nine 'new coverings of my ladies makyng'.

(I guess a Tudor Nicky Haslam might have found this decor – single colour-themed rooms with lashings of velvet and satin and the family coat of arms all over the place – a tad 'common' or 'nouveau riche'. Mind you, the 'make-over' done by my grandfather in the 1930s, still visible at Plas Newydd, did include all the light switches being gold-coloured versions of the coat of arms. By repute, the light switches of Woodrow Wyatt, flamboyant tycoon and Labour Party politician who was a friend of my parents, went one further – made of real gold and featuring mini-sculptures of his own and his first wife's heads.)

The inventory gives many small clues as to what life was like in the Paget household. An exotic imported ivory desk at one end of the spectrum, and a great number of chamber pots at the other. This is the only direct evidence about the toilet arrangements for the household. The biographer of Sir William Petre, Paget's co-Secretary who built a manor in Essex, Ingatestone Hall, which is likely to have been similar to West Drayton, offers a bit more information on this very important subject. Ingatestone Hall did have pipes supplying water for various kitchen, laundering and washing activities, and we can assume this was also the case in West Drayton. But it is unclear whether the water supplies were also used in toilets; probably not. Petre's house had at least five 'houses of office' or 'stool houses', containing seats covered in leather or velvet on top of pewter pans. There's no such reference in the Paget archives; but these matters might not have been deemed worthy of mention. Mediaeval manors or castles generally had a draughty 'garderobe', often in a turret with a hole in the floor above a groundpit. Petre's biographer concludes, 'the evidence suggests that the sanitary arrangements ... were roughly midway between the garderobe and the water closet invented by Sir John Harrington before 1600 but not in general use until much later.'[2] Returning to the West Drayton inventory, for entertainment there was a chess set and a 'payr of tables', which means a backgammon board rather than two tables. (The expression to 'turn the tables' comes from this usage.) Also 'maskying' coats and 'visards' (masks), probably for dressing up at Christmas festivities. An enormous quantity of crockery, cutlery, pots and pans and utensils are listed in the kitchen and buttery, ranging from silver and gilt plate marked with the coat of arms and/or the initials WP, to twenty-four leather buckets. Among interesting items were 'pwdrynge tubbs', in which meat was salted to preserve it, a barber's basin for shaving and a pair of stocks for punishment.

The size of the enterprise is revealed by the rooms with specialised functions: a bake house, pastry house, brew house, milk house, 'Slauter' house, 'Wheate lofte', 'Chaundrie' for making candles and a 'Stylling' house, where perfumes and cordials were distilled. Much of the foodstuff came from Paget-owned farms near West Drayton, at Harmondsworth, Iver, Uxbridge and Heathrow, and also from land near Burton-on-Trent in the Midlands. Many household necessities were homemade. The kitchen clerk's accounts indicate a huge well-controlled household, largely self-sufficient and needing few things to be bought from outside. Records for the winter of 1546/47 show seventy-seven hens being sent from the Staffordshire estates to West Drayton and the household there receiving seven oxen and sixty sheep. Homemade candles were an important by-product from sheep and ox fat, as were 'winter felles' (fleeces) and ox hides.

The rich and powerful of Tudor England exchanged a lot of food, and especially drink, as presents. The Pagets received £15 worth of wine as presents that winter, including Clarets, Rennyche (Rhine), 'Mustadell' (muscadet), and, somewhat surprisingly, 'Sake'. (While considering, for a millisecond, the exciting possibility that this establishes a previously unknown link between Tudor England and Japan, it is probably a phonetic spelling of 'Sack', which was a fortified sweet wine, similar to sherry, imported from Spain.) The previous Christmas, in 1545, when William had been away from home negotiating with the French, his friend Thomas Chamberlain, the English agent in Antwerp, had shipped to Anne Paget 'an ame of Rhenish wine, which after my taste I think ye will not mislike'[3] (I have not been able to find out what quantity an 'ame' was). Plenty of beer was also drunk in the Paget household, much of it home-brewed but also bought in from breweries in Windsor and London. 'Small beer', a virtually alcohol-free ale, was widely drunk by all, including children, because it was much safer than water. (From Shakespeare on, it has also been used metaphorically to mean 'of relatively little importance'.) Stronger and bitterer beers that used malt and hops were newly invented and gaining ground in Tudor England. These were sometimes criticised as a new-fangled cause of moral decay, for example by one of Henry VIII's doctors, as being 'to the detryment of many Englysshe men'. A view not shared by the Pagets. The beers they bought differed greatly in strength, quality and price. In the winter of 1552, the records show beer of three different types being bought in, ranging in price, per barrel, from 3 to 7 shillings.

What did they eat? Tomatoes and potatoes had yet to be imported from America, awaiting, in myth at least, for Sir Walter Raleigh to bring them back, along with tobacco, as in the Beatles song:

> I'm so tired, I'm feeling so upset
> Although I'm so tired, I'll have another cigarette
> And curse Sir Walter Raleigh
> he was such a stupid git.

But imported spices were already in use. The kitchen clerk records provision of 'Spices of Dyvers sortes' and specifically mentions the use of saffron on Christmas Day 1551. The Tudor diet did not include cooked vegetables, although it did allow for some salads, fruit and veggie soups. Fruit and veg do not feature much in the accounts but this is probably because the produce from the West Drayton kitchen gardens and orchards, which were extensive, was not recorded in the same way as meat and fish. There is occasional mention, in menus or as purchases, of oranges, 'aples to rost', 'radishe roots', 'peason' (peas?), 'onyons', 'cabages', 'wallnutts' and 'chesnuts'. But the big thing was meat, either fresh or preserved in salt and spices. Great quantities were eaten of beef, veal, mutton, lamb, pork and bacon. Also plenty of venison, of which the 'umbles' (intestines, etc.) were made into pies for the lower orders. Thus the expression to 'eat [h]umble pie'. 'Wilde boore' and rabbit were often on the menu. All this heavy meat was supplemented, particularly in winter, by a huge variety of birds: chickens, turkeys, mallards, teal, snipe, plovers, quails, woodcock, pheasants, partridge, curlews, gulls, peewits, blackbirds, sparrows, larks, herons, cranes, swans and hawks.

And by fish. 'Fish days' were every Friday and Saturday as well as all of Lent and several other occasions, and they were taken very seriously. This arose not only from religion but also from reasons of State, to aid the sea-fishing industry and thus the navy, which relied on the support of their ships. Severe penalties could be inflicted for eating meat on 'fish days'. However, as with all such things, you could get round the regulations if you really wanted to and had sufficient pull. Meat was served in the Paget household on 'fish days' because there were always those who were excused on 'medical grounds', and anyway children could be exempted. When Sir Edward Warner, the gentleman who had been particularly helpful in providing damning depositions to convict Henry Howard (Earl of Surrey), visited West Drayton, he came with a royal licence for himself and his wife to eat meat during Lent and other fasting days for the rest of their lives. The same thing is recorded for the visit of Sir Thomas Chaloner, a successful diplomat, soldier and much-admired poet who was a protegee of Somerset. But a lot of fish was eaten, both fresh and salted, with thirty different types listed, including, in the kitchen clerk's spelling: whytings, sprottes, gunnell (eel-like 'butterfish'), bryll, floanders, playces, sea breame, solle, shrimpes, thorneback (a ray), oysters, ling, cod, sturgeon and herring. The last, fresh and pickled, feature a great deal. Cod and similar fish might be fresh, salted or just dried hard in the sun. Lamprey eels and freshwater crayfish were another part of the fish diet, and were sourced very locally. The Domesday Book has 1,500 eels as part of the valuation of the weirs and fishpond at Harmondsworth and there is elsewhere mention of a flourishing export trade in 'lamprons' caught at Heathrow and Teddington, supplying Dutch fishermen with bait. Crayfish were apparently still being fished in the waterways of the area at the beginning of the twentieth century. Meals sometimes had a 'sweet finish', with deserts known as 'subtleties', either sugar confections, jellies or marchpane (marzipan) made from ground almonds. There is a story of William trying to secure the services of a pastry chef in Antwerp.

We have a detailed account of the massive feast consumed on 21 September 1551 when the Lord Protector, 'The Duke of Somerset and his Trayne' came to dine at West Drayton. It is not known exactly how many were at table, but the kitchen clerk records that they were served with five and a half mutton carcasses, twenty-six pieces of beef, one veal carcass and six pigs. Fowls and birds included thirty-six pigeons, twenty-six chickens, eleven baked and four roasted capons, six quails, a swan, a heron, two gulls and forty-eight sparrows. Three hundred eggs were used along with 1.5 gallons of cream. Seventy-eight loaves of bread were eaten and seven bushels of 'ffurmite wheate', which was wheat, with the husks removed, boiled in cinnamon and sugar. Four barrels of beer and a kilderkin (16 gallons) of ale (the 'old-fashioned' beer without hops) were drunk. Ten pounds of candles were used and a quantity of plants (we do not know what type), known as 'Saunders', were bought to be burnt to scent the air.

This was obviously an exceptional occasion. Ordinarily there could be as many as eighty people eating in the household, with most of the servants and retainers in the great hall, their meal referred to by the clerk as a 'mease' (mess). The family, their guests and the higher servants are referred to as the 'familia' and eat in a smaller, more luxurious, dining room. Mealtimes were earlier than now, presumably because, despite the use of candles, daylight was a defining factor. (Breakfast is seldom mentioned in the clerk's accounts, but according to one reference, then, as now, eggs were a breakfast 'thing'; twelve eggs were served for the children's breakfast in the London house on 12 January 1551.) Dinner, or lunch was at 11.00 am and supper was at 5.00 pm. Entertainments, such as music, dancing or plays followed supper. In *A Midsummer Night's Dream*, the artisans' hilarious play, *Pyramus and Thisbe*, is performed 'between our after-supper and bed-time' and Bottom suggests that they leave 'a casement of the great chamber, where we play, open, and the moon may shine in at the casement'. We do not know for sure that plays were performed at West Drayton or in the London house, but it is likely.

There is plenty of evidence that music played a big part. At West Drayton, the parlour (essentially the sitting room) contained a virginal (a harpsicord-like keyboard instrument) and a lute; the adjoining servants' chamber had three viols (predecessors of the violin), another virginal and 'gret syngying boks'; the great hall had two more virginals; and there were two 'gyttornes' (guitars) in the house. In the Pagets' London house there was 'a case of violls' (a set of six instruments) and 'a case of regalls' (a small portable organ). In Chapter 7, we have seen how William imported musicians from Antwerp. And Thomas

Tusser was employed by the Pagets as a musician. Tusser was an influential sixteenth-century cultural 'all-rounder', famous for his 'instructional poem' *Five Hundred Points of Good Husbandry*, which was an expanded version of his original *A Hundreth Good Points of Husbandrie*, published in 1557. This book is the origin of many well-known sayings, such as 'A fool and his money are soon parted', 'At Christmas play and make good cheer, For Christmas comes but once a year', 'Seek home for rest, for home is best' and 'Sweet April showers do spring May flowers.' The full title of this best seller was:

> *Five Hundred Points of Good Husbandry*
> *As well for the Champion or Open Country as for the Woodland or Several together with A Book of Huswifery*
> *Being a calendar of rural and domestic economy for Every Month of the Year And exhibiting a picture of the Agriculture, Customs, and Manners of England in the Sixteenth Century.*

On the title page Tusser described himself as 'Servant to the Honorable Lord Paget of Beaudesert' and dedicated the book to Thomas, William's son, with a poem praising his father, including the stanzas:

> Your father was my founder
> Till death became his wounder,
> No subject ever sounder,
> Whom prince advancement gave.

and:

> His neighbours then did bless him,
> His servants now do miss him,
> The poor would gladly kiss him,
> alive again to be;
> But God hath wrought his pleasure,
> And blest him out of measure,
> With heaven and earthly treasure,
> So good a God is he.

Not the greatest poetry and who knows whether it reflected a genuine affection for William from this servant or merely sycophancy for the rich and powerful. A later edition of the book adds that 'We are not to understand that he [Tusser] was a menial servant, but only a retainer; of whom persons of rank, in those days, kept a number proportional to their opulence, or their love of ostentation.'[4]

As well as being a talented musician, Tusser was a horticultural expert and his *Good Husbandrie* titles are early examples of successful gardening books. It is certain that the large gardens and orchards at West Drayton will have been worthy of this top horticulturist's involvement. As with the decorating, there's a clue that Lady Anne was 'hands on' in the garden – in the form of a letter from Lord Cobham in Calais to William saying, 'I have sent to my lady your wife, according to my promise, some asperges [asparagus] seed.' The interior decorating, the gardening, managing large households at West Drayton, London and Staffordshire, and the lavish entertainment of guests; Lady Anne may well have been controlling it all. As is often the case with the hidden history of women's involvement, there is not a lot to prove it in the written records. But there are hints that here may be yet another example of 'Behind every great man…'

Before returning to the story of the political shenanigans of the reigns of Edward and Mary, a final, and darker, example from the local archives shows what life was like in those days: one Giles Feverell was hanged in 1554 for stealing six of Lord Paget's oxen at Drayton.

Francis I of France. (*Wikipedia commons, public domain*)

The Emperor Charles V. (*Wikipedia commons, public domain*)

Bishop Gardiner, Paget's first patron. (© *National Trust*)

Thomas Cromwell. (*Wikimedia commons, public domain*)

Thomas Wriothesley. (*Wikimedia commons, public domain*)

Edward Seymour, Duke of Somerset. (*Wikimedia commons, public domain*)

John Dudley, aka Lisle, Warwick and Duke of Northumberland. (*Wikimedia commons, public domain*)

Lord William Paget, 1st Baron Beaudesert. (© *National Trust*)

Baby 20th Baron Paget, along with his grandfather, the author and 8th Marquess of Anglesey, and his father, the Earl of Uxbridge, in front of the portrait of the 1st Baron in the Gothic Hall at Plas Newydd. (*Photo Katherine Uxbridge*)

The author in the Great Barn at Harmondsworth, called 'the Cathedral of Middlesex' by John Betjeman. Owned by William Paget. (*Photo Susie De Paolis*)

The author in front of the Gatehouse to William Paget's West Drayton Manor. (*Photo Susie De Paolis*)

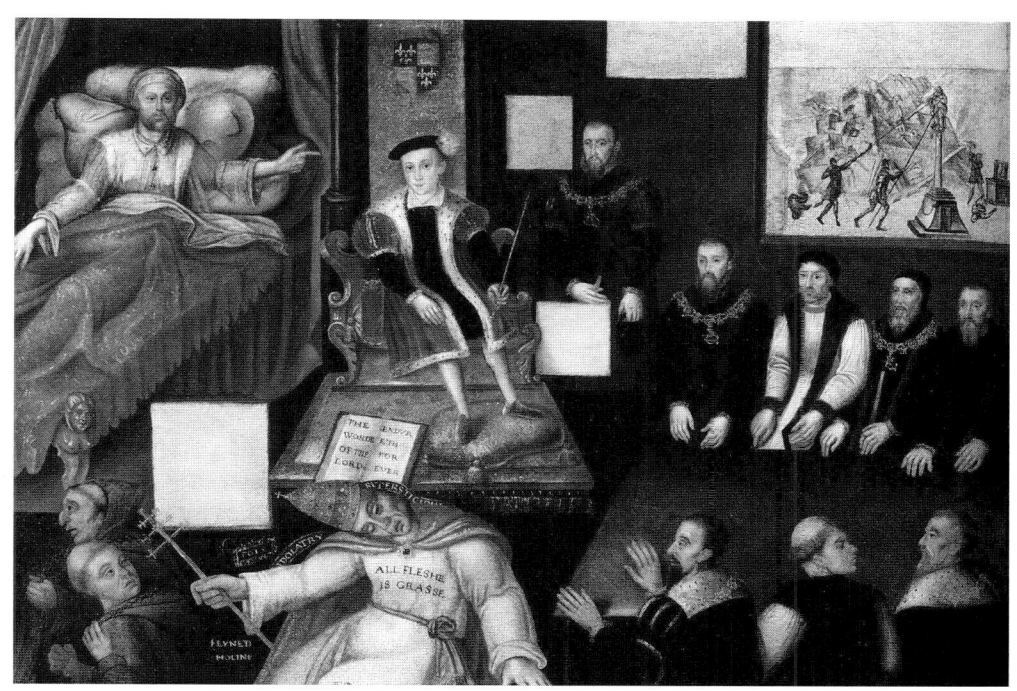

Henry VIII on his deathbed, pointing to Edward as his successor, while the Pope and Papistry are destroyed. Edward Seymour (Somerset) next to Edward; William Paget on the far right. (*Wikimedia commons, public domain*)

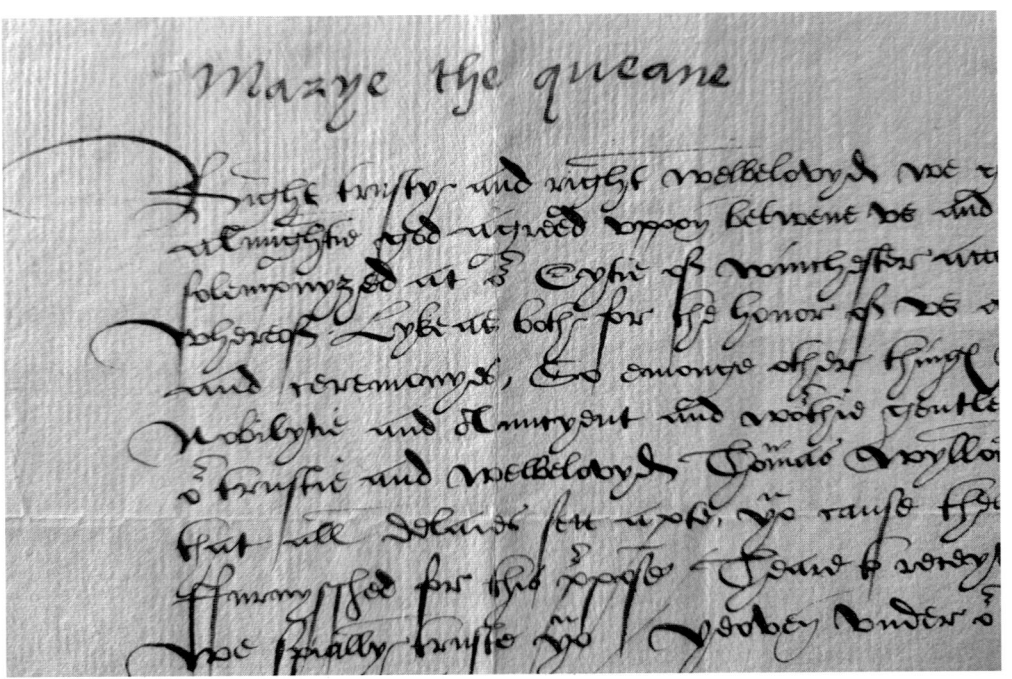

Letter from 'Mary the Qeane' to William Paget. Shows the difficulty of reading 16th century handwriting. (*Owned by the author*)

Signature of Princess Elizabeth, in a letter to Paget thanking him for his help during Mary's reign. (*Previously owned by the author*)

Mary of Hungary, Charles V's Regent in the Netherlands. (*Wikimedia commons, public domain*)

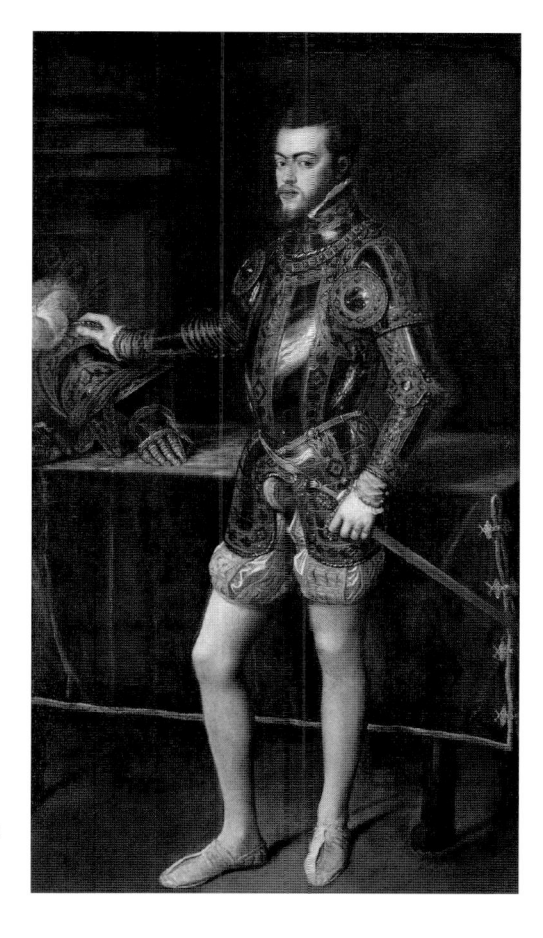

Philip II of Spain, in the portrait by Titian shown to his bride to be, Mary. (*Wikimedia commons, public domain*)

An illustration, somewhat romanticised, of fortifications and soldiers in 16th century France. (*From a french history of Francis I, Paris 1909. Courtesy of Octavian von Hofmannsthal*)

Part II
Edward, Mary and Elizabeth

Chapter 15

Somerset's Right-Hand Man

> The Protector governs absolutely, but always on the advice of Secretary Paget.
>
> Ambassador van de Delft to the Emperor Charles V, 1547

Henry VIII's demise brought out contradictory emotions in his subjects. Some felt sorrow at the death of a great and strong ruler, and no doubt feared for what the future might hold. For others it was 'good riddance': according to the sarcastic commentary of the early nineteenth-century historian, Patrick Fraser Tytler, who made a collection of key Tudor letters, many people 'were unnatural enough to rejoice once more feeling their heads secure upon their shoulders'. A letter from Bishop Gardiner to Paget, from Tytler's Collection, illustrates this vividly. Gardiner pompously complained that, on the very day that he and the parishioners of Southwark were to hold 'a solemn dirige [dirge] for our late sovereign lord and master', a certain troupe of theatrical players employed by the Earl of Oxford, 'lewd fellows', intended to perform with 'mirth' in the same borough. (Incidentally, the son and heir of this Earl of Oxford, who continued his father's interest in the theatre, is the prime alternative candidate for authorship of the plays by 'Shakespeare deniers' – prominent among them the actor Mark Rylance who plays Thomas Cromwell in the adaptations of the Hilary Mantel books.) Gardiner goes on to say that he had already spoken to the Justice of Peace for the area but that the same, 'answereth neither yea nor nay as to the playing … and therefore I write unto you, wherein if ye will not … meddle, send me so word, and I will myself sue to my Lord Protector.'[1]

We do not know whether the bishop succeeded in banning the players. But the letter shows the very contradictory reactions to Henry's death, and is also one of many examples showing the hierarchy of power in its immediate aftermath: Somerset at the top, Paget in the number two slot.

Somerset consolidated his hold on power in the first few months of 1547, so, as has been said, 'his status changed from that of a chairman of a governing committee to that of a viceroy with a panel of advisors, whom he might consult or not as he pleased.'[2] His autocratic power is established in the records of the

Privy Council for 21 March 1547 in an entry which repeats over and over his authority to

> do, procure and execute, and cause to be done, procured and executed, all and every such thing and things, acte and actes, which a Governour of the Kinges persone of this realm during his minorite and a Protectour of his realmes, domininions and subjectes ought to do, procure and execute, or cause to be doone, procured and executed...

And so on: on and on. That is a tiny extract from an entry that goes on for pages in exactly the same vein. You get the sense that they felt that if only they said it over and over, it would be so. The tone is one of insecurity bred of an awareness that their legitimacy was thoroughly dubious.³ For the moment, however, it went largely unchallenged. Somerset and Paget made it clear to foreign ambassadors that they should deal with them and not the Privy Council. Somerset now had the power to appoint new Privy Councillors: a particularly notable change in that Henry VIII had attempted to lay down who the councillors should be for the duration of his son's minority. The Lord Protector also changed his coat of arms to resemble the royal one his sister Queen Jane Seymour had borne: an arrogant act confirming his king-like status. (It is difficult for us to credit just how significant such matters were: but their importance in sixteenth-century culture and politics is shown over and over again. For example, it was the attempt by the Howards, a few months earlier, to make their coat of arms more regal that sealed their fate.) Paget's own status was also enhanced at this time when he was installed as a knight of the prestigious Order of the Garter. A curious footnote to this, revealing William as a conscientious, if not positively pedantic, civil servant, is that he apparently promptly set to work collecting the arrears of fees owed by other knights of the Garter.

Whatever the formal position, Somerset and Paget also had to make sure that the residual power of the more conservative figures from the last days of Henry VIII, Wriothesley and Gardiner, was broken. Wriothesley had probably been against Somerset's elevation from the start. Charles V's ambassador van der Delft claimed that the Lord Chancellor had 'refused to consent to any innovations in the matter of government beyond the provisions of the [Henry VIII's] will'.⁴ Nonetheless, it had initially seemed that Wriothesley was happy with the new order as were they with him: he had been re-instated as Lord Chancellor and even rewarded with the earldom of Southampton. But an opportunity to unseat him arose when he made an error of judgement, legally and politically. Some lawyers, probably concerned about their own status or job security, complained that he had appointed 'civilians' to hear Chancery cases in his absence, and that he had done so without first obtaining authority from the Privy Council. This was not quite a trumped-up charge but most commentators at the time and since reckon that it was really just an excuse to get rid of a man who had been reluctant to endorse Somerset's new powers, had failed to seek the Lord Protector's permission to act and who might prove a threat in the future. The Privy Council meeting of 5 March stripped him of this post and placed him under house arrest, 'as in pryson'.

An interesting aspect of Wriothesley's fall is the light it throws on the importance of the Great Seal of State as a symbol of government authority. He had physical possession of this in his capacity as Lord Chancellor and the ruling of the Privy Council stressed what danger

> might ensue to the Kinges moste ryall persone, and what hindrance, detriment and subversion to his affayres, if the Greate Seale of Inglande, whereby the King and the realm might be bownde, shuld continew in the handes of so stowte and arrogant persone as durste ... to seale with oute specialle warraunt from the Kinges Majeste by the advice and consent of us, the Lord Protectour and Counseill.

And the Council very specifically stated that the Great Seal should be removed from Wriothesley on that day, 'after supper' at his London home, Elye Place, by Thomas Seymour (Somerset's brother) and two others.[5] Custody of the Great Seal of State was significant at other critical moments later in this story. In October 1551, one of the triggers for the arrest of the Duke of Somerset, in the 'coup' that also resulted in Paget's imprisonment, was the rumour that 'Somerset and his accomplices had prepared to seize the Great Seal of England'. And it was important that the then Lord Chancellor, Richard Rich, deserted Somerset and brought the seal with him to join Warwick's coup, as it was also, in July 1553, when William Paget physically delivered it to Mary to confirm her, rather than Lady Jane Grey, as sovereign.

When authority is questioned and the winner in a game of power is uncertain, certain objects seem to gain great symbolic significance. One thinks of the Crown itself when Richard III was replaced by Henry VII at the battle of Bosworth Field – at any rate as told by Shakespeare; or, later, the Mace that Oliver Cromwell had snatched away from Parliament to assert his rule. The incidents involving the Great Seal of State in addition show how very personal and small-scale the business of government was in Tudor England. Three men went to collect the Seal from Wriothesley's home, 'after supper'; thirty men were to accompany Paget when he delivered it to Mary. It has been claimed that Tudor government only employed about 1,500 people, including the most menial jobs, and that there were only about 175 posts at Court which could support a gentleman.[6] So everybody pretty much knew everybody else; which is why contemporary historians of the sixteenth century rightly place much greater emphasis on personal networks than on institutions.

But networks of personal relations did not always survive in the face of serious political or religious disagreements. William may have been close to Wriothesley from school and to Gardiner from university, but disagreement with the one about the necessity for a king-like Protector and religious differences with the other effectively ended those friendships.

Paget also fell out with Bishop Gardiner early in Edward VI's reign over the issue of bishops' powers. Royal Commissions renewing episcopal jurisdiction had to be issued when there was a new monarch. Gardiner wrote angrily to Paget about the wording of these commissions because bishops were described as 'delegates': whereas he believed that bishops should have jurisdiction in cases of ecclesiastical law 'in their own right', not as a result of delegated powers. He accused Paget of being 'a pyncher of the bishoppes and amonges them me', and he reasserted his determination to defend 'Goddes truth against that they cal Goddes Worde'. The primacy of God's truth, interpreted by the institutions of the Church, as opposed to that of God's Word, as revealed to individuals by the Bible, was perhaps the defining religious difference between conservatives and Evangelicals. William replied pretty sharply,

> I malign not Bishops, but would that both they and all other were in such order as might be most to the glory of God and the benefit of this realm … I wish either that you were no bishop, or that you could have such a pliable will as could well bear the reformation that should be thought meet for the quiet of the realm.

And he signed off curtly, 'No man wisheth you better than I do … if you wish me not like, you are in the wrong; and thus I take my leave of your lordship.'[7]

This was about as close as the florid politeness of sixteenth-century correspondence gets to a 'get lost' letter. Gardiner was frozen out of a government which was leaning more and more in the Evangelical direction as the year went by. By October, he was imprisoned for his resistance. Paget reported to van der Delft that, 'I have had several long discussions with [Gardiner], as his friend, to persuade him to mitigate his attitude. But he is quite intractable and entirely different from what he used to be.'[8] As Gardiner's biographer has pointed out, when detailing the theological disagreements, this was not really the case. It was, rather, that Somerset and his allies such as Paget had moved the religious goal posts, while it was Gardiner who was consistent, arguing that no radical religious innovations should be enacted during the King's minority.[9]

* * *

In the last months of Henry's and the first months of Edward's reigns, Somerset had needed Paget's support to gain and consolidate his position. Paget had been able to offer the institutional power of the Secretary of State and, equally important, the influence that flowed from his close personal relationship with Henry. But, more than this, it appears that William was also Somerset's political mentor. In a letter back in April 1544, he had been advised by 'the Master of Practices' how to enhance his political connections with those whose influence was crucial at that moment. Paget had said, 'His Lordship will do well to salute now and then with a word or two in a letter my Lord of Suffolk, my Lord Wriotheseley, and others, forgetting not Mr Denye.' Paget and Somerset were close at the personal and family level as well as in matters of politics, as is shown by a revealing 'ps' that the latter added in his own hand to a letter to the former in June 1545. Half jokingly, he accused William of criticising him for failing to write to his (Somerset's) wife. One assumes that either Somerset's wife had told Paget this, or, more likely that she had complained to Anne Paget, who then passed on the complaint to her husband. Somerset then went on to 'josh' his friend, 'as though you would be noted a good husband and that no such fault could be found in you. I would advise you to leave off such quarrels, or else I will tell my lady [Anne Paget] such tales of you as you would repent the beginning.' In their confab in the gallery at Westminster while Henry was dying, the future Lord Protector had, in Paget's words, promised 'to follow mine advice in al your procedings, more than any other mans.'[10] The role of intimate political advisor that Paget had played for Henry VIII now continued with Somerset, who made sure, as had Henry, that his advisor was by his side most of the time. Even when he went to campaign against the Scots in the summer of 1547, Paget accompanied the Lord Protector for the first three days travelling north and William was the only Privy Councillor to go with him on inspection tours of Dover and Portsmouth in 1548.

There are many examples of Paget's great power at this moment. A letter from John Dudley (Viscount Lisle, Earl of Warwick, future Duke of Northumberland), who was later to replace Somerset as effective ruler of the country, shows that Paget is seen as the man, the one who could deliver. Dudley wanted to add the castle and land at Warwick to his earldom, 'because of the name, I am most desirous to have the thing ... to have the same castle, meadows and park; wherein I pray you to show me your friendship, to move the rest of my lords to this effect.' In the same letter he asked Paget, 'further to be friendly to Mr Denny, according to his desire for the site and remains of Waltham, with certain other farms adjoining'. And he throws in a request on behalf of Sir Anthony Browne, 'The Master of the Horse would gladly ... have the lordship in Sussex that was the Lord Laware's; which in my opinion were better bestowed upon him.' As pointed out by the nineteenth-century historian, Tytler, whose collection included this letter, many Privy Councillors evidently 'thought it proper to enrich themselves during the minority of the sovereign' and it was 'through [Paget] much of the patronage seems to have flowed.'[11] Incidentally, William replied favourably to Warwick's begging letter in July 1547, although apologising for his delay in dealing with it because he was 'Absent from the court by reason of the meseles werwith all my house is troubled one after the other'.[12] Nor was the academic world backward in knowing on which side their bread was buttered; the University of Cambridge chose this moment to name their powerful alumnus, Sir William, to be High Steward of the University.[13] Paget naturally did not exclude himself from the benefits of office. One particularly good perk was getting his hands on Exeter House, the London palace which was the residence of John Vesey, Bishop of Exeter – when he was deprived of his see for his Catholic sympathies. This grand mansion on the Strand, between what is now the Royal Courts of Justice and Middle Temple Gardens on the Thames, then became Paget House, which also allowed William to increase his wealth by selling his London house in Canon Row. In Elizabeth's reign, Paget House continued as a benefit for those enjoying royal patronage. It became first Leicester House, when Robert Dudley, Earl of Leicester was the Queen's favourite and later Essex House, when her favourite was Robert Devereux, Earl of Essex. The Devereux pub is one of the buildings now on the site.

That power flowed as much from personal 'networking', and influence with the ruler as from any formal position, is further shown by the fact that Paget chose to give up being Secretary and also refused the job of Lord Chancellor in the summer of 1547. This was probably due to a combination of a personal desire to avoid the heavy burden of routine administrative work and a political need to be available as Somerset's close advisor. van der Delft reported to Charles V on 17 June that Paget had turned down the Lord Chancellorship, 'in order to avoid undertaking more work. He is, indeed, continuing to lighten his work as much as he can, and he even thinks of giving up his post as Secretary and to accept instead two or three other offices of comparatively light responsibility, but of great emolument...'[14]

Indeed, the jobs he took on, Comptroller of the King's Household and sole Chancellor of the Duchy of Lancaster, involved less work, were prestigious, well paid and were anyhow not without direct influence. The Comptroller of the King's Household was in charge of a budget of about £40,000 a year and received a salary of £107. The Chancellor of the Duchy received £142 and had huge powers of patronage, including appointments to seventy-three church benefices. A list of the direct employees of the duchy shows that many of them were friends and retainers of Paget. (The Duchy of Lancashire exists to this day as a separate Crown body, owning half a billion pounds' worth of land – not just in Lancashire – and other assets, and providing the monarch with £20 million a year income.) There is also a hint that William may have wanted to spend a bit more time at home or managing the estates he had acquired at West Drayton and in Staffordshire. Both van der Delft and the French ambassador, de Selve, mention Paget's absences from Court as occasional inconveniences when dealing with the English government: pointing also to his central role in foreign policy.[15]

The duchy in addition controlled many parliamentary boroughs and it helped William consolidate his influence in Staffordshire, where he was responsible for Lichfield receiving parliamentary representation. The official history of Parliament suggests that he organised the whole of the elections to Parliament in 1547 and 'began to play the part of government manager and spokesman in the Commons, and liaison officer with the Lords', being responsible for a lot of what happened in Parliament up until the spring of 1549. The great issues of the day – religion, dynastic and family power, war with Scotland, foreign policy vis à vis France and the Empire, government finance – will be considered below. But it is important to realise that, whatever drama and intrigues were played out in the sphere of higher politics, the more prosaic business of government continued in the background, then as now. For example, Paget's name was associated at this time with bills to do with the control of cattle breeding, with sewers, with abstention from eating meat at certain times (an issue referred to in Chapter 14) and an Act for the regulation of Curriers (curers of leather), Cordwainers (leather shoemakers) and Girdlers (makers of leather belts). Worshipful companies of these three trades still exist in the City of London, mainly as charitable institutions, supported by the leather or shoe industries of today, by companies such as Jimmy Choo or L. K. Bennett. (I have, incidentally, found it fascinating to discover, while researching this book, just how much of contemporary British life is still quite closely connected to our history from way back – whether it be the leather industry or the financing of the Crown through the Duchy of Lancaster.) Back to Paget and Parliament, it is notable that one of only about thirty Acts of Parliament in 1549 was a private one for the 'Creation of a churchyard at West Drayton', re-locating it to enable him to expand his property.

The official History of Parliament is of the opinion that, while Somerset was away campaigning in Scotland, Paget was 'the effective head of the government'.[16] It is certainly the case that, as in the previous reign, and irrespective of his official job, he continued as a, if not the, main player in the formulation and execution of English foreign policy. Both the French and Imperial ambassadors considered him to be the man they had to deal with. The latter was of the view that 'his authority in the country is great', that he was 'the principle manager here now' and 'the Protector governs absolutely, but always on the advice of Secretary Paget'. There is an interesting entry in van der Delft's report to the Queen of Hungary (the Imperial Regent in the Netherlands), showing not only how important Paget was considered but also how readily he was looked to for political advice, even by a foreign ambassador:

> as during the last few days God has blessed me with a new born son, I thought it would afford me a good opportunity to render my relations with Paget more intimate ... if I asked him to favour me by standing godfather to my child. He took the invitation in very kindly fashion, but he advised me, since it was my intention to ask Lady Mary to stand godmother, to invite the King and the Protector to be the other sponsors. I followed his friendly advice...

By September 1547, van der Delft was writing to the Emperor that although Paget 'intended to withdraw from the active management of business [he] is still in charge of everything' and 'seeing that the Protector himself does nothing of importance without him, Your Majesty may perhaps think it advisable to confirm him in his attachment by a gracious word or two in a letter.' The Emperor obliged, expressing to his ambassador a worry that Paget might have shown 'some signs of jealousy' because a previous letter had been addressed to Somerset rather than to him. His letter then heaped praise on Paget, calling him 'very dear and well beloved', thanking him for his support and assuring him that 'on my side the most sincere and active reciprocity shall always exist, and if at any time it may happen that I can give you pleasure I will do so.'[17]

Chapter 16

Balancing Act – Home and Abroad

> The foreign ambassadors had quickly become accustomed to dealing with Paget. It was apparent that he and Somerset worked closely together and that Paget exerted enormous influence.
>
> Margaret Scard's life of Somerset, *Tudor King in All But Name*

English foreign policy continued to be about balancing Valois France and the Habsburg Empire. At the very beginning of Edward's reign, an unofficial French envoy, Captain Paulin, was in London negotiating an early return of Boulogne and the possibility of an Anglo-French alliance, to be cemented by Edward's marriage to a French princess. The Empire was naturally concerned about this, with Paget needing to reassure them that no Anglo-French dealings would be detrimental to their interests. van der Delft remained nervous, for example about a rumour that Paget's visits to Staffordshire might be 'a pretext for him to get away and quickly cross the sea' to negotiate with the French.[1] But the ambassador need not have worried too much. It was true that, after Charles V defeated the German Protestants at the decisive Battle of Muhlberg, in April 1547 (immortalised in the portrait by Titian that hangs in the Prado), there was concern among Paget and other English policy-makers that the European balance of power had swung too much in the Imperial direction. Specifically, there was a fear that, with the Continental Protestants dealt with and with Charles V apparently all-powerful, he might turn his attention to intervention in favour of Mary and English Catholicism. As the perceptive writer of the Preface to the *Calendar of State Papers, Spain, 1547–49* puts it,

> The Battle of Muhlberg pleased the English no better than it did the French. Besides the fact that their sympathies were with the Protestants, the young king's mentors sincerely believed in the danger of Imperial intervention in the Lady Mary's favour, which might bring with it such an event as the restoration of the Orders of the abbey lands, of which they all enjoyed a share.[2]

This was indeed a real worry for Somerset, Paget, and all the other new nobility and official class who had profited by the Dissolution of the Monasteries. But, for the moment, it was no more than a background fear. In the foreground was the issue of subduing the Scots, which inevitably meant English hostility to the traditional ally of Scotland, France. This mutual hostility increased when the King of France, Francis I, died in March 1547 and was replaced by Henry II, at whose Court the Guise influence was dominant. Mary of Guise was Queen Dowager of Scotland and her only child was the Queen (Mary, Queen of Scots). As a result, 'the Guises cared for nothing else while Scotland was threatened with annexation by England'.[3] In April, de Selve, the French ambassador, reported that 'there has been a marvellous amount of noise that the [French] King is resolved to make war on the English.' Paget could therefore honestly reassure van der Delft that the French 'will never deceive us, for we never have any trust in them'.[4] Commercial interests, as before, also pointed towards continued alliance with the Imperial Netherlands. From 1363 onwards, Calais had been designated the 'Wool Staple', meaning that all wool exports, which nearly all went to the Netherlands, had to pass through the town, with the Crown having a customs point there and levying a tax. There was concern in both the Netherlands and England – voiced in discussion between Paget and van der Delft – to make sure this arrangement continued.

The military campaign against the Scots that dominated policy was an obsession for Somerset, who had fought them before in Henry's reign and who again led the invading English army in person. Paget was one of many landowners ordered to provide troops. One of the recovered 'royal letters' owned by my family is from Somerset ordering him to provide, 'x [ten] grete horses or good geldings ... well trimmed to serve in the felde', along with their riders, to assemble at Newcastle on 23 August. The letter also gives instructions as to their uniform, 'bycause moche diversities of colours in the cotes ... would appere very unseemly we have resolved to have their cotes all of redde'. This is interesting as most authorities record the very first use of the English 'redcoats' as being in Ireland and in Elizabeth's reign and the official adoption of red uniforms for the English army as occurring a century later.[5]

As the purpose of this campaign against the Scots was to force a marriage between Edward VI and Mary, Queen of Scots, it was dubbed the 'Rough Wooing'. And rough it was, with 14,000–15,000 Scottish casualties at the battle of Pinkie, a major English victory, but known in Scotland as 'Black Saturday'. The slight respect that the English elite had for the Scots is vividly illustrated by what Paget told van der Delft in the aftermath of Pinkie:

So you see that Scotsmen always will remain Scotsmen with neither loyalty or law. Nevertheless the earl of Huntly who is a prisoner promises to do wonders for our advantage if we allow him to return to his own country to carry on negotiation with the nobles, amongst whom he possesses great authority. But warned, as we have been, by so many examples of the unreliability and vanity of such promises, we are nevertheless disposed to prove Huntly's good faith in the matter on condition that he leaves here as hostages his three sons and his wife. The latter we are insisting upon because he holds her in such high esteem, and the Scots are naturally little regardful of their children.[6]

Paget's anti-Scottish and anti-French rants may have been exaggerated because he would have been well aware that this was the sort of stuff that pleased the Imperial ambassador. But one suspects that the feelings were also real, and, if so, and in that they continue in the England of today, it supports the hardly surprising theory that national prejudices against the nearest neighbours are often the deepest and most long-lasting. Despite the victory at Pinkie and the high hopes that Somerset and Paget had of subduing the Scots, they refused to come to terms. The wooing may have been rough but it was unsuccessful. The young Mary, Queen of Scots escaped to France and the continued occupation of much of the Lowlands and Borders, without peace, remained a huge drain on the English treasury.

Although Somerset's war with the Scots made peace between England and France unlikely, he and Paget nonetheless continued to explore that possibility. At about the time of the battle of Pinkie, the French ambassador wrote to his king that he had been 'asked down to Hampton Court to hear the word of the King as delivered by Paget'. English and French commissioners had been meeting to resolve an issue to do with the boundary river around Boulogne when the French had suddenly departed without making any agreement. De Selve reported that Paget 'played outraged' about this behaviour and hoped it did not mean war. In addition, de Selve wrote that the Protector and Paget wanted to explore a deal on Boulogne without the other Privy Councillors initially knowing about their negotiations. He tells how, Paget and he having dined earlier, they met alone in the Council Chamber while the other Privy Councillors were still eating and Paget started to make proposals that he (de Selve) noted down on the menu. At which point, the other Councillors entered the room wanting to get involved and the ambassador recorded

> that Paget was not pleased with this interruption and that he quickly put the letter from the Protector that he had been showing Selve into his

pocket and drew out another one which he later on showed to them all, while speaking loudly in French 'Gentlemen, Mr Ambassador was just asking me for news of the Protector.'[7]

The letter Paget concealed made it clear that Somerset and he were prepared to contemplate returning Boulogne but that they needed to win over the Privy Council – in particular Somerset's great rival, Warwick – to which end it would greatly help if the French king could pretend that it was he, not the Protector, who opened the negotiation. Nothing in the end came of this because of continuing and deepening Anglo-French hostility over Scotland. But the incident is revealing of how foreign policy was being managed by Somerset and Paget independently of the Privy Council – indeed, where necessary, by manipulating its members.

The interconnection between British domestic politics and the complexities of European geopolitics, which had been such a feature of Henry's reign, continued under the Protectorate. With French troops being sent to help the Scots, the English wanted to employ mercenaries, to be raised from Imperial dominions. The Emperor initially refused, not wanting to antagonise the French and being unhappy about the too aggressively Evangelical direction of English religious reform. Somerset responded furiously, asking Charles's ambassador

> what sort of friendship I called that, and then, getting into a passion, he cried, 'I see very well that we must settle our affairs, so that we can live on good terms with everybody … I am everyday being approached by the French … Everything could be settled by Boulogne, and the King would be the gainer by the extent of more than two hundred thousand pounds…'

And Somerset complained of 'the undue confidence I have reposed in the friendship between the Emperor and my master the King. It seems to me that I am learning fresh wisdom every day against my own inclination.'[8]

This was at least partially bluff on Somerset's part. Nonetheless, Charles V would have been embarrassed at this time, when his hands were full with German affairs, if a peace between England and France had left the latter free to interfere with his schemes. Paget, as usual, poured oil on the troubled waters of Anglo-Imperial relations, and the Emperor relented and allowed the English to raise their mercenaries.

In the second half of 1548, another bout of the plague hit London, with the Imperial ambassador reporting in October that 'London is still so dangerous that those who frequent it are not allowed to go to Court, or to the Protector's house.'

And a bit later that

> The King still remains at Oatlands [the royal palace near Weybridge in Surrey] without holding any Court, this being a consequence of the death of some of his officers very suddenly. The Protector also has recently lost some of his household, and Controller Paget some of his neighbours in the village [of West Drayton] where he was living.⁹

Meanwhile, the unwinnable war against the Scots and increasingly open hostility towards the French continued to be combined dangerously with further friction between England and the Empire over commercial relations and religious policy. In January 1549, when English officials detained and searched Dutch ships to make sure no French goods, particularly weapons, were on board, Charles had a 'convenient grievance' (in the words of the Preface to the *State Papers, Spain 1547–49*) to lay 'an embargo on the property of English merchants in Flanders. His object in making such a commotion was merely to render the English Council anxious to appease him by refraining from disturbing the Lady Mary on account of religion.'¹⁰

However, this occurred at just the moment when the plot by Somerset's brother, Thomas Seymour, Admiral of England, was uncovered, apparently causing Charles to backpedal for fear of being accused of complicity in the intrigue. Relations between the Protector and his brother had been strained for some time. Thomas was jealous of his brother's king-like position and felt himself undervalued. He had plans to marry royalty, whether Mary, Elizabeth or Katherine. Edward had not approved when he did marry Henry VIII's widow, Katherine Parr, and there was a dispute as to whether the jewels the King had given her were loans (i.e. State property), or gifts (i.e. her own). Then there was the issue of Thomas's possible 'overfamiliarity' with the 14-year-old Princess Elizabeth who was living with them at this time.

Paget explained to van der Delft what had happened. The ambassador's report is worth quoting at length, as it reveals – though with uncertain accuracy – the detail of a *Game of Thrones*-like 'palace coup', in this case a failed one. Paget said,

> He [Thomas Seymour] has been a great rascal [ce a este grand meschant], I then asked ... if it was really a criminal case as I had been told at Calais. Paget answered that as he hoped to reach his own house safely it was plain in every respect that the Admiral had intended to kill the King and the Lady Mary, and marry the Lady Elizabeth; that he had more greed than wit or judgement ... [it was explained that] the origin

of the quarrel between the Admiral and the Protector ... [was when] his brother was made Protector of the kingdom and the King's person, he went to him and asked him to countenance his plan to marry the Lady Mary. The Protector was displeased and reproved him, saying that neither of them was born to be King, nor to marry King's daughters; and though God had given them grace that their sister should have married a King, whence such honour and benefit had redounded to them, they must thank God and be satisfied; besides which he knew the Lady Mary would never consent.

Paget apparently then continued the story, explaining that

> the Admiral went off and married the widow of the late King [Katherine Parr] showing his resentment against his brother openly ... The Earl of Warwick, to end the matter, had used strong language to the Admiral, remonstrating with him that he had come to occupy such a high position through the favour of his brother and the Council, who had admitted him amongst their number against the late King's wish; who, being on his deathbed, and hearing his name amongst those elected to the Council, cried out 'No, no', though his breath was failing him ... [Thomas Seymour then] turned to other means to satisfy his great cupidity. He won over to his side several gentlemen of the King's [Edward's] Chamber, and by kindness and gifts, succeeded in gaining preference over his brother in the King's affections ... Since then the Admiral has tried to negotiate his own marriage with the Lady Elizabeth ... The council was informed of all of this, and when the Admiral was finally discovered within the palace late at night, with a large suite of his own people, and the dog that keeps watch before the King's door was found dead, they determined to summon him to appear before them. He refused to obey, and sent word to the Protector that Controller Paget must be sent as hostage to his house if they wanted him to answer the summons ... He was [nonetheless] taken to the Tower at eight o'clock in the evening. I will inform your Majesty of the details of his examination and of the evidence against him, after I have seen the Protector and Controller Paget.[11]

Paget drew up the precise list of 'Interrogives for the Lord Admiral', which included asking him whether he had tried to change the people in attendance on the King, had made promises to get them 'to take his parte' and whether he talked about his idea of marriage to the King's sisters? Somerset then authorised the execution of his brother, adding the Seymours to the list of notorious fratricides, which began with Cain and Abel.[12]

Chapter 17

Somerset's Cassandra

> Make me not to be a Cassandra, that is to saie, one that told the trouthe of dangers before and was not beleved.
>
> Paget to Somerset, 2 February 1549

Although acting as his right-hand man, Paget had, by 1548, become highly critical of Somerset's policies and style of government, and he attempted to change it in a long series of letters of advice which he sent to the Protector. The first, in February, cautioned him to go easy in the area of religious reform, to only 'alter such thinges as upon great and deep consideration [were] agreeable bothe to Goddes Lawe and to the preservation of the pollicie of the realm ... otherwaies be uncertayne subdayne and dangerous to you and yours, and Go knoweth to what confusion of things.'

William was well aware that the majority of Englishmen were still adherents of the 'old religion', that the argument that radical religious change should not be attempted during a minority reign was widely respected, and that aggressive evangelism sat uneasily with his preferred European alliance with the Holy Roman Empire of Charles V. The letter also criticised Somerset's Scottish war policy. 'I besech your grace for Goddes sake', he wrote, 'to passe over this summer with out newe fortifications' as there were not the resources to sustain them and they would also encourage 'the commynge of France'.[1] Somerset paid a bit of attention to this advice with respect to religious reform, pushing on slightly less aggressively at this time than he might otherwise have done. But he totally ignored the counsel about Scotland, where his policy was both financially unsustainable and did indeed result in the arrival of 6,000 French troops in June. The Franco-Scottish army then besieged the English position at Haddington, a major town to the East of Edinburgh, and, when Somerset foolishly urged an English force under Sir Thomas Palmer to try to relieve it, the English were annihilated and Palmer captured. He was a close personal friend of William Paget and this prompted the next letter to Somerset, in July, accusing him of provoking Palmer 'to [too] much forward with lettres accusing his stillness, slackenes and slepinge', thus bringing on the disaster.[2]

The next letter, sent 'on Christmas Day, at night, 1548', combined further criticism of Somerset's foreign policy with a general complaint about his style of government. It pointed out that at the beginning of the Protectorate, Somerset was 'being but in an entry to war with Scotland, in peace with France, in amity with the Emperor, and in an indifferent concord with all the rest of the world [except Rome].' Whereas, now, he was in open war with Scotland and 'entering into war with France, ready to have the Emperor fall out with you, and in discord with all the rest of the world, besides dissension at home now at liberty to burst out ... You are in beggary, in debt, in scarcity of men to serve, in unwillingness of men to serve...'

Paget made recommendations for shoring up the nation's finances, suggesting particular appointments to manage the Royal Mint and to handle the victualling of the army and the navy. He urged that in matters of religious reform, the Protector should watch out that 'the world [be] little offended' as much as that 'God be pleased'. He reiterated a belief in moderation: 'Extremities be never good, and for my part I have always hated them.' He admonished Somerset for having 'cared to content all men (which is impossible)' and for being 'loth or rather afraid to offend any'. Comparing the Protectorate with Henry VIII's reign, he said, 'Then all things were too straight and now they are too loose; then was it dangerous to do or speak though the meaning were not evil; and now every man hath liberty to do and speak at liberty without danger.'

While thus warning against indecisive or 'weak' government, Paget balanced this by signing off with a plea for Somerset to listen to the advice of others: 'before your grace show your opinion in matters, to hear other men's'.[3]

In a culture where the exchange of gifts was a central part of what we now call 'networking', William's 1548 New Year's gift to the Lord Protector reveals his position as close friend and respected political guide. He wrote:

> considering the favour of your Grace to be special toward me, and my love is reciproque toward you, methought it best to send your Grace, though no rich gift, yet a token of my heart ... My token is this schedule here enclosed, wherin, as in a glass, if your grace will daily look.

His gift to the ruler of England was a distillation of his political wisdom; it reads,

The Schedule
Deliberate maturely in all things. Execute quickly the determinations. Do justice without respect. Make assured and staid men ministers under you. Maintain the ministers in their offices. Punish the disobedient according

to their deserts. In the King's causes give commission in the King's name. Reward the King's worthy servants liberally and quickly. Give your own to your own, and the King's to the King's, frankly. Dispatch suitors shortly. Be affable to the good, and severe to the evil. Follow advice in Council. Take fee or reward of the King only. Keep your ministers about you uncorrupt. Thus God will prosper you, the King favour you, and all men love you.

W. P.[4]

More letters at the beginning of 1549 reminded Somerset of a whole list of specific government actions that he needed to do: to appoint someone to manage Boulogne 'in lieu of the Admiral', his brother; to decide who was to be in charge of the army of the north and with how many men; to sort out their pay; to deal with issues concerning the navy; to get knowledge of what was happening in France, by spies or ambassadors; to hurry up with getting money out of Parliament, 'for time goeth awaye'; and to stop the theft of bells and lead from churches. These detailed lists, along with 'The Schedule' rather confirm the view of one historian that, 'If one reads between the lines, it is difficult to avoid the conclusion that Paget believed that Somerset had not even mastered the rudiments of government.'[5]

In a February 1549 letter, Paget continues with more of the same: 'you are in playne ware with the Scottes, and ever ready to the same with the French' and, above all 'there is cause to doubt the emperor'. Always the advocate of an Anglo-Imperial alliance, Paget stressed the link between that and domestic religious policy: 'if the emperor do square with us, it is good to se whether here at home some thincking it be for religion, will peradventure thincke it also their duties for surety of the King and the realm to take his parte and then your force at home is too weake.'

And, as often, a connection was made between finance and commerce and the Imperial alliance: 'we have no money at all to speak of' and 'if the emperor _arred with youe there can be none levied. For the merchant shall have no vent [sales], the clothier shall have no vent, nor your sheepmaster no vent of his wolle.'

In another letter, the advice is again very specific: appoint Wotton, Mildmay and Wriothesley (now back in the Council) to deal with matters of finance; send Warwick to the army of the north; send Lord John Russell to the West Country; send me (Paget) north, south, east or west – wherever you want.[6]

Somerset seems to have largely accepted receiving this barrage of criticism and advice – and there was plenty more to come later in the year – even if he seldom acted on it. But there is a March letter in which William did seem worried that he may have gone too far, because he reassured the Protector that, while he always said 'Franckely to your grace what I thought', that was 'the somme of my sayenge' and he would never criticise him in public, in the Council or elsewhere. There is reference to a rumour that envious people were trying 'to prevail with your grace against me', in particular that one of those people might have been Somerset's wife, something which 'went to my harte like a dagger'. In this instance, Paget said that he was immensely relieved to discover that this rumour was not true.[7] The supposed malicious influence of the Duchess is, however, a topic to which we will return.

Meanwhile, in April and May 1549 the flow of letters continued: 'For Goodness sake time devise for remedie.' 'We have not nor shall not have this yere sufficient money to mainteyne us in the warre honorablie.' 'The common people too liberal in speech, too bold and licentious in their doings and too wise and learned in their own conceytes.' 'All things in maner going backwarde and unfortunately and every man almost out of harte and courage, and our lackes so well knowen as our enemies despise us and our friends pitie us.'

Somerset's autocratic behaviour was becoming more and more evident. Paget told him how one of his (Somerset's) advisors had come to him in tears after he had been admonished 'too much more than needed' by the Protector. Somerset had, in Paget's opinion 'grown in great choleric fashion, when soever you are contraried in that which you have conceived in your head', and he needed 'when the whole Council shall move you, or give you advice in a matter ... to follow the same, and to relent sometimes from your own opinion.' Once again, it was relations with the Emperor that particularly worried William because the latter was 'undoubtedly in his herte displeased with your proceedings in religion' and there was the danger that 'thempereur agreing with France ... will then travail in some purpose ... contrarye to our purpose'. That France and the Empire might jointly gang up against Protestant England remained the nightmare fear.[8]

To avoid this, Paget went, in June 1549, on another one of his many missions to Charles V's court. In this respect at least, Somerset seems to have responded to the avalanche of advice from Paget. The mandate was to prevent a further deterioration in relations, to discuss a possible marriage between Mary and Don Luis of Portugal, Charles's brother-in-law, and to try to get the Emperor to agree to aid the English if the French attacked them in Boulogne. An incident that occurred just before Paget's departure shows how closely connected domestic religious policy was with foreign policy and how the resolutely Catholic Mary therefore still had leverage. Rich (Chancellor) and Petre (Secretary) visited Mary to get her to provide a letter of recommendation to the Emperor for Paget to take with him, and to obtain her consent to the

Portuguese match. At the same time, they threatened her that Parliament had enacted certain dispositions regarding religion that had to be obeyed by her household. But Mary saw them off without too much trouble, saying she would not change the religious practices of her household if her life depended on it and then warning, unless they left her alone, that she would tell in Paget's letter to Charles of the bullying treatment she was receiving. Outwitted, Rich and Petre left, with the letter for Paget, but having had to accept that Mary would not shift her religious stance.

Notwithstanding Mary's letter and Paget's diplomatic assurances over religion – in general and about Mary's situation in particular – Charles remained unconvinced. Although Paget prevented further deterioration in the relationship, he got nowhere with the Don Luis marriage idea, and the Emperor explicitly ruled out support for England if the French attacked Boulogne. Which they proceeded to do, with some force, resulting in the loss of various forts around Boulogne in August: a further blow to Somerset's prestige.[9]

In the late spring and early summer of 1549, while Paget was away, all hell was breaking loose back home, Somerset's policies provoking a breakdown in law and order all over the country, with particularly serious rebellions in the South-west and in Norfolk. Paget directly blamed Somerset for the revolts, writing to him that 'society in a realm doth consist and is maintained by religion and law'. He had failed in upholding both. As for the first, 'the old religion is forbidden … and the use of the new is not yet printed … in the stomachs of the eleven or twelve parts of the realm'. As for the second, 'your too much gentleness [is] an occasion of so great an evil as is now chanced in England by these rebels.'[10] There were several causes for the rebellions. There was serious resistance to the imposition of the new religious practices, particularly in Devon and Cornwall. The currency had been debased as a result of the financial needs of Somerset's wars. Taxes on sheep and woollen cloth, imposed for the same reason, were unpopular. There was a bad harvest. Prices rose.

Another issue was the enclosure of common land, the resistance to which Somerset initially encouraged. On this subject, the modern historian might have some sympathy with him because the enclosures tended to benefit the rich landowners at the expense of the poor. But the Protector certainly did not regard the unequal English social structure which caused this as in any way on the agenda, and when rebels, who did, took the law into their own hands, his initial encouragement and weakness was in the end replaced by brutal repression. As Paget warned the Protector, speaking of similar rebellions in Germany, 'when the very like tumult to this began first, it might have been appeased with the loss of twenty men; and after with the loss of an c. [100]

or cc. [200]. But it was thought nothing … [they] suffered the matter to run so far, as it cost, ere it was appeased, they say, a thousand or two thousand mens lives.'[11]

It proved the same, or worse, in England. When Somerset did eventually listen to Paget and others and, to restore law and order, authorised expeditionary forces under Lords Russell, Herbert and Warwick – using foreign mercenaries and troops diverted from the war in Scotland, over 5,000 rebels were eventually slaughtered. As the historian John Guy puts it, Somerset purported

> to champion the poor against the rich, but his true opinions were always those of his time: aristocratic, acquisitive, authoritarian … If Somerset was slow to respond to revolt, this stemmed not from charity but from irresolution and his urge not to be distracted from his consuming obsession: the conquest of Scotland.[12]

Even Somerset's championing of the anti-enclosure movement had a less than altruistic motive connected with this obsession, because he feared that rural depopulation encouraged by enclosures would deplete the pool of strong and fit men available for English armies – particularly to fight the Scots. He is said to have owned 2,000 sheep himself and to have enclosed land for them and for his parkland – though acting as a reasonably good landlord by offering tenants alternative fields to grow their crops on.

Similarly, on the question of enclosures as it directly affected him, Paget certainly furthered his own interests. But on this, as with other matters, he favoured compromise. There is a document that shows thirty-five of his tenants in Middlesex accepting his enclosure of 150 acres in exchange for his agreement that no further common land should be enclosed and with him waiving his right to pasture his cattle on the remaining common land. We do not, of course, know whether this really was a reasonable deal for the tenants and how voluntarily they entered into it.[13]

One of the leaders of the of the religiously inspired Western rebellion was William's brother Robert. I have been unable to find out much about him beyond the fact that he was Catholic and lived in the West Country. The Paget family, probably like many others, did not have a unified position on religion. As we shall see later in the story, it is pretty clear that William's wife Anne was a committed Roman Catholic and two of his sons undoubtedly were. Despite his power and status, he was evidently unwilling or unable to impose his own moderate views on his family. Somerset's response to Paget's brother's rebellion reveals the Lord Protector's guilt-ridden and solipsistic character. He wrote to Lord Russell, instructing him to show no mercy to Robert Paget for William's sake, 'consydering that we have not spayred our owne brother', adding 'It shuld much Import us yf we should spare any other mans brother' and that the issue touched his honour because many people 'have not lefte unspoken that we shuld consent to the death of our owne brother, and now should wink at him'. Indicative of how Somerset's haranguing was resented and his power waning, it appears that Russell ignored this order and Robert's life was spared.[14]

Chapter 18

Somerset's Fall

[Somerset] failed to appreciate that his position was not an inalienable right but one that was dependent upon the support of king, council and nobility. The privy councillors had lost confidence in his ability to govern responsibly ... Even Paget had become disenchanted with his master's government.

Margaret Scard in *Tudor King in All But Name*

Edward VI's six-year reign from 1547 to 1553 can be conveniently divided into two roughly equal halves. Somerset ruled as Lord Protector in the first; but the second was more muddled. Confusingly, in this second three-year period, there were two 'coups' against Somerset, both of them led by John Dudley, Earl of Warwick. The first, in 1549, removed Somerset from his position as Lord Protector. Then, in 1551, after he had partly regained power and was seen as a renewed threat by Dudley, came the second coup that resulted in Somerset's execution. William Paget was in the thick of these events, bouncing up and down between the House of Lords and prison.

By the autumn of 1549, Somerset's policies were wholly discredited and, when a coup was launched against him, most of the charges were the same as those made in Paget's letters. Commentators, at the time and since, blame Somerset's personality, an unfortunate combination of vacillation and arrogance. There is also the suggestion that his second wife, Anne, was a proud and difficult woman who encouraged her husband's autocratic tendencies and was widely detested. Paget, speaking to van der Delft, put the Protector's failures down to the fact that 'he has a bad wife'.[1] Her snobbish pride was apparently shown in her attitude to Henry VIII's widow, Katherine Parr, over whom she unsuccessfully claimed precedence – always a matter of great importance to everyone at Court. It was said that having failed to get official approval of her primacy, she on occasion physically shoved Katherine out of her place at the head of entrances and exits at Court. Some of the stories about her may have been exaggerated by Catholic historians who resented her support for Evangelical religious reform. Another common cause for complaint was Somerset's excessive personal building projects. He considered the Seymour house in the country, Wolf Hall, to be inadequate and so embarked on major work in Wiltshire as well as conspicuous projects at Syon House and Somerset House in the Strand, neither of which were completed in his lifetime but from which Londoners have benefited ever since. Although large and expensive, these building enterprises were small compared to Henry VIII's: but he was the king. Indeed, Somerset might well have got away with much of his behaviour if he had been a legitimate hereditary monarch; but he was not.

The coup unfolded during the first two weeks of October and ended with Somerset, probably on Paget's advice, purchasing his life in exchange for the complete sacrifice of his power. In addition to all the other complaints about the Protector, Dudley (Warwick) had a few of this own. His park had been ploughed by protesters against enclosure, he was aggrieved that he had been inadequately supported in dealing with the Norfolk rebellion, he had various requests turned down and he felt his services had generally not been appreciated. He was also an ambitious conspirator who saw his moment had come when he returned to London as a hero in the eyes of all who wanted the restoration of law and order, at the head of a victorious army, and with many in the Privy Council thoroughly fed up with Somerset's rule.

At the beginning of the month, two centres were in competition for power: at Hampton Court, with the young king and Somerset, was Paget along with Cranmer, and Petre and Sir Thomas Smith, the co-Secretaries; in opposition, gathered round Warwick in London, were many of the Privy Council, with the Catholic-inclined peers Wriothesley and Arundel supporting him because of their opposition to religious reform. They were soon to be joined by St John and Rich. Knowing his authority was threatened, it was Somerset rather than the dissident councillors who rather foolishly escalated the situation into a showdown. He issued orders for troops to disperse from London, appealed to Russell and Herbert to assist him with their troops from the South-west and, a bit later, commanded all the King's subjects to come to Hampton Court to defend the King and his Protector. He was wholly unsuccessful in the first two ventures and the 'peasants' who came to Hampton Court were considered pretty useless from a military point of view. On 6 October, the Privy Council were meeting at Warwick's house, Ely Place in Holborn, and about to send further criticism to Somerset about how he ignored their advice and was 'minding to follow his own fantasies', when Petre arrived from Hampton Court. He initially warned them they might be arrested as traitors but was soon converted to their cause. As was the Lord Chancellor, Rich, who arrived with the Great Seal of State. They were therefore no longer 'the Ely Place faction' but now a clear majority of the Privy Council and, crucially, they knew

– as did Somerset and those around him such as Paget – that if push came to shove, they held the military advantage.²

Not yet ready to concede defeat, Somerset that night moved the Court from Hampton Court to the more easily defensible Windsor Castle. (He had first thought to move to the Tower, but learnt that the conspirator councillors had already seized it.) As the most detailed history of Edward's reign puts it, the move was,

> a frightening experience for the still very young King, and it was one for which he never forgave Somerset. Not fully informed by his aloof uncle, not certain of his role in what was occurring, slightly ill with one of his periodic colds, and probably sound asleep when he was routed from his bed, the royal child was handled more like a piece of infinitely valuable baggage than the fledgling Tudor monarch that he was.³

On 7 October, the Privy Council in London wrote to Paget and Cranmer protesting their loyalty to the King and making it clear they were willing to treat with Somerset if he would submit, absent himself from Edward and disperse his forces. As often during the crises in Tudor history, we do not have clear proof of Paget's role. In matters of policy, he was on the side of the conspirators rather than Somerset. Although he remained with Somerset physically, this was probably more to do with persuading him to surrender than to support him. There is a suggestion that it was very nearly Paget, rather than Petre, who was sent from Hampton Court to Holborn. Would he have acted in the same way? Very probably.

Somerset's wife, Anne, wrote to William begging him to resolve the differences between her husband and the Privy Councillors: she failed to see, 'What hath my lord done to any of these noble men or others that they should thus rage and seek the extremity to him?' It is likely that this was the decisive moment when Paget persuaded Somerset to give in. On the next day, the 8th, the Privy Council were sent a dispatch, signed by Paget, Cranmer and Sir Thomas Smith, informing them that Somerset was now prepared to resign the office of Lord Protector. This letter was delivered by Sir Phillip Hoby, the recently returned ambassador to Charles V who was trusted by both sides, and was accompanied by two other letters indicating that Somerset was prepared to surrender without violence so long as he was treated reasonably. One was from Smith to his co-Secretary Petre calling for 'moderation in all things' and against the need to 'require with blood that which may be had with persuasion and honour'. The other was from the young King Edward himself to his Council hoping that the present 'uproar' could be brought to an end and that they did not intend 'with cruelty to purge' his uncle Somerset and his associates.[4]

Letters on the 9th confirmed that Somerset was losing: the Privy Council instructed Sheriffs and Justices in the counties to ignore directions to levy forces, made with the King's hand, stamp and signet, as these were being abused by Somerset; they also wrote to the Princesses Mary and Elizabeth about Somerset's malpractices and expressed trust that they would adhere to their party against him; Russell and Herbert confirmed to the Council that their forces were not going to the Protector's assistance – a crucial decision of which Somerset soon became aware. Meanwhile, the Court of Common Council of the City of London, a body which had been directly elected from the city's wards since 1384 and which is still the local authority for the city today, convened to decide on the issue of legitimacy. After considerable debate, and although with some support for Somerset, they eventually came down on the side of the Privy Councillors in London and committed their 500 to 1,000 armed men.

Although it now appeared likely that the Warwick coup was going to prevail, it was not yet 'all over', because Somerset still had the King in his power and was surrounded by his own armed servants and those of the royal household. It was Paget who liaised between the two centres of power to confirm the success of Warwick's coup while ensuring that it remained bloodless and that Somerset, and others such as Smith and Cecil, were spared – if temporarily imprisoned. This required delicate management of the situation but also a degree of deception to make sure that Somerset and his supporters 'went quietly'. It presumably helped that Paget, as Comptroller of the Royal Household, was the official boss of most of the servants at Court. On the 9th, he sent his private servant, Master Bedell, almost certainly without Somerset's knowledge, to meet Warwick and the Privy Councillors. We do not know exactly what was said. But, on the 10th, Sir Philip Hoby returned to Windsor bearing two private letters from the Council, one for the King and one for Paget and Cranmer, both blaming Somerset's tyranny and requiring that his forces which still surrounded Edward be sent away. At the same time, Hoby made a public declaration on behalf of the Privy Councillors to reassure Somerset and his supporters that they would be treated fairly. The only account of what was said in this declaration is the report by Sir Thomas Smith, a committed supporter of the Protector who was subsequently imprisoned: so it may be biased by bitterness. Smith claims that Hoby announced on behalf of the Council a guarantee that they would in 'no manner hurt' Somerset, that they promised not to take away his lands or goods and that they reassured his supporters that they could keep 'their rooms and places' The report continues:

'Upon this, all ... wept for joy, and thanked God, and prayed for the Lords [the Privy Councillors]. Mr Comptroller [Paget] fell down on his knees, and clasped the Duke [Somerset] about the knees, and weeping said, Oh! my Lord, ye see now what my Lords be.'

The nineteenth-century historian and Tudor letter collector, Tytler, continues the narrative:

> Relying on the honour which had been pledged, and the tears that had been shed by Mr Comptroller [Paget], he [Somerset] entertained no suspicion, but permitted his guards to be removed, his servants disarmed, and the young Monarch to be once more attended by those officers of the household who had been suspected of leaning to Warwick and the conspirators.

This news was sent to the Privy Council in London, who, announcing that they were pleased with the 'diligent travail' of Paget and Cranmer, dispatched Sir Anthony Wingfield with an armed party to Windsor to arrest Somerset, Smith and others.

Wingfield, Paget and Cranmer wrote to the Privy Council on the 11th that they had successfully arrested Somerset, who was now held in 'a very high tower: and a strong and good watch shall be had about the same'. They also reported that the King was troubled with a 'rheum, taken partly with riding hither in the night' and was not enjoying being at Windsor. Paget, master of administrative detail for the Court even in the midst of organising a coup d'état, added, 'I, the Comptroller, have spoken for provision to be made at Richmond, where there is already five tonnes of beer and five tonnes of wine. But the physician dispraiseth the house, and wisheth us rather to Hampton or London.'

In the end they stayed a bit longer at Windsor, while Warwick and the other councillors arrived there to present themselves to the King and arrange for Somerset to be taken to the Tower. The coup was over.[5]

Paget's action, in removing Somerset's servants from about the King at Windsor, had been critical in assuring the success of this coup d'état. But because he had initially been in the Somerset camp and was closely associated with him, it was not certain that he would be part of the new regime. van der Delft reported to the Emperor that when Warwick and the other Privy Councillors first appeared at Windsor,

> they showed Paget no favourable countenance, which disturbed him greatly, but after he had been with them in Council he came out very

joyful and showed quite a different face from before. Since then he has had long conversations with the Earl of Warwick ... So, Sire, all the Councillors are now of one mind, and conduct affairs unanimously and in good order, and it may be hoped things will look better than they have in the past.[6]

Does Paget's part in this coup prove him to have been villainously deceitful, as some, such as Tytler, would have it? Was Somerset expecting to be imprisoned in the Tower after ordering his armed men to stand down? Not if Smith's account of the promises of Hoby and the subsequent joyful weeping is accurate in detail: but it may well not be. In addition, it seems unlikely that Somerset would have fought to the bitter end even if he had not been deceived, because he already had little support. So, if there was some deceit, it may have been more a matter of saving Somerset's face than outright perfidy on Paget's part. It also has to be relevant that bloodshed, even the possibility of civil war, was avoided. Furthermore, Somerset was not imprisoned for long and was soon free, and powerful and rich enough to be soon plotting against Warwick: and he stayed friendly with Paget – in part the story of the next chapter.

Chapter 19

Peerage and Prison

> The dividing line between the House of Lords and Pentonville Jail is very very thin.
> Ralph Richardson, playing a captain of industry, when his young assistant, played by Malcolm McDowell, is arrested as the fall guy when a dodgy arms deal falls foul of the law: from the 1973 Lindsey Anderson film *Oh Lucky Man*

For a very brief period in the immediate aftermath of the coup, it appeared there might be a restoration of Catholic influence. van der Delft was hopeful in his reports to the Emperor. But it soon became clear that Warwick had simply used the support of those who favoured the old religion, such as Wriothesley, Arundel and Southwell, to help overthrow the Protector. They were excluded from power, dismissed from the Privy Council and, in some cases, arrested: while others of reformist inclination were appointed to the Council. It was decreed on Christmas Day 1549 that the *Book of Common Prayer* must be used by all persons in the realm. It was apparent that, although the individual at the top had changed – a Dudley replacing a Seymour, the ruling elite, under a staunchly Protestant king who was beginning to make his influence felt, continued in power. In addition, Warwick soon brought Somerset back, aware that he still had many friends and supporters. He was released from the Tower at the beginning of February 1550 and was back in the Privy Council and in possession of much of his land by April. William Paget, along with several others who had enabled the coup, received his reward. There was a £6,000 cash handout and he was made Baron Paget of Beaudesert. The barony was supported by a grant of local land obtained from the confiscated estate of the conservative Bishop of Lichfield.

His first significant job for the new regime was, not surprisingly, to lead a team to negotiate peace with France. Events began to unfold in a wearily familiar manner. They had a nightmare crossing the Channel: driven back by a storm and finally getting to Calais weeks after leaving London. William's seasickness was by then a joke in the Privy Council, who sent condolences for 'some of your company that are no seamen'.[1] Next there was the usual haggling over where to meet the French. Then, when they managed to meet, although a truce was agreed, both sides began by setting out extreme positions necessitating references back to London and Paris. However, thereafter, events moved quite fast as Paget persuaded London that, because war with France and Scotland had been the cause of many of the domestic difficulties, peace should be gained by selling Boulogne for whatever they could get for it. When Paris came back with an improved offer, of 400,000 crowns, he recommended acceptance. He wrote to Warwick that they could have got better terms 'if peace and war had been so indifferent to us as we might have adventured sometime to have broken off'. But that was not the case, because peace for the English was 'the first degree of it'.[2] Peace was then agreed – with France and Scotland. Paget acceded to most of the French demands, though he put up a fight for the right to evacuate English artillery from Boulogne before its return. His friend and protege, John Mason, was made ambassador to France and Paget was back in England at the end of March. He was then involved in tying up the details of the treaty, making sure they actually got the money out of the French. He had to cross the Channel again in April and, in May, to receive the French ambassadors and their cash in London.

* * *

In April 1550, Paget had a small part in the fascinating story of Sebastian Cabot. Sebastian, and his father John, were explorers who have gone down in history as competition to the far more famous Christopher Columbus, to Amerigo Vespucci who is remembered because of the continent's naming and to the somewhat less well-known Leif Erikson – all of them considered as the European 'discoverers' of America. The Cabots, initially from Venice, but operating sometimes from England and sometimes from Charles V's dominions, went on extraordinary pioneering expeditions across the North Atlantic. While Columbus and Vespucci were reaching the Caribbean, they were exploring the northern seaboard of America. But, although the Cabots were perhaps the more obvious candidates, they made less good national heroes for the USA of the eighteenth and nineteenth centuries which was keen to develop a founding myth without ties to Britain, than did Columbus who had no such unwanted connection. As a result, it was Columbus who became the founding father of choice for the USA. He still is in many parts of America, though less so now because of his treatment of 'natives', his links to slavery and other crimes. In the 'woke' USA of today, the Icelandic/Norwegian Leif Erikson, whose expeditions dated from much earlier, is now preferred, probably because, as is the way with such matters, with less known about him, less bad is known about him.

Whose expeditions discovered what and when is still a matter of much controversy – and was from the mid-sixteenth century. Then it was already disputed as to whether the first discovery of North America by the Cabots at the end of the previous century had been under the auspices of the Tudors or the Habsburgs – an important factor in determining the ownership of territory. Henry VII definitely funded a Cabot expedition in the 1490s. But notes attached to Sebastian's famous maps of North America, published in the 1540s and 1550s in countries ruled by the Habsburgs, claimed, probably falsely, that he discovered America with his father in a prior expedition, which was funded by Castilians or Portuguese, not by the English. Throughout the first half of the sixteenth century, Sebastian alternated between England and Spain and was involved in expeditions originating in, and financed from, both countries. He led a particularly notorious one from Spain in the 1520s and 1530s. During it, when he decided to change its purpose and direction after he had heard rumours of the huge wealth of the Incas, several of his officers mutinied and he then left them marooned on an island – where they died. On his eventual return to Spain, he was arraigned on charges of causing their death and of disobeying orders. His relationship with the Imperial authorities from then on was ambiguous: he was convicted but his sentence was not fully enforced because Charles V remained interested in information he might have about the New World and for the services he might offer. In 1548, he moved back to England, which is where he became a problem for discussion between the Privy Council and Charles V, between Paget and van der Delft.

The issue was whether Cabot was to remain in England or return to the service of Charles V. How keen Charles was to have him, whether Sebastian wanted to go and whether the English would let him go were all in question. In a discussion of 22 April 1550, relayed to Charles by his ambassador, 'Paget affirmed that Cabot had begged that on no account would they send him to your Majesty' but that 'if he wishes to go he may do so, and we are pleased to give him leave'.[3] However, in a dispatch six weeks earlier, van der Delft had written the opposite, that although Cabot was keen to go to the Emperor, the English were stopping him. This letter is worth quoting in full as it also reveals a bit of what Cabot thought he had to offer:

> As for Sebastian Cabot, I believe I can truthfully assure your Majesty that he desires nothing so much in the world as to be able to speak once to your Majesty, and he often comes to me secretly to ask me to write to your Majesty so that he may be delivered from this captivity: and

although they offer him high wages here, his only wish is to die in your Majesty's service. He is trying to persuade me that a million in gold is at stake in his being able to give your Majesty some secret information. He also says that it would be well if the charts that are now being made at Seville were suppressed until he can furnish the explanation to your Majesty. He declares it is of the highest importance.[4]

What Cabot had to sell could have been one of many things: either detailed information about the Americas – about Inca gold or the possibility of a North-west Passage; or maybe his certification, on maps, of the Cabot late fifteenth-century discovery of North America having been an Imperial rather than English project – the controversy referred to above; or his delineation, to the Imperial benefit, of the exact position of the Line of Tordesillas which the Pope had decreed to determine which lands were Spanish, which Portuguese. In the end, Cabot seems to have remained in England, whether willingly or not. But he does appear to have helped the Imperial claim to part of North America, in that a Spanish map of 1551 has a text reading that the land was discovered by the Cabots in MCCCCXCIV (1494) – earlier than the date of the English expedition which Henry VII had funded.

In van der Delft's words, Sebastian, who was probably as much a self-publicising con artist as an explorer, was evidently trying 'to make his own profit out of both sides'.[5] He was still at it two years later. Although heavily involved in English attempts, under the auspices of the Muscovy Company, to open a trading route to the spice islands and China via a North-west Passage, he continued to try to sell his information and services to the Emperor. van der Delft's replacement as ambassador, Jean Scheyfve, reported that Cabot told him about English plans to send three vessels to

> navigate by the Frozen Sea towards the country of the great Chamchina. The English opine that the ancients passed by that sea and joined the Ocean, as Pliny and others wrote; and they believe the route to be a short one, and very convenient for the kingdom of England, for distributing kerseys [jerseys? – at any rate some kind of cloth or clothing] in those far countries, bringing back spices and other rich merchandise in exchange ... I then remarked that it appeared to me that the country of the great Chamchina formed part of the Emperors' conquest. He [Cabot] said it was true; but that view only interested the Emperor and the king of Portugal, while the others would probably claim that the land would belong to him that first occupied it. Nevertheless, he knew a means of thwarting them if

he could go to his Majesty's court, and he would then unfold other great secrets to him concerning navigation, in which millions were at stake.⁶

The North-west Passage never materialised as the great trading route between Europe and the spice islands and China. (Though, with global warming melting the icecaps in the twenty-first century, it may yet.) Paget was one of the original investors in the Muscovy Company, which achieved rather more limited success by trading with Russians, including selling them arms. Sebastian Cabot is thought to have died in England in 1557.

* * *

Returning from this exotic subject to the less romantic but very important business of the organisation of English government, Paget was responsible for a significant memo outlining 'Rules for the conduct of business in the Privy Council'. The Council should meet at least three days a week with sessions from 8.00 am until lunch time and from 2.00 to 4.00 pm, with a special session on Sundays to hear private suits. There should always be at least six Councillors in attendance at Court, with the Secretary always there along with at least two of the holders of the great offices of State (the Lord Chancellor, Lord Privy Seal, Lord Chamberlain, etc.). Various other detailed suggestions to make the functioning of the Privy Council more organised and efficient were listed. In addition, as well as a plea that Councillors should 'love one another as bretheren, or dear friends', he proposed all recommendations for offices and benefices should be decided by a majority of attending councillors voting by secret ballot with black and white balls and that no councillor should speak or write for his friends in any matter of justice. One imagines that these latter ideas would not have been wildly attractive to Warwick and his friends, and the proposals anyhow feel like the wise advice of an ex-office holder that might not have been so enthusiastically endorsed by Paget when he was himself at the centre of power and patronage. There is no evidence that the more controversial recommendations were adopted. However, this memo can be seen as a small link in the national progress from arbitrary ad hoc government towards a more ordered and business-like structure. It even contained a miniscule shift towards more democracy and less corruption – in aspiration at least.⁷

Meanwhile, the political intrigues of the Dudleys and Seymours continued to dominate the first half of 1550. It was unclear whether the partially rehabilitated Somerset and his supporters would be able to co-exist with the increasingly powerful Warwick and his faction. Initially there was some hope that they might, as, in June, Warwick's son married Somerset's daughter. But there remained little love lost between the fathers. Knowing that Somerset had many supporters in Parliament, Warwick made sure it met as little as possible. It did not help that he told Somerset to bury Margery, his mother, who was also the King's grandmother, without pomp or ceremony. By November, Scheyfve, the Imperial ambassador, was reporting home that there was 'deep discord among members of the Council. Some take Warwick's side, others my Lord Somerset's.'[8]

One of the issues, about which Paget strongly disagreed with Warwick, was the tilt of policy away from an Imperial alliance to greater friendship with France. A major bone of contention for the Empire remained the treatment of Princess Mary. Whereas Paget and Somerset had assured Charles V that attempts to force her to conform to the new religion would stop, Warwick and his government increased the pressure on her. In addition, Paget and Warwick appeared to have clashed in a Privy Council meeting in January 1551. What exactly this was about remains obscure and is hardly made any clearer by the words Warwick wrote to Paget after the meeting. He told him that he had wished, 'as well for the King's surety as for the truth of the matter, that men should not be against the perfect reforming of it, especially as it has been thus far debated, which I reckon a happy thing.'

The 'it' probably refers to a proposed reform of the legal basis for Warwick's authority, which was opposed by Paget and others. But, as W. K. Jordan, the historian who has covered Edward VI's reign in greatest detail, dryly comments, the meaning is not helped, 'by the fact that Warwick was not a truly literate man. Many of his memoranda, especially when he was angry, are very murky in language.'[9]

Throughout 1550 and 1551, Paget's influence in the Warwick-dominated Privy Council was still considerable, but waning. In the spring of 1550, he continued to attend most meetings. In March, he was appointed to a commission to look into the accounts, 'of the tresaures of warres, vittaylers and others' and, in May, to another small group to examine government finances in general. But later in the year and in 1551, he was often away from the Council. However, if Scheyfve is to be believed, he certainly had not given up his desire for power – if for the moment without much success. The ambassador wrote to Charles V in September 1550, 'They say that Paget tried hard to get the Chancellorship, but did not succeed.'[10] And he was part of the trial of Bishop Gardiner which had endless sessions at the end of 1550 and the beginning of 1551. Indeed, one of the twenty-two sessions, which involved eighty witnesses in all, was actually held in Paget's house in the Strand. The exchanges between Gardiner and Paget were personal, bitter and largely irrelevant to the case in hand. That was supposed to be about whether the bishop had disobeyed government rulings on religious matters. But what the two men argued about was whether Henry VIII had respected Gardiner and whether Paget was ungrateful to his former patron. We do not have any objective record of what was said, but Foxe's *Book of Martyrs*, although clearly anti-Gardiner, is a sufficiently detailed account to have some credibility. He says:

> behold in the depositions of the Lord Paget, and there you shall see, that the King [Henry VIII], before his death, both excepting him [Gardiner] out of his pardons, and quite striking him out of his last will and testament, so detested and abhorred him as he did no Englishman more.

And Foxe goes on to say that Gardiner replied:

> Lord Paget hath, in his deposition, evidently and manifestly neglected honour, faith, and honesty, and showeth himself desirous, beyond the necessary answer to that was demanded of him, (only of ingrate malice) to hinder, as much as in him is, the said bishop, who was in the said lord's youth his teacher and tutor, afterward his master, and then his beneficial master.[11]

We have seen how Paget and Gardiner had previously fallen out. But, after this, their relationship became, not surprisingly, one of rancorous enmity. Their reciprocal loathing for each other played a major part in the story of Mary's reign.

If Paget's behaviour towards Gardiner was aimed at ingratiating himself with the ruling Warwick, it was not successful. He was largely out of power and continued to be closely associated with his former associate, Somerset. As shown in the household records, detailed in Chapter 14, on 21 September the Pagets lavishly entertained Somerset and his retinue at West Drayton. For once, they were backing the wrong horse. Warwick was getting ready to eliminate the danger to his rule that Somerset still threatened because of his rumoured alliance with either populist discontent or with the old conservative nobles – despite the fact that these two threats were essentially contradictory. First Warwick consolidated his power by handing out prizes to those whose support he needed. At the beginning of October 1551, the Marquess of Dorset was made the Duke of Suffolk, the Earl of Wiltshire (William Paulet, previously Lord St John) was created Marquess of Winchester and Sir William Herbert became Earl of Pembroke. At the lower level, knighthoods were dished out to Nevilles, Sidneys, Chekes and the increasingly powerful William Cecil. With his own status also enhanced – Warwick from now on is Northumberland, Duke of – he was nearly ready to strike down Somerset. But it is significant that, before he did so, he felt the need to place his rival's influential associate, William Paget, under house arrest.

Scheyfve reported to the Emperor on 10 October: 'I have heard from a trustworthy source that the Duke of Somerset is going to be accused and arrested, and that the plot is being very secretly woven by the Earl of Warwick and his party. Moreover, Lord Paget has already been commanded to keep his house.'[12]

Chapter 20

Survival

Steal a little and they throw you in jail; steal a lot and they make you king.
Bob Dylan, in his 1983 song 'Sweetheart Like You'

The ambassador's sources were correct. Paget was placed under house arrest and, soon after, Somerset and others of his party were taken prisoner. The Duke himself was taken unawares and was arrested just after dining with the King, or, possibly, actually in his presence. Edward, now a very mature 14-year-old, seemed to have had little sympathy left for his uncle. The initial charges against Somerset were trumped up, including one from a servant, Crane, who served Somerset in some capacity and was probably tortured to get a confession. He claimed that a 'feast of assassination' – aimed at killing Northumberland (Warwick) and others – had been planned to take place at Paget's house. This, and other absurd claims, were dropped when Somerset eventually came to trial, in favour of slightly more realistic charges. Meanwhile, most of Somerset's supporters were taken prisoner easily in what must have been pre-planned moves. One, Sir Ralph Vane, tried to flee but was found hiding under the straw in the stables of one of his servants. There's no record of the circumstances of Paget's arrest, but that detail of Vane's capture perhaps gives a flavour of how traumatic these events might have been for a man and his family who were so used to a life of comfort, wealth and power. Although the Pagets had seen such things happen often enough to friends and political associates, this turn of events must have nonetheless been a great shock when it happened to them. Five days after the house arrest, things got worse. Scheyfve explained to the Emperor what was going on:

> My Lord Paget was confined for a few days to his house, and on the 21st instant [of October 1551] was taken to the Fleet, which is a prison in London, but much less ominous than the Tower. Some say that he had some understanding with Somerset, or at least was inclined in that direction, because he saw that Northumberland and his party treated him with constant coolness. Others think – and this is most probable – that Paget gave the conspiracy away, and is only being kept in prison in order

to divert the suspicions Somerset and his party might nourish of him. There are people who assert that Paget was arrested in connection with the affairs of Lady Mary, Princess of England, and that the Council are charging him with the promise made to your Majesty, in virtue of which the Lady Mary was to be allowed to continue in the practice of the old religion, on the ground that he went beyond his power in giving it.[1]

The ambassador's idea that Paget betrayed Somerset, was party to Northumberland's plot and that his arrest was merely a cover was soon disproved by his incarceration in the 'much more ominous' Tower from 8 November and by the fact that he was stripped of his Chancellorship of the Duchy of Lancaster. That he had promised to the Emperor that Mary would be allowed to go on practising the old religion was true, but was in line with what had been English policy at the time. Whatever his guilt, or lack of it, he remained in prison and in limbo, uncertain of his ultimate fate, while Northumberland consolidated his position and brought Somerset to trial and execution. Northumberland secured his military position, first in London by dispatching gendarmery and 'bands of horse' to control the gates to the city and then, as backup, by gaining an assurance from Montmorency, Constable of France, that 'there is a good store [of troops] in France' in case the Emperor were to use the occasion to advance the interests of 'some that are nearer of kindred unto the King than the Duke' (i.e. Mary).[2] Somerset was brought to trial and, although the wilder changes of treason and attempted assassination were dropped, he was convicted of the felony of inciting an unlawful assembly – without any real evidence for even this – and condemned to death. He was beheaded on 22 January 1552.

Would William also lose his head, and what would life in the Tower have been like for him? Conditions varied hugely – from the horrific to the luxurious. When Anne Boleyn arrived as a prisoner, she immediately and nervously asked where she was to lodge and was immensely relieved that she was to go to the well-appointed Beauchamp Tower. At the other extreme was 'Little Ease', the vilest dungeon in the Tower, known to be dark, damp, rat-infested and with not enough room to stand up or lie down. In between, and Paget's likely destination, were quarters such as the Bell Tower – where Thomas More had been held. Conditions there could be made less or more unpleasant. In More's case, adjusting the rigour of the detention was deliberately used as a method of pressure. Sometimes he was allowed servants, a good diet, books, writing materials, other luxuries, walks outside, contact with other prisoners and family visits. At other times, all these privileges were revoked and he was denied adequate heating, clothes and food.

Paget's conditions were also varied, though perhaps not so extremely.³ The initial instruction from the Privy Council to the Lieutenant of the Tower, for the general treatment of those arrested along with Somerset, was that they, 'be kept in prison surely, secretly, without any other lybertie of walks, or going out of their prisones, or speaking or writing, or any other manner of lybertie' except by specific order of the Council. The Lieutenant was also to assist the Council's commissioners 'for the putting the prisoners, or any of them, to such tortours as they think expedient'. We do not know who actually interrogated Paget and it is unlikely he was tortured. Fifteen days after he was sent to the Tower, the Privy Council drew up an instruction authorising two people, the names left blank, 'to confer together and devise such interrogations [of Paget] as they shall think fyt'. He was probably allowed his own servants, food, light and fuel during most of his imprisonment. But privileges were used as a means of pressure: on 27 February 1551, the Council authorised 'that Lady Paget may visyte the Lord Paget at tymes convenyent', whereas on 11 March, likely at the moment when William was resisting signing an abject confession of guilt, that privilege was suspended.⁴

There is a letter early in his imprisonment, from the Council to the Lieutenant, telling him to ask Paget 'where the Privie Seales of his office of the Duchie of Lancastre is, and to send hither the same if he have it with hym'. This shows again how small-scale, personal, and in this case inefficient was the business of sixteenth-century government. Outside the Tower, moves were afoot to deal with sequestrated Paget assets: one Richard Cooper was appointed 'Receyvour to the Lord Paget'. But it appears that the Privy Council was at least acting to protect his property from opportunist squatters, because they sent a letter to the local Justice of the Peace, 'to remove suche as have by force, sence the Lorde Pagetes committing, entred the mannour of Great Marlowe [a property he had acquired] and to put suche other in posssession againe therefo as were in it before the sayd Lord Pagetes sequestracion.'⁵

Paget's fate hung in the balance. There was little evidence that he had actively conspired with Somerset. However, as we have seen repeatedly in this history, proof of guilt was seldom the crucial factor in determining Tudor trials. On 12 February, with it not yet decided whether Paget was to be included in the conspiracy charges, Scheyfve reported that various of the prisoners in the Tower, including Paget, were in danger of going 'the same way' as Somerset. Two weeks later, things were looking up, as Scheyfve could report, 'Four gentlemen who had been condemned for their share in Somerset's plot were executed here the other day ... but my Lord's Grey and Paget are no longer feared for.'⁶

As Somerset's biographer says, Paget's guilt and conviction, 'became less important if Warwick intended to drop the charge of planning to murder the lords at Paget's house'.[7] But we can only speculate as to what really swung it for William. Was it past favours done for Northumberland (when he had been Dudley, Lisle or Warwick); continuing support from friends still in power and in the Privy Council – such as Cranmer, Cecil, Petre, Sadler and Mason; value as an experienced member of the ruling elite; Anne's advocacy; direct bribery; or even, just conceivably, his innocence?

While his life was no longer in danger, release from prison and a return to anything like his previous life remained in question. There was a humiliating removal of his Order of the Garter. For Paget, as for Wolsey and Cromwell when they fell from grace, their humble origins were thrown in their faces. The King stripped Paget of the Garter, 'for divers his offences and chiefly because he was no gentleman either on his father's side nor mother's side'. His name was physically erased from the parchment book of the Garter and replaced by that of Sir Andrew Dudley, Northumberland's brother. After much umming and erring, it was finally decided to charge Paget with corruption in administering the Duchy of Lancaster. What Northumberland required was an abject admission of guilt, irrespective of the truth, which also served as a way of signalling total submission. He rejected Paget's first confession as lacking sufficient servility as it was couched 'with subtlety and dissimulation'. What he demanded, and got, was that Paget

> confessed how he without commission did sell away my [the King's] lands and great timber woods, how he had taken great fines of my lands to his said peculiar profit and advantage, never turning any to my use or advantage ... For these crimes and others he surrendered his office and submitted himself to those fines that I or my Council would appoint.

Was the charge justified? Not really. Did Paget reward himself out of the Duchy? Yes. To a greater extent than anyone else? No. The profits to the Crown from the Duchy certainly did not suffer while he was Chancellor.[8]

Paget appeared before the Star Chamber at the end of June 1552 and his confession, along with an agreement to pay a heavy fine and to lose various stewardships and keeperships, bought his release from prison.[9] In the days of the Tudor kings, as now in present-day Saudi Arabia, Russia and China, while it was and is the case that the whole system runs on corruption, when an individual falls out of favour with the currently powerful faction, they are often imprisoned for corruption. Essentially it is a combination of a 'shake down' with a brutal reminder of who is the boss. In Paget's case in the 1550s, as with the out of favour Saudi officials imprisoned in the Ritz-Carlton hotel in Riyadh in 2017, servile acknowledgement of guilt and payment of a large fine were enough to ensure release and eventual rehabilitation.

While free from the Tower, William had to work tirelessly and with his usual skill to get back his position in society. First, he had to lift the banishment to Staffordshire that had been an additional part of his sentence. He pleaded that he suffered from a fistula and Lady Paget from a liver complaint and a 'stitch in her side' that all necessitated a London doctor and that his Staffordshire establishment was so small that his large family would soon find it 'unsavoury', 'and then he shall have no place to remove unto but to some inn'. The sob story worked and at the end of September the Privy Council officially released him from the order of provincial exile. Next, he needed to ameliorate his fine. By subtle networking, the detail of which is unrecorded, he achieved a reduction of the face value of the fine from £8,000 to £4,000. But also, of equal significance, he obtained agreement that it could be paid off gradually, in land, to a theoretical value of £200 a year.[10] At this point, as usual when a rich and powerful figure fell, the vultures were circling. The chronicler Strype reports, though with unproven accuracy:

> And when order should be taken for the delivery of any of the lands of the Lord Paget, in satisfaction in part of his fine, they prayed the Council, that the Earl of Huntingdon and the Lord Chamberlain [Sir John Gage] might not be forgotten; the one to have the custody of his house at Drayton, and the other of that at London.[11]

But William Paget, who after all had much experience himself of 'not being forgotten', saw off these threats.

Another crafty move, having first got it agreed that the fine could be paid off in land, was to then reverse the procedure and get it allowed that the 'land debt' could be paid off in cash – because William knew that land was massively undervalued and the coinage debased. That this way of reducing further an already halved fine was accepted does seem quite extraordinary. But it was agreed by the Privy Council in November.[12] In the same month, Scheyfve reported that he was well on his way back, even if his health had suffered from his imprisonment and although the ambassador remained doubtful that he would regain all his power:

> Paget has for some time been troubled by a discharge from the head, but is now better. I know not whether it was caused by durance vile (squalore

carceris) [i.e. the effect of prison]. Some believe he may return to favour and become Chancellor, but I fear his fortune will be less good.[13]

By the end of February 1553, he had somehow managed to pay a total of £1,744 to the Crown and have that accepted as payment in full of his fine. He kept most of his property including his houses. In March, his rehabilitation was confirmed by an audience with King Edward. The proof of his complete restoration to favour is the illuminated Patent on vellum, signed by the King with seal and dated 25 March 1553 that restored the Baronial Coat of Arms to the family, which had been removed when he was sentenced. This magnificent document, normally on display at Plas Newydd, toured the USA in 2022 and 2023 as part of the Metropolitan Museum's 'Art of the Tudor Court' exhibition.

William Paget and his family had suffered the most serious attack on their lives, liberty and welfare from October 1551 until March 1553, with eight months of prison and a further eight months before their position was restored. But they had survived. This crisis had occurred when William was in his forties, mid-life in contemporary terms but much later in a typical sixteenth-century lifespan. In the few remaining months of Edward's reign, when Paget remained remote from the intrigues of Court, one can imagine him reviewing the arc of his life to date. Coming from 'nowhere', this consummate political fixer had risen to the heights, becoming the closest advisor to first King Henry and then Protector Somerset. He was the acknowledged expert in foreign policy, the 'go to' figure in English diplomacy for the European ambassadors. He had forged a close relationship with the most powerful man in the Western world, the Emperor Charles V, and with his associates, particularly the ruler of the Netherlands, Mary of Hungary. In his personal life, he had married 'well' and probably with love to a woman who proved a strong and stable support in the Paget family enterprise. They had been very lucky by the standards of the times to be blessed with many children who survived and were healthy. The family had grown very rich, with several significant properties and large land holdings. All this had been achieved not only by luck and William's intelligence and administrative skills, but also by astutely building up a wide and effective network of friends, acquaintances, patrons, proteges and supporters – over a twenty-year career.

In this he had undoubtedly learnt both positive and negative lessons from his early mentors and exemplars, Gardiner, Wolsey and, above, all the 'master', Thomas Cromwell. Cromwell evidently had a genius for cultivating not only the noble, rich and powerful, but also their families – particularly the women. His biographer comments on how he 'had a way with dowagers' and an 'ability to charm widows'. Directly, and through his wife, Paget also realised the importance of family networks. When their husbands were threatened or needed favours, wives wrote to him when he was in power, as they had to Cromwell. Anne Somerset's letter to Paget when her husband was in danger during the 1549 coup is an example. William and his wife will have looked for similar help when the wheel of fortune had turned against them. Anne Paget was clearly a very good friend of Anne Petre – she was godmother to the Petres' eldest son – and Petre was still at the centre of power as joint Secretary when Paget fell. One interesting snippet of information is that on the very day that her husband was moved from the Fleet to the Tower, Anne entertained the Earl of Huntingdon – who was a close political associate of Northumberland – to dinner at West Drayton. It is difficult to know quite what to make of this, particularly in view of Strype's report that Huntingdon was trying to get his hands on the property. We do not know what happened. But we can be pretty certain that Anne was loyal and helpful to her husband and we do know that the Earl failed to get West Drayton.

Her powerful advocacy is shown in an undated letter to the Privy Council. Although it is the only written evidence we have of her intervention, it suggests that she repeatedly pleaded to the Councillors on her husband's behalf.

In mooste humble wise besechethe our good lordships, youre daily oratrice Anne Paget to be good and gracious lords unto her husband ... please you to be mediators unto his highness [the King] to have pity upon him and me and our poor children, and to determine a gracious and merciful end of our trouble...[14]

When it all came crashing down, survival and rehabilitation would have been made possible by using personal and family networks to the full – Anne's intercessions and connections being very important. Unfortunately, there is not much more in the archives to show exactly how this networking was done, but there is one further significant clue – in the hard evidence of financial records. William's debts at this time were large. Who he had borrowed money from to buy his way out of trouble is a pretty good indicator of the support network he had built up to save him in his hour of need. It started close to home. In the chapter on the West Drayton household, we have seen how he had acquired rich wards of Court who subsequently married two of his daughters. By 1553, he must have added two further wards to the family because the record shows that he owed four of them a total of over £1,000. Other debts reveal the wider support network he had been able call on: £204 owed to Thomas Chamberlain of the Merchant Adventurers, interestingly, £380 to the wife of Richard Cox – his friend, tutor to Prince Edward and vice-chancellor of the University of

Oxford, and the biggest single sum, £900 to 'Ralf', whom we can assume was Ralph Sadler, the Cromwell protege who had remained rich and powerful and was evidently a very good friend – and he, like several other good friends of the Pagets, was still an active Privy Councillor.[15]

After the shocking events of 1551 to 1553, William may have been tempted to pursue a safer and more peaceful life for himself and his family. By the standards of the time, he was getting old and he had growing health problems, not helped by his stay in prison. But repaying these debts alone would have argued for remaining at the centre of power in a world where political influence and financial strength were inextricably entwined. His actions anyhow make it clear that his appetite for power was little diminished. The next ten years were certainly not to be safe and peaceful. In the immediate future, further dramatic upheavals were on the way, with the death of Edward, the short-lived reign of Lady Jane Grey and the triumph of the Catholic Mary Tudor.

Chapter 21

'Long Live the Queen' (Jane or Mary?)

> And, though I liked not the religion
> Which all her life Queen Mary professed,
> Yet in my mind that wicked motion
> Right heirs for to displace I did detest.
> Sir Nicholas Throckmorton in his
Poetical Autobiography

In the words of one historian, John Dudley, Duke of Northumberland was, by early 1553, 'sick, very tired and almost completely disillusioned'. This combined during the last months of the reign with the serious illness of the King to produce a 'partial paralysis of government'.[1] The cleverest politicians, sensing trouble ahead, kept their heads down. Cecil, on whom Northumberland had become increasingly reliant, chose to absent himself from Court as much as possible with the excuse of illness, real or more probably invented. Paget also, though with less choice in the matter, wisely remained inconspicuous. As he became more gravely ill, Edward VI, along with Northumberland, became desperate to prevent Mary's succession. The Dudleys wanted to continue in power, while others, particularly King Edward, were mainly motivated by religion – to avoid a return to Catholicism. Northumberland's son, Guildford Dudley, married Lady Jane Grey in May and a month later the dying King drew up a will leaving her the Crown. This change to the succession, which clearly went against Henry VIII's will and any accepted norms, was initially resisted by many in the ruling elite. (Of course, when Mary eventually won, they all chorused 'We was made to do it'.) But the King and Northumberland forced it through. When, on 21 June, the dying King required them all to witness the will, 'Paget added his name far down amid the lesser knights of the realm and carefully apart from the others of his estate.'[2] The Privy Councillors, of which luckily Paget was not one at this point, were forced into signing an additional pact swearing them to stand by the will. On 6 July, the King died and a few days later, Lady Jane Grey was proclaimed queen.

But Mary was having none of it. When she heard rumours that the King was dying and that there were plans for denying her succession, she left London, where she might have been more easily threatened. From Kenninghall in Norfolk, she proclaimed herself queen and began to gather support. The country was on the brink of civil war. Even before the King's death, Scheyfve had reported that all the Privy Councillors were buying up weapons and armour. Now everyone who had access to any kind of military force was being obliged to take sides. To begin with, it looked as if Queen Jane might prevail. Her supporters had the capital, the Tower, the royal guard, the fleet, the symbols of power such as the Great Seal, the treasury, and the unanimous support of the Privy Council. And the French! Even Mary felt she could not win without the support of her uncle, Charles V, who was reluctant to get involved. However, Mary had two huge advantages: legitimacy and, partly because of that, popular support. Even Lady Jane Grey, when offered the Crown, reputedly said, 'The crown in not my right and pleases me not, the Lady Mary is the rightful heir.' Legitimacy could actually trump religion for many, as the Protestant Sir Nicholas Throckmorton makes clear in his *Poetical Autobiography*, which I have quoted at the head of this chapter. Mary was popular and the rule of the Dudleys unpopular. Even in London, the proclamation of Queen Jane had been met with surly silence by the crowd. Whereas there was wild enthusiasm for Mary, particularly in East Anglia. On 12 July she moved from Kenninghall to the larger and more defensible Framlingham Castle in Suffolk and was joined by various nobles and their supporters, including the Earls of Bath and Sussex and Lord Wentworth.

Meanwhile, on the same day at the Tower, a decision to send Jane's father, the Duke of Suffolk, to lead the forces to confront Mary was reversed when Queen Jane requested, with tears, that her father stay with her. The Council then persuaded Northumberland to go instead, flattering him that he was 'the best man of warre in the realm'. One imagines that he was thoroughly suspicious of their motives, knowing as he did that it was only he who held together the Council in pro-Jane unanimity. However, hoping that they would keep 'fidelity to the quenes majestie' and warning them of the 'feare of Papestry's re-entrance',[3] he left on the 14th to lead the troops against Mary in Suffolk. At this point, or a day later, Paget was centrally involved in what may have been a crucial intervention on Mary's side. The very first entry in the Acts of the Privy Council of Queen Mary reads as follows:

> Reporte ys made by Mr Smyth, sente from Mr Brende, that Sir Edward Hastyngs, Sir Edmunde Pekham, Sir Robert Drewrye, Mr Leonarde Chamberlayne, with others of the force of the shyres of Oxforde, Buckyngham, Berks, Myddlesex, were resolved at nyght, being the 15 of Julye, at Drayton, at my Lorde Paget's house, being in nomber

tenne thowsande, and this day to mershe forth towards the Palaice of Westminster, wher there purpose ys to apprehende Mr Jobson, and to tayke the armure and munytyone that they there shall fynde, for the better furnysshyng of theym selfs in the defence of the Queen's Majestes person and here tytle.[4]

As this report was probably written up after Mary's victory and would reflect well on the participants, including Paget, it has to be treated with caution, and the figure of 10,000 men may be exaggerated. But that Sir Edward Hastings was raising forces for Mary in Buckinghamshire at this time is independently verified and, given that the troops that Northumberland could muster came to a maximum of 2,000, even if this report is half true it would have been significant. It is possible that Lady Anne or one of Paget's sons, who as we will see later in this story were more definitely sympathetic to Catholicism than William, had something to do with this gathering at the Paget house.

This report of the muster at West Drayton, combined with news of further support for Mary from elsewhere, including an important switch by some of the navy, will have made members of the Privy Council, who were already lukewarm, waver in their support of Jane. The 19th was the critical day when the tide turned. In the early morning, Paget was summoned to the Tower, and appeared to have rejoined the Privy Council, where he and the other Councillors performed their last (or, in Paget's case, only) act in favour of Queen Jane – an instruction to the Lord Lieutenant of Essex to support her. But by the late morning most of them, reportedly led by Paget and Arundel, had left the Tower, where they claimed that Northumberland had kept them locked up until his departure, and reconvened at Lord Pembroke's London house, Baynard's Castle. There the Earl of Arundel lectured them:

> The Crown belongs rightfully, by direct succession, to my Lady Mary lawful and natural daughter of our King Henry VIII ... If by chance you should feel somehow guilty proclaiming now our Queen My Lady Mary, having acclaimed Jane only a few days ago, showing such quick change of mind, I tell you this is no reason to hesitate, because having sinned it befits always to amend, especially when, as in the present circumstances, it means honour for your goodselves, welfare and freedom for our country, love and loyalty to his King, peace and contentment for all people.[5]

The hard-nosed members of the Privy Council did not hesitate – evidently sensing which way the wind was blowing; nor did they feel particularly guilty about their 'quick change of mind' or about 'having sinned'. They were indeed much more concerned with the honour, not to mention the interests, of their 'goodselves'. 'Love and loyalty' to one dead king, Henry VIII, and his will, in the end carried more weight than 'love and loyalty' to the other one, Edward VI. They therefore changed their allegiance and proclaimed Mary Queen, which was excellent news for the Imperial ambassadors, who reported,

> All the Council, except the Duke of Suffolk and the Lord Chamberlain [Northampton] who remained at Court, met at the Earl of Pembroke's house, my Lord Paget being for the first time of their company, and together adopted a decision which one may say they could not help. At two o clock in the afternoon part of their number went to the ambassadors and told them that they had decided to proclaim the Lady Mary Queen. Most of them, they said, had been compelled by force to proclaim the other, for they had truely desired to remain friends with the Emperor and turn their backs on the French, and the Lady Mary was true heiress to the Crown.[6]

It was good news too for most of the population who greeted it with great rejoicing, as the ambassadors reported:

> Men ran hither and thither, bonnets flew into the air, shouts rose higher than the stars, fires were lit on all sides, and all the bells were set a-peeling, and from a distance the earth must have looked like Mongibello [Mount Etna]. The people were mad with joy, feasting and singing, and the streets crowded all night long.[7]

Paget and Arundel rode to Framlingham Castle in the company of thirty men and bearing the Great Seal of State, to deliver the Crown to Mary and, according to a further message to the Emperor from his ambassadors, to

> ask her pardon for the offense committed in the reception of the Lady Jane of Suffolk, and perform the ceremonies usually gone through in England when pardon has to be demanded for so heavy a crime, which are said to consist in the guilty party appearing on his knees with a dagger turned towards his stomach in recognition of his offence and submission to the penalty deserved.[8]

Northumberland, much of whose force had already deserted him, realised the game was up, and surrendered. He was sent to the Tower, where he was later beheaded. Among the many rebellions against central government in sixteenth-century England, this was the only successful one. England had come very close to a religious civil war and Lord William Paget, by helping Mary to victory, had played an important part in avoiding one.

* * *

Paget and Arundel, their kneeling knife-to-the-stomach apology accepted, returned to London. As Charles V's ambassadors relayed to him, 'In this beginning Arundel and Paget are carrying on the government, until the Queen reaches London.'[9]

One of our retrieved family 'royal letters' was sent by the Queen to the two of them from Colchester – halfway on her slow and triumphant progress to the capital.

It referred to their letters to her of the previous day, 'Movinge us by our Mercye to Suspende and forebeare the arestynge and commyttinge of the duke of Suff[olk] [Lady Jane Grey's father] all contrarye to thinstruccions delyvered unto you by us as you the Lord paget dothe knowe.'

From the start, Mary here made it clear that there were limits to her mercy and, furthermore, that she expected to be obeyed at the first time of asking. She continued, 'We marvayl not a Lyttell, of this your so soden mutacyon and chaunge in a matter of suche weight so Nerelye towchynge the state and Suertie of our persons in the present case. And for that we hetherunto perceyve no cause whye to alter our former Determination.'[10]

The letter also instructed them to arrest Sir John Cheke along with the Duke of Suffolk. Cheke had been involved in producing the documents that excluded Mary from the succession and backed up Northumberland's coup. He was a prominent Protestant humanist scholar and tutor to Edward VI and was a good friend of Paget's.

During the early days of the reign, the Queen's attitude was a mixture of conciliation and punishment, of change and continuity. In an audience with Renard, Charles V's ambassador who was to become her closest advisor, and in the presence of Paget and a few other Privy Councillors, she concurred with the ambassador's view, 'not to hurry where religion was concerned, not to make innovations nor adopt unpopular policies'. She said, 'she wished to force no one to go to Mass'.[11] Although Northumberland and two of his supporters went to the block, Guilford Dudley and Lady Jane stayed in comfortable imprisonment and the Duke of Suffolk was actually released from prison very soon after he had been arrested as per the instructions to Paget. On the issue of Edward's funeral, she compromised: he was buried in a Protestant service conducted by Cranmer, while she held a requiem Mass for his soul in a private chapel.

Whatever Mary's views, it was clear that at this point 'the body politic', and Parliament in particular, while agreeing to return religion to that of the final years of Henry's reign, was not willing to abolish the royal supreme headship and reinstate the authority of the Pope, and, above all, would not sacrifice their property and revenue from ex-monastic lands. Mary also compromised in her choice of Privy Councillors and close advisors, adding experienced men such as Paget, Arundel and Petre to her existing group of loyal Catholics. However, the power of the committed Catholics was boosted by Paget's old friend and recent enemy, Gardiner, who was released from the Tower along with the very ancient Duke of Norfolk. Gardiner was then appointed Lord Chancellor.

Tension between the two groups was evident, with reports that discontent was rife, 'especially amongst those that stood by the Queen in her days of adversity and trouble, who feel they have not been rewarded as they deserve, for the conspirators have been raised in authority'.[12] Disagreements about forgiveness and revenge and moderation and extremism in religion crystallised around Gardiner and Paget, with the Imperial ambassador writing, 'It is said quite openly that Paget cannot get on with the Bishop of Winchester, and that they are jealous of one another.'[13] The other major issue which they fought over was the plan for a royal marriage. As the rivalry between the two played out – up until Gardener's death in November 1555 – it became clear how each had strengths and weaknesses when it came to their influence with the Queen. Gardiner had the advantage of his committed Catholicism and the badge of honour of imprisonment for his beliefs under Edward VI; whereas Paget was suspected of being a heretic and remained a moderate in matters of religion. But Paget had the advantage of being a long-term supporter of alliance with the Habsburgs against the Valois, of having a close relationship with Charles V – who was much admired and deferred to by Mary – and of being a passionate advocate of the Queen's marriage to his son Prince Philip; whereas Gardiner had always been more pro-French and anti-Spanish and was a proponent of marriage to an Englishman, Sir Edward Courtenay – the only Englishman with sufficient royal blood to be a contender.

Chapter 22

Marrying Mary to Philip

> Lord Paget had spoken to her at great length on the question of marriage, going as far as to advise her not to look on it merely as a marriage but as a solemn alliance which might be made to the greatest of advantage to her Kingdom and subjects.
>
> Queen Mary to Renard, 1553

It is to the royal marriage that we now turn. Paget was at the centre of the negotiations, which were opened at the start of the reign and ended in the actual wedding to Philip a year later.

> Paget talked with me [ambassador Renard] the day of the Queen's entry [into London 3 August], and after various remarks said it [Mary's marriage to a Habsburg] would be the finest match in the world, but that the time had not yet come to speak of it. I replied in such a way as not to make him suppose it had been thought of on our side.[1]

Paget would certainly have guessed that it had already been thought of by the Habsburgs. A letter from the Emperor to his son from a few days before made that clear. In it he said that, although 'the English will do all in their power to prevent our cousin from wedding a foreigner', the advantages 'are so obvious that it is unnecessary to go into them'.[2] If the Emperor could get Mary to marry a Habsburg, France would be encircled, with the sea route between the Netherlands and Spain made safe. It would also balance the threat from the proposed marriage of Mary, Queen of Scots to the son of the King of France. The hegemony of Europe was at stake. On 14 August, the Bishop of Arras, Charles V's chief advisor, wrote to Renard to say that, if Mary was inclined towards such a marriage, she would no doubt get someone such as Paget to speak about it to him. Having had previous encounters with the 'Master of Practices', he warned his ambassador about 'Paget, who is a match for you, for he spoke to you as he did to find out your opinion. As he is so sharp, you must watch yourself more when you talk to him, and try your best to make him talk himself.'[3]

This diplomatic jousting continued into the autumn of 1553, as a long report from Renard to the Emperor on 5 October shows. At this stage, the two sides were still feeling out each other's positions and there were other Habsburg candidates for marriage being considered as well as Philip. The ambassador told Charles that

> having heard from the Queen that Paget was in favour of a foreign alliance, and knowing, moreover, that Paget wished to make good the loss and damage he suffered at the hands of his enemies; ... that he was a man of wit and stood well amongst those who governed and administered the affairs of the country ... especially as he has always professed his devotion to your Majesty ... I requested him to give me his opinion and tell me in confidence if it would be suitable that your Majesty should make any overtures or proposals to the Queen concerning her marriage, in what terms, by what means.

Before answering, Paget cautiously wanted to confirm the status of the negotiations, and his own part in them:

> He desired to know if your Majesty had named him personally as one to whom I should address myself. I replied, Yes. Then, he said, on that assurance, he would tell me in confidence and all sincerity how matters stood ... [Everyone] considered it necessary for the good of the kingdom that the Queen should enter into an alliance and marry; and the sooner the better, because of the state of her affairs and her years.

The councillors were divided as to whom she should marry. As well as Courtenay there were Don Luis of Portugal and Emmanuel Philibert, Duke of Savoy, in addition to Philip. Paget continued,

> [The Queen] would accept a marriage for the good of her people and in the hope of begetting heirs, rather than from any private inclination or amorousness of disposition ... the Queen's happiness ought to be taken into consideration, as well as her age and comfort; that a husband should be proposed to her suitable in these respects, with whom she could live in happiness and content, and who would remain at her side...

Paget was worried about Philip having 'so many kingdoms' that he would not stay very much in England (as proved to be the case), about his young age (26), and the fact that he only spoke Spanish. 'If the marriage were to come off, it would be expedient for him to learn to speak and understand English, otherwise it would prove a dumb marriage.' William had direct knowledge of that – the disaster that was Henry VIII's marriage to Anne of Cleves. Because of the 'so many kingdoms' problem, he wondered whether one of the other two candidates might be more suitable.

Both Paget and Renard agreed to keep these negotiations secret, as the ambassador's letter reveals:

> The next day I repaired to his [Paget's] house at the appointed hour, early in the morning. He let me in by the back door of his garden to prevent my being noticed by anyone. He said he had no leisure for a lengthy conversation, as the Queen had sent for him to deliberate on the articles concerning religion, to be brought before Parliament, that might give some trouble.

Paget wanted Renard to clarify the Emperor's intentions for the marriage, as the Queen would not marry without his advice, and he wanted a further description of Philip's 'character and parts'; to which Renard replied that he was 'a prince possessed of natural gifts as great as his acquired qualities'. Renard's report ends by stating that the 'matter is a weighty one' and that he foresaw 'difficulties in the way of its achievement: intrigues and contrary efforts, because of the Bishop of Winchester's partiality, of the objections to a foreigner, and the various considerations that will be entertained, such as those Paget indicated, and others too.'[4]

The Emperor replied, thanking his ambassador for this 'full account of your conversations with Lord Paget' and surmising from it that Paget, 'would not disapprove' of a proposal from Philip. Charles then proposed on his son's behalf. He instructed Renard to tell the Queen of the communication with Paget, adding the somewhat convoluted sentence, 'If her opinion of him [Paget] is such that she approves of using him to counterbalance the Bishop of Winchester's designs in favour of Courtenay, you will adopt the tone with Paget that the Queen shall approve of.'

Rather more straightforwardly, Charles said that he had followed Paget's advice in sending individual letters to the important Privy Councillors telling them that he had 'made certain proposals' to the Queen, he enclosed a personal letter to Paget thanking him and another rather bossy one to Mary advising her to marry 'and the sooner you make up your mind the better'.[5]

Renard then had an audience with the Queen in which he knelt before her and formally offered the hand of Prince Philip. Her reply was, in essence, the often used, 'I'll think about it.' According to the account relayed back to

Charles, she had quite a few concerns: 'she did not know how the people of England would take it'; Philip 'would have many realms and provinces which he would be unwilling to abandon to come and live in England'; 'if he were disposed to be amorous, such was not her desire, for she was of the age your Majesty knew of and had never harboured thoughts of love'; and finally, 'if he wished to encroach in the government of the kingdom she would be unable to permit it, nor if he attempted to fill posts and offices with strangers.'[6]

Despite these doubts, Paget and Renard got busy trying to win over the Queen and her other advisors. Mary reported to Renard that

> Lord Paget had spoken to her at great length on the question of marriage, going as far as to advise her not to look at it as merely a marriage, but as a solemn alliance which might be made to be of the greatest advantage to her kingdom and subjects. Let her consider the future and realise that if she married Courtenay or some poor Prince the country would not benefit by the match, but if she chose a puissant and exalted husband she and England would enjoy security and repose.[7]

Before coming to an audience with Mary and her Privy Council, Renard 'had, on Paget's advice, privately given Winchester his letter [from the Emperor] to show him that your Majesty had a great regard for him and realised his importance ... he imagined I had letters for him only.'

The ambassador thought that Gardiner and other members of the Council were now 'well enough aware of the Queen's small liking for Courtenay, and are now working against each other not to let slip the honour and profit that will attend the successful negotiation of the other match.'[8]

On Sunday, 29 October 1553, Mary decided to say 'yes'. She told Renard she had not slept and had continually wept and prayed to God to give her an answer. As he told Charles,

> She had considered all things ... had also spoken to Arundel, Paget and Petre. She believed what I had told her of his Highness' [Philip's] qualities, and that your Majesty [Charles] would ever show her kindness, observe the conditions that were to safeguard the welfare of the country, be a good father to her as you had been in the past and more, now that you would be doubly her father, and cause his Highness to be a good husband to her. She felt herself inspired by God, who had performed so many miracles in her favour, to give me her promise to marry his Highness.

In retrospect, even though it was another two months before the marriage treaty was signed and a further six months before the wedding happened, this can be seen as the decisive moment, mainly because Mary was so determined, then and subsequently, that 'her mind, once made up, would never change'. But this would not necessarily have been obvious at the time. Paget told Renard that people were still trying to put Mary off the marriage by telling her that Philip was 'very voluptuous and has bastard sons and daughters'. There was still much opposition to be dealt with, not least from Gardiner, Parliament and the French. The terms had to be agreed, very complex arrangements made and the connected issues to do with religious reforms and the succession resolved. As Renard told the Emperor, he was off to 'consult Paget as to what shall now be done'.[9]

* * *

Renard's next letter to Charles warned that Gardiner was still rooting for a marriage to Courtenay and opposing one to Philip on two grounds – that it would force England into a war with France and that 'the people and nobility will never put up with Spaniards in this country'. However, the ambassador was confident that 'Paget, who has undertaken this business, has used it to obtain the Queen's confidence and now has state affairs in his hands. He assured me that the Queen will not change against her word.' Paget was also advising Mary to 'be content with re-establishing mass and religion as they were in the late King Henry's lifetime' and to delay bringing home Cardinal Pole, the Pope's envoy, at least until after the royal wedding. On the question of monastic lands, he was urging her not

> to revoke all the liberalities given by the Crown under the late Kings Henry and Edward, consisting of Church and other property; but as this matter nearly touches all the nobility and most of the people [by which he obviously meant the ruling elite, including himself], it cannot be put into execution without arousing a mighty tumult.

Then there was the problem of the succession, if, notwithstanding the marriage, Mary were to die without issue. To avoid the Crown going to Mary, Queen of Scots – about to be married to the Dauphin – 'the best thing to do in order to please nobles and commons would be to cause the next Parliament to confirm the Lady Elizabeth's right to succeed'. Paget suggested that Elizabeth should marry Courtenay. William, the great survivor, may have been thinking of his own future as well as of the benefit to the country of continuity of government, when he advised Mary and the ambassador, 'Were the succession arranged in this wise all sides might be satisfied and all possible trouble avoided. He thinks it better to keep in with Elizabeth than to antagonise her, and entirely disapproves of those who wish to put her in the Tower.'

On this issue he was predictably once more in conflict with Gardiner, telling Renard 'that the Bishop of Winchester had a spite against him for having advised the Queen not to imprison Elizabeth because of religion, but to reduce her with kindness.'[10] Paget's arguments about Elizabeth's succession were repeated in a discussion he had with the Queen and Renard at the end of November. Eventually, just before her death five years later, Mary would accept them. But, for now, she angrily stated,

> it would burden her conscience too strongly to allow Elizabeth to succeed, for she only went to mass out of hypocrisy, she had not a single maid of honour who was not a heretic, she talked every day with heretics and lent a ear to all their evil designs, and it would be a disgrace to the kingdom to allow a bastard to succeed.

Henry VIII's rejection of her mother for Anne Boleyn evidently still rankled. However, as 'time did not press as yet', Mary, Paget and Renard all agreed to shelve the question for the moment. Renard shrewdly commented that Paget's attitude towards Elizabeth may have been partly 'for private reasons of his own, in order to provide for his and his family's future'. Paget's advocacy of Elizabeth's right to the succession was, however, balanced by warnings to her not to make trouble. He and Arundel visited her and threatened, 'if she left the straight road and intrigued with the heretics and the French she might have reason to regret it'.[11]

He stressed the need for speed in progressing the marriage, with English commercial interests being an additional incentive; Renard to the Emperor, again:

> Paget tells me that English merchants at Antwerp write saying that there have been quarrels between English and Spanish merchants in that town, and that they have fought on two occasions. He is amazed that your Majesty does not see to stopping all occurrences that may alienate the English, and has again said that the sooner you send to England to have the [marriage] treaty concluded the better.

Despite everyone's insistence that it was not expected to be a love match, it was thought advisable to send Mary a picture of Philip. Mary of Hungary, the

Emperor's Regent in the Netherlands, who we have encountered earlier in this story as a great art collector, sent over a beautiful Titian of the prince, which, she said, 'will serve to tell her what he is like, if she will put it in a proper light and look at it from a distance as all Titian's (tyssien) paintings have to be looked at.'

As someone who appreciated great painting, she sent the portrait 'under one condition; that I am to have it again, as it is only a dead thing, when she has the living model in her presence'.[12] It appears that the pious 37-year-old virgin queen was not put off by this picture of the 26-year-old prince, with his smouldering look and codpiece to the fore.

William was heavily involved in many aspects of the marriage plans. He was worried that too many 'objectionable Spaniards' might remain in Philip's service when he came to England. Charles V, who had grown up in the Low Countries and had himself had great difficulty adjusting to Mediterranean ways, was sympathetic to this concern and was happy to give an assurance, though diplomatically adding that, 'it would be better to have the promise given separately rather than to include it among the articles [of the marriage treaty], in order to avoid wounding national susceptibilities.' It was Paget who advised Renard, who advised Charles V, who then advised his son: for example, that the Queen did not want to be married during Lent, that Southampton would be a suitable place for Philip to land, and that he should send Mary a present as a token – a large diamond was sent. Paget tried, without much success, to reassure the French ambassador that his country had no reason to fear the match. Meanwhile the Queen's definite commitment had seen off the opposition from Parliament and Gardiner. It was reported that she had confronted her Lord Chancellor in a fury about his encouragement to the parliamentarians who had promoted Courtenay's suit. When Gardiner replied in tears that he was fond of Courtenay because they had been in prison together – obviously expecting her sympathy for 'suffering Catholics' – 'in reply the Queen asked him whether it would be suitable to force her to marry a man because the Bishop had conceived a friendship for him in prison.'

It is thought that the terms of the treaty were largely Paget's work. They were generally very favourable from the English point of view. If Mary were to predecease her husband, his interest in the country would end. If there were children from the marriage, of either sex, that heir would inherit England and the Low Countries but have no claim on Spain. Particularly significant was Philip's commitment to take an oath before the ceremony to preserve the laws and customs of England, to keep Englishmen in his household, not to make the country go to war against France and not to remove the Queen from the realm. These terms were agreed with Charles's negotiators and Philip himself was not too happy with them. But he eventually agreed, although adding a secret disclaimer. The treaty was signed at the beginning of January 1554.

William's role in steering the match to a conclusion bought him thanks from Charles, who wrote him an effusive personal letter of gratitude – as well as giving him material rewards, which we will examine later. It had also made him very influential with the Queen. She restored to him three of his manors which he had lost as part of his fine and, importantly, his Order of the Garter, declaring it had been removed 'neither justly, nor in due order'. Although most of his rehabilitation had been achieved in the previous reign, this completed the process. Mary's favouring of Paget followed from the Emperor's high regard for him and her enthusiasm for the marriage he had arranged. But given his close association with the Protestant establishment, it will have come as quite a surprise to many and naturally led to much jealousy. Renard had reported to the Emperor:

> Paget is envied because the Queen listens to him. The Catholics and those who stood by the Queen during her troubles are being tempted to withdraw their allegiance because she is favouring heretics ... and doing nothing for the men who were faithful in her hour of need. Paget has been suspected of heresy because he ruled King Henry and influenced him in a heretical direction.

Sir Robert Rochester, a long-time ally of Mary and controller of her household, told Renard, 'in confidence, that many regretted to see that Paget had the Queen's ear'. And, on the last day of the old year, the ambassador reported to the Emperor, 'Waldegrave, Inglefield [Englefield], Southwell and others who supported Courtenay's suit have been trying to arrange the Cardinal's [Pole] coming, now that they see themselves out of favour, in order to discredit Paget and prepare their own return.'[13]

Chapter 23

Rebellion and Repression

[The Emperor] praised clemency, in order to think that Paget might not think he advocated violence, and stated that he had advised the Queen to govern by mild methods rather than by the show of authority and the letting of blood.

[Paget told the Emperor] Most of the nobility were greatly concerned about Church property, which had come into their hands as a reward for services rendered ... wherefore it would be necessary ... to leave them undisturbed in their possession.
Account of Paget's November 1554 audience with
Charles V, Spanish Calendar

The ruling elite may have been reconciled to the Spanish marriage, but many in the country were not. The Imperial delegation that came to sign the marriage treaty were pelted with snowballs. Paget reported that Sir Peter Carew and others in Exeter were warning the Queen that Philip had better not disembark in the West Country with Spaniards as it was suspected they would 'do as they pleased, and violate their daughters'. A plot was being hatched by Carew, along with the Duke of Suffolk and Sir Thomas Wyatt in Kent and backed by the French, to block the marriage and reinstate Protestantism. When it was uncovered, the conspirators were forced into early action before they were ready, forcing Carew to escape to France and Suffolk to flee to Leicester. But Wyatt successfully raised a force and marched towards London. This was a serious rebellion, made more so when some of the troops sent to confront them changed sides influenced by the cry of 'We are all Englishmen' who needed to fight against Spanish designs 'to spoil us of our goods and lands, ravish our wives before our faces, and deflower our daughters in our presence'.[1] The Queen felt herself in danger, complaining to Paget that her Council was ineffective and split and that

> they were to have supplied her with a body guard four days ago, and she had not yet received a single man except for the 200 archers of her usual

guard ... Paget, sinking to his knees, replied that for the last fortnight and more he had been doing his best to raise troops, but that as he was only one voice in the Council he could not do everything by himself ... there were in the Council suspicious persons, ill-disposed towards your majesty, and of evil intention. The Queen then commanded Paget to tell the Council that they must immediately raise troops in order to safeguard her person.²

Another of our recovered 'royal letters' was from 'Marye the quene' to Paget in his role as a landowner and Baron with a large number of retainers – ordering him 'to Leavie all the power and force of horsemen and footemen that yow can'. He raised thirty cavalry and 100 foot soldiers who contributed to the Queen's victory, which was achieved as much as anything due to her brave and impassioned speech to Londoners in which she swore that, although she intended to marry the Prince of Spain, she had been, at her coronation, 'wedded to the realm [of England], and to the laws of the same, the spousal ring whereof I wear here on my finger, and it never has and never shall be left off'.³

In the aftermath of the rebellion, Mary was no longer inclined to show mercy. Not only were those who fought for Wyatt hanged, but Lady Jane Grey, her father the Duke of Suffolk and her husband, Guilford Dudley, were now executed. Elizabeth was also threatened. As before, Paget was the voice for moderation, while Gardiner advocated severity. It was reported at the beginning of March that the princess was to be cross-questioned about her involvement in the rebellion by both of them, along with Arundel and Petre, and that 'her fate should depend on her answers'. Gardiner succeeded in getting her sent to the Tower at the end of the month, but by mid-May she was released into civilised housing near Woodstock – though under the supervision of a reliable Catholic gentleman. Paget was arguing

> that if sufficient evidence to put her to death were not discovered he saw no better means of keeping her quiet than to marry her to a foreigner, and if a match with the Prince of Piedmont could be arrange, Parliament and the Council would readily consent that the Succession should go to them in case the Queen had no children.

Emmanuel Philibert, Prince of Piedmont, Duke of Savoy, cousin of Philip II of Spain, comes about number sixteen in the thirty-plus suitors proposed for Elizabeth throughout her lifetime. According to Renard, Paget still felt able to try to move the Queen in the direction of mercy and moderation. He told her that enough blood had been spilled. When Mary 'remonstrated with Paget for having spoken as he did', he justified himself by saying that the nobles did not want another tyrannical figure such as the Duke of Northumberland had been, and Gardiner was in danger of filling that role.[4]

Two other stories, involving Paget, from the Imperial ambassador's dispatches in the spring of 1554 reveal the spirit of the times: essentially, corruption and superstition. William had previously suggested to the Emperor and his advisors that it would help ease the acceptance of the marriage if English officials were 'rewarded' – preferably with a gift seen to come directly from Prince Philip. In March this was confirmed, as Paget conferred with the Queen about 'the names of men who might have pensions, or receive chains [of gold]'. By this stage in the proceedings, Gardiner and Sir Robert Rochester, Controller of Mary's household, were sufficiently converted to the match to be allowed to also submit lists of names. The Imperial authorities accordingly had '4000 crowns melted down for chains' and allocated another 1,000 crowns to 'be distributed in money'. The full list includes not only the 'good and great' but middle-level officials such as the Captain of the Tower of London, right down to heralds and archers. The other story is an anecdote Renard thought worthy of reporting to Charles V:

> The heretics have put up a man and a woman in a house here in London to rouse the people by asserting that a voice was to be heard in a wall, and it was the voice of an angel. When they said to it, 'God save Queen Mary' it answered not; but when they said 'God save the Lady Elizabeth' the voice replied, 'So be it.' Then was asked another question, 'What is the mass?' and the reply came, 'Idolatry'. And this fraud had so much success that by eleven in the morning there were over 17,000 people collected round the house. The Council sent thither the Admiral, Paget and the captain of the Guard, and the man and woman have been arrested.

Although the figure of 17,000 must be exaggerated and the whole episode has the whiff of the kind of far-fetched 'urban myth' beloved of the modern tabloid press, it serves to remind us how very important religious superstition was in the sixteenth century.[5]

The discord between Paget and Gardiner came to a head in April with the latter introducing a bill in Parliament, the exact details of which have not survived, but which was reported as, 'concerning religion and the Pope's authority, establishing a form of Inquisition against the heretics, setting up again the power of the Bishops and dealing with the Pope's authority'. Paget was strongly opposed to this, writing to Renard, 'for the love of God, Sir, persuade the Queen to dissolve Parliament at once… the weather is beginning to be warm and men's tempers will wax warm too'. Gardiner's proposals, he said 'will heat the people altogether too much'. Only two bills should have been introduced 'one on the marriage', 'the other confirming every man in his possession [i.e. of Church property]'. Paget's opposition to Gardiner's bill led to its rejection in the House of Lords. The Queen was furious. Unusually for him, Paget had miscalculated the royal mood, apparently being unaware of the strength of Mary's commitment to the measure. As Renard was the man with the Queen's ear, both Gardiner and Paget came to see him in order to influence her. Gardiner was triumphant, stressing to the ambassador that, 'the act had failed to pass because of the opposition organised by Paget' and adding 'the Queen had better realise who was her good and faithful servant, and who was not'. Paget was worried that he had fatally blotted his copybook – even fearing a return to prison. Renard wrote, 'When Paget heard that the Queen knew of his doings he came to see me and begged me to obtain for him leave to go away to the baths in Cornwall. He was suffering from pains in his leg, he said and he saw that the Queen was not pleased with him.' He was concerned to find out just how angry Mary was and 'whether there was any intention of shutting him up – a prospect which terrifies him'.

It seems clear that his sojourn in prison had rattled him badly – as it would, and he was very keen not to repeat the experience.[6]

On 13 May, Renard reported to the Emperor:

Paget, moved by a bad conscience, presented himself before the Queen on the way from Mass, and begged her pardon for his efforts during the last session to prevent the passage of the Bill providing for the punishment of heretics, and the proposal to make it a treasonable offence to take up arms against His Highness. As for the first point, Lord Rich had persuaded him that what was aimed at was the expropriation of those who held Church property. In the second matter, he had acted out of ignorance and inadvertency; but in future he meant to serve her truly and loyally. The Queen, after remonstrating with him on his conduct, pardoned him, admonishing him to do better hereafter.[7]

There seemed no doubt Gardiner's star was rising and Paget's falling in the spring and summer of 1554. Part of the long report on every aspect of English life sent to the Venetian Senate by their observant ambassador, Giacomo Soranzo, reads,

> Paget, both because he is a very experienced statesman [molto pratico della ationi del mondo], as also having been the person who negotiated the marriage with the Prince of Spain, took precedence of all of them until now, when, as an acknowledged anti-Catholic, he is out of favour with Her Majesty. The Bishop of Winchester, on the contrary, who at the commencement opposed the marriage and ran great risk of disgrace, until being convinced of the Queen's firm intention he diligently aided its accomplishment is now paramount to everybody.[8]

There were rumours that Paget was actually conspiring against the government, particularly with Mason, his protegee, and the current ambassador to France, and also that Arundel and Paget might be thrown into the Tower. However, these rumours proved unfounded and Paget had not completely lost power and influence. He still had support from many in the Imperial court. 'Notes for Prince Philip's guidance in England', produced in June by an unknown hand in Charles V's court, recommended to the bridegroom that he 'put his trust in Paget, who was the Ambassador's instrument in negotiating the marriage and is a man of understanding'. Philip finally arrived in England on 19 July at Southampton. Paget's concerns about English sensitivities probably influenced the careful choreography of public relations. The prince made a speech to the assembled English councillors saying that he had come to live amongst them not as a foreigner but as a native Englishman. He publicly advised his entourage to conform to local customs, and then symbolically raised his lips to a flagon of English ale. After his first meeting with Mary, where they sat hand in hand and talked for half an hour, he said on his departure, 'Goodnight, my Lords all' in English – words that the Queen had just taught him. The wedding took place in Winchester Cathedral on 25 July.

Although playing a less important role than Gardiner, Paget and his wife Anne were part of the welcoming party and wedding celebrations. On the day after the wedding, William 'kissed the King's hand and departed well satisfied'.[9] That satisfaction, recorded by Renard, may have been caused by confirmation that he was to receive an annual pension of 1,500 crowns from the King which was accorded him around this time. Renard had somewhat turned against Paget and become more of a Gardiner supporter, but others in the Imperial camp, such as Ruy Gomez de Silva, an important figure in the King's entourage, were more favourable to Paget. He wrote:

> our Ambassador's attitude has not always been wise ... he has taken sides for one of the parties here, and as his influence with the Queen is great, he is able to be of use to some and do serious harm to others. The result

is that those who are out of favour are resentful and one of them is Paget, who, as the Ambassador himself confesses, helped him more than anyone else during the marriage negotiations. The King has already done much to remedy this.

Philip was evidently impressed by Paget and/or by those advisors who favoured him. One of these was the remarkable and influential ruler of the Netherlands, Mary, Queen of Hungary, who wrote to Charles V's minister, Arras,

> It seems to me that Paget's complaints … are not altogether unreasonable, as he now sees all hope vanish of obtaining his reward for the pains he took to bring about the marriage, of which he was certainly the principal artisan … it would be a good thing … to tell Paget that he is embounden to him … [and] give him a substantial proof of his favour … and persuade the Queen to make it up with Paget and employ him … and I fail to see why … an attempt should not be made to come to terms with Paget, for of whatever religion or leanings he may be, there is no denying that he has been too valuable a servant in the past to be turned so lightly away.[10]

In addition, the Emperor himself remained a Paget supporter, writing in October that King Philip 'is making ready to treat the religious question with the assistance of Paget who has returned. He is the right man, and is hopeful of the result on condition that Church property is not touched.'[11] Paying attention to these promptings, Mary did indeed employ him – describing him to the Emperor as 'my dear and well-beloved Lord Paget' – as one of the two envoys dispatched in November 1554 to collect the papal envoy, Cardinal Pole, from Brussels. An account of his audience there with Charles has the Emperor thanking him profoundly for bringing about the match and being pleased to hear that he was 'once more in favour' with the Queen.[12] One indicator of that is another of our recovered 'royal letters' to Paget, signed by Mary and Philip in January 1555, ordering him to act as one of the two commissioners for the installation to the Order of the Garter of Lord Howard of Effingham and of Emmanuel Philibert – the Duke of Savoy and cousin to Philip whom we have encountered as a suitor for Elizabeth's hand and who was about to replace the Queen of Hungary as Governor of the Netherlands.[13]

In their conversation, Charles and Paget praised clemency and moderation and wanted the Queen and King 'to govern by mild methods' rather than by 'the letting of blood'.[14] But this was not to be. At the beginning of 1555, with the Gardiner faction still very influential with the Queen and Paget acting increasingly as Philip's advisor ('often in the King's apartments'), the burnings of heretics for which 'Bloody Mary' became infamous accelerated. Commenting on the continuing rift between Gardiner and Paget and Arundel, Renard wrote to Charles that the bishops 'are so hot and hasty about religion and the papal authority, causing heretics to be burnt every day, that I fear their rashness may cause the people to rise up in arms this spring.'[15]

While not wanting to dwell on the gory details, it is the historian's duty to give an idea of the horrors really inflicted by burning people at the stake. One example will suffice. John Hooper, former Bishop of Worcester and Gloucester was brought before Gardiner and other bishops for denying the papal supremacy and the real presence of Christ in the bread and wine and was condemned to be burnt. Anna Whitelock's excellent biography of Mary takes up the story:

> Standing on a high stool and looking over the crowd of several thousand that had gathered to watch him, he prayed. An eyewitness described how 'in every corner there was nothing to be seen but weeping and sorrowful people'. Faggots were laid around the stool and reeds place in between Hooper's hands. Then the fire was lit. The wind at first blew the flames from him and having burnt his legs, the fires were almost extinguished. More faggots and reeds were brought and finally the two bladders of gunpowder tied between his legs ignited. In the end he could move nothing but his arms, then one fell off and then the other, with 'fat, water and blood dropping out at his fingers' ends', stuck to what was left of his chest. It had taken forty-five minutes of excruciating agony to kill him.[16]

Similar scenes to this were repeated 300 times over the following year, culminating in the burning of Cranmer in March 1556. William Paget was opposed to these barbarities. But it cannot be denied that he was a central figure in a government that committed them: as indeed he had been in the government of Henry VIII, which behaved with equal brutality.

Chapter 24

Serving King and Queen

> Lord Paget, both now and ever, will always be the mediator and regulator [compositore] between the most Serene Queen and the King; he thus establishing himself in the closest confidence of both one and the other, and increasing his repute to an unlimited extent, warranting his hopes of every possible reward from their Majesties.
>
> Venetian ambassador in England to the
Doge and Senate, 7 April 1556

Away from the horrors at home, Paget's next mission was to lead the English delegation that attempted to mediate a peace between the Habsburgs and Valois. A peace conference was held in May 1555 at La Marque, on the border of the English territories in France. The Venetian ambassador reported that Paget was heavily involved in the logistics – arranging the accommodation and food supplies – and dealing with the diplomatic niceties of getting two nations at war to talk to each other. He organised it so that, 'wooden lodgings had been prepared for all the aforesaid personages [the French and Imperial commissioners], who were separated from each other by a centre hall in which to meet on the days of the conference.' Predictably he had trouble with the French grandees, as he had

> arranged that neither the Imperialists nor the French were to have more than a hundred horse, with one single [running] footman for each, which arrangement greatly displeased the French lords, as they had come fully attended, accompanied both by noblemen and prelates, and by gentlemen and servants.

He got agreement to an armistice – 'Lord Paget proposed a suspension of hostilities on the frontier there at least during the conference' – and on the method of negotiation, whereby 'he and his colleagues will spend four days in visiting the Imperial and French commissioners' separately, in order to avoid face to face confrontations between the warring parties.[1] While he was acting to some extent as an honest broker, there was little doubt that he favoured the Imperial camp, keeping them, but not the French, informed, and not offering much hope of success. The Imperial delegation wrote to the Emperor on 25 May:

> Lord Paget said to us, aside, not having time to go into more details, that his impression was that if we wanted a peace lasting two or three years, during which the King of France would be able to gather strength again and afterwards do even worse things than before, we would succeed in obtaining it, but that if we were out for a good and lasting peace, as we said, we would not achieve anything.

News of two significant events reached the conference at the beginning of June, strengthening the French position and making them even less likely to want peace. Mary's pregnancy failed – or proved to have been a phantom, and a new Pope was elected who was a sworn enemy of the Habsburgs. On 8 June the Imperial delegation were told that nothing indicated that the French 'were really desirous of negotiating. As far as Paget could see, it looked like goodbye.'[2] The next day, the English left to return home. While the conference had been going on, William's son and son-in-law were visiting Brussels. An indication of the Emperor's respect for their father/father-in-law is revealed in a dispatch of the Venetian ambassador in Brussels. 'The Emperor gave orders for refreshments to be sent to Lord Paget's son and son-in-law' and said 'he wished to see them before their departure, as he did, showing them many marks of good will out of regard for Lord Paget'. The Venetian's nose for the nuances of power and class is shown by his additional remark that there were 'no such demonstrations' towards Lord Courtenay (also visiting Brussels), 'who is infinitely superior [in aristocratic status] to the Pagets'.[3]

In August, with Mary clearly no longer pregnant and a multitude of calls for his attention from elsewhere, the King departed, leaving his wife in tears. A Council of State, which included Paget, was to keep him in touch with English affairs. However, once back on the Continent, Philip found he had little time for England, particularly as Charles abdicated from his lordship of the Netherlands in October 1555 and from the Spanish crown in January 1556. Paget's return to influence in the Tudor Court was boosted by the death in November 1555 of his great rival, Gardiner. The two were in fact reconciled at the bishop's deathbed. Who was now to become Lord Chancellor became an important question. The French ambassador, Noailles, reckoned that 'Paget would much like it' but that, although 'he will make a case', he would not succeed. He was right. While King Philip supported his candidature, the post eventually went to the more reliably Catholic Nicholas Heath, Archbishop

Serving King and Queen 171

of York. Although Paget's power during Mary's reign was considerable, there would always be a limit to it because of his 'dubious' religious history. As the canny Venetian ambassador in Brussels, Badoer, remarked, he 'will exert himself more willingly than anybody else, from the hope, by doing good service, of getting into greater favour with the Queen than he is, by reason of his favouring the Lutheran opinions.'

Although failing to get the Chancellorship, he was happy to be appointed Lord Privy Seal, one of the great offices of State. It was prestigious and well paid: he received £1 every day from customs receipts plus other official remuneration valued at £800 a year. Cromwell had apparently preferred this office to the Chancellorship because it avoided a lot of time-consuming mandatory judicial duties.[4]

When it came to sending someone to the Netherlands to persuade her husband to return – the most important thing in Mary's life – Paget was the overwhelmingly obvious choice. As the Venetian ambassador said, she 'could not send any person of more subtle intellect, or more dear to the King'.[5] He left at the beginning of April 1556 with a letter from the Queen to the Emperor offering best wishes for his recovery from gout, congratulating him on the peace with France (achieved by the Treaty of Vancelles, but which was to be short-lived), and hoping that, 'now the abdication was over' and 'the truce concluded', he would persuade his son to return. She begged him on account of 'the unspeakable sadness I experience because of the absence of the King'.[6] The Venetian ambassador reckoned that 'the chief object of his [Paget's] discourse was to inspire the King with the hope, on his return to England, of being crowned which has not yet been given him by the Queen.'

In addition, Paget emphasised to Philip that, as far as 'conception for the succession' was concerned, there was 'no time to lose … as she is not of an age to be able to delay'.[7] He hoped to accompany the King back to London, though meanwhile having time for a visit to the baths at Aix-la-Chapelle to restore his health. But by 12 May, which was when Paget left to return home, it was apparent that Philip was not coming immediately. Badoer interestingly recounted how 'Lord Paget received from the King [Philip] a chain worth 1200 crowns, which his attendants said was a recompense the precise equivilent of the expenses incurred by him during this brief mission, as he spent 170 crowns weekly for his table alone.'

He continued that at the farewell banquet that Paget gave for 'several Spanish cavaliers', they expressed worries over conspiracies aimed at killing Philip if he returned to England. William reassured them there was no such danger. It was reported that Paget's return, although without Philip, 'has wonderfully comforted the Queen, the King having sent to tell her that at the latest he will be with her by the end of next month'.[8]

Philip's arrival was nonetheless repeatedly delayed for the next nine months. Mary, like Madame Butterfly scanning the horizon for Pinkerton's ship, became more and more fraught, plagued by anxiety, rumours, and, the worst, false hope. At the end of August, 'so great was her anxiety and desire for the coming of the King' she sent Paget and Pembroke to Calais to receive him; a wasted journey.[9] Again, at the end of September, when there were further rumours that Philip might be coming, 'Owing to such good news, the Queen in a transport of delight, wished instantly to send the Earls of Pembroke and Arundel and Lord Paget towards the seaside, and also to march thither the archers of the guard.'[10]

Meanwhile, further Protestant plots were unearthed in March and July 1556. Elizabeth's possible involvement and the general question of what to do about her and the succession was again reviewed. In May, the Queen sent a courier, Francesco Piamontese, to ask Philip's advice. As before, the King agreed with Paget's opinion that, failing any children of his own, Elizabeth should succeed, preferably after being married to a Habsburg such as Philibert. The prospect of Mary, Queen of Scots, married to the French Dauphin, succeeding to the English throne was the result to be avoided at all costs. Piamontese therefore returned to London with a clear message to Mary that no further enquiries should be made into Elizabeth's guilt in plotting, nor any evidence unearthed to implicate her servants.

Despite taking the baths at Aix, William's health at this time was not good. It was reported at the end of November that 'Lord Paget has been confined to his house by indisposition for upward of a month'.[11] But he was well enough in the new year to be once more involved in the long-delayed return of the King. Mary had continued to try every argument, including the less than convincing one that, if he wanted Elizabeth to marry Philibert, he needed to come to England, as the marriage could not happen in his absence. What actually got Philip to return was that, when the Treaty of Vancelles with France had broken down and war resumed, he desperately needed England's financial and military support. At the start of February 1557, he sent one of his chief advisors, Ruy Gomez de Silva, with instructions in advance of his arrival, to 'inform her [the Queen] when I intend to be there … explain how the French have broken the truce', and how he was obliged 'to raise an army to prevent his Holiness [the Pope] and the French from waging war in the kingdom of Naples.' He then added, there seems to be a good prospect that the English will break with the French, and I am confident that they will do so, you will not take this matter up with the Queen or anyone else, except Paget. You will explain the matter fully to him, in order that he, as if of his own accord, may prepare things so that when I arrive in England they may be sufficiently advanced.[12]

Finally, on 20 March, Philip set foot on English soil again, for what one cynical observer described as a 'warmed over honeymoon'.

Initially the Privy Council was reluctant to support the Habsburgs in their war with the French, despite the efforts of Philip and Paget. However, like the attack on Pearl Harbour and Hitler's declaration of war against the US – though obviously on a microscopically smaller scale – the enemy foolishly solved the problem for the 'war party'. Thomas Stafford, a Protestant exile, landed at Scarborough from two French ships with a mixed English and French force, aiming to depose Mary, who they said had forfeited her right to the Crown by the Spanish marriage. This rebellion was easily put down but, in the words of one of the Spaniards, 'the French have spared us the trouble' of persuading the English to join the war.[13] War was declared at the beginning of June and Philip, having got what he wanted, left his wife again a month later. The English sent a small expeditionary force under the Earl of Pembroke to help the Imperial forces on the Continent. Paget had a central role leading the war council.

However, he was experiencing serious health problems at this time. He wrote to the Bishop of Ely from a spa, 'I am enforced to remain here for sum rest, being as evil in all the parties of my body ... as I was at my going to the baines.' He had previously visited medicinal or therapeutic baths, going to them when on diplomatic missions to the Continent. Balneology had become very fashionable in the sixteenth century, in part explained by the Renaissance revival of all things Classical, in this case Roman baths. A Venetian-published 1553 encyclopaedic work, *De balneis*, was a best seller. Visits were, then as now, supposed to be somewhat of a holiday, with luxurious accommodation and accompanied by good food, wine and music. And bath houses throughout history have been linked with sexual excess. A contemporary Italian proverb gave a nice twist to their reputation as a cure for sterility: 'If you want your wife to conceive, send her to the baths, and stay at home yourself.' But whether they actually cured anything was a very open question. William, although a regular visitor to baths, was evidently quite sceptical, reporting that he had been told that the visits had two effects, one that, for a time, the person would feel very ill, 'and the other that after a month he shall find great ease and benefit'. To which he wittily commented, 'The first property I am sure I feel: I pray God I may find the other.'[14] We do not know whether he did, even temporarily. His overall health was certainly deteriorating.

Perhaps his ill health was undermining his usual efficiency, as indicated by an uncomplimentary reference to his logistical work contained in a dispatch from King Philip's military representative in Calais. Pembroke had told him that the force could not move to engage the French until they obtained more carts for transport, 'and if Lord Paget had said 12 were enough, he had been talking about something he did not understand'.[15] If truly reported, Pembroke's analysis of Paget's poor logistics in this case is borne out by a report from the 1544 English campaign against the Scots, which claimed that an army of 16,000 would need 500 carts; so, proportionately, the 1,000 troops of Pembroke's expeditionary force in France would have needed thirty-one. Once the English got going, they did have some early success, taking part in the capture of the city of St Quentin. But it was short-lived. On New Year's Day 1558, a large French force attacked Calais and seven days later it fell. This was England's last Continental possession. The importance of its loss led to the famous story that Mary feared, when she died, Calais would be found engraved on her heart. Whether Paget, who throughout his career had tended to favour peace, had really approved of English involvement in the Habsburg campaign which led to this disaster, or whether he just felt the need to go along with Philip's policy, remains a moot point.

Much of the failure of English arms could be put down to a paucity of resources, illustrated by the lack of carts or the fact that the English expeditionary force numbered about 1,000 whereas the French, according to reports, attacked Calais with 27,000 troops. That paucity followed from the dire state of royal finances. Just how bad the situation is shown by the fact the English Crown's credit rating was so poor in Edward's reign that the foreign mercenaries who provided Court security demanded to be, and succeeded in being, paid monthly in advance. Paget was a leading figure in various attempts to improve the position during Mary's reign. Despite the inevitable opposition, some effort was made to reduce the royal household expenditure. There was a serious attempt to face the issue of the repeated debasement of the currency. It failed, but can be seen as laying the groundwork for the recoining which was actually accomplished under Elizabeth. More successful was Paget's action in increasing the customs rates. He had suggested this to the Queen in 1556 and from May 1557 he sat on a commission for a year which resulted in approximately tripling the customs take for the next reign. Of more immediate concern to King Philip were efforts to get hold of large sums to continue the war against France and retake Calais. One of his representatives in England, Count Feria, wrote to him in February 1558 that Paget had told him, 'members of Parliament had met to discuss the money and that if your Majesty wished, 800,000 crowns might be found there, over and above the Parliamentary grant', but that Philip need to write to Mary 'urging her to collect money'.[16]

In March, Feria complained of 'these incompetent Councillors who say that the country is rich and then add that they do not know how to raise the necessary money to defend it and recover its lost reputation'.

He detailed the financial position, reporting that Paget

> told me that over and above the £100,000 which Gresham was going to raise on loan in Antwerp, they were trying to borrow £50,000 or £60,000 more from merchants in London. When Paget said this, he was trying to wreak vengeance on those who had made such a mess of the Queen's affairs, because those affairs had not been entrusted to him.[17]

The Gresham referred to was Sir Thomas, a leading merchant and negotiator for the Crown who was involved with Paget and others in various attempts to restore the English currency. 'Gresham's Law', which states that 'bad money drives out good', was only explicitly formulated in the nineteenth century but takes its name from him.

At the beginning of May 1558, Feria further reported that Paget and the Admiral, Lord Howard of Effingham, 'consider it would be possible to set up a land-force, and that the Calais undertaking would not be as difficult as other people think', if 'your Majesties were determined to avenge the insult of Calais' and as, 'no prince ever begins a war with all the money he is going to need to finish it'. Paget then suggested various men as suitable to lead the army.[18] In the end, nothing came of this. In fact, whether even Paget, with his pro-Imperial sympathies, was really keen to continue the war with France at this point is doubtful. A treaty was anyway signed between Philip and the Pope in September and negotiations were begun for peace between England and France. William was again unwell in his bed at West Drayton at this time, although he was consulted about these peace moves. Mary's health was rapidly deteriorating and on this occasion the Tudor succession was to be straightforward. Ten days before her death, the Queen bowed to the inevitable, which Paget and others had been pleading for throughout her reign, and accepted her sister as heir. On 16 November 1558, she died at night and the next day Elizabeth was proclaimed queen – accompanied by church bells and bonfires.

Chapter 25

Elder Statesman Under Elizabeth

> There was no one she could marry outside the kingdom nor within it.
> Paget on Elizabeth's marriage prospects, reported in
> Feria's dispatch to Philip II, 14 November 1558

Just before Elizabeth's accession, the Count of Feria sent a lengthy dispatch back to his master in Madrid. Elizabeth, he reported, 'is a very vain and clever woman. She must have been thoroughly schooled in the manner in which her father conducted his affairs ... She is determined to be governed by no one.' He was right. She would also, he correctly surmised, want to 'maintain good relations with both your majesty and the king of France without tying herself to either party'.

What, if any, role would Paget have in the new reign? He had been so closely associated with King Philip that the new queen's attitude would undoubtedly be coloured by the complex relationship she had had with that king. From Philip's point of view, her role in the English succession had presented him with a dilemma. While her religion and Queen Mary's hostility to her sister had made him unsympathetic to Elizabeth, he also had had good reason to avoid alienating her. Unless Mary had a child, he needed to support Elizabeth's succession. The alternative was Mary, Queen of Scots, whose reign would have linked England and France in an alliance disastrous to Habsburg interests. Philip, and Paget to the extent that he was closely linked with him, had therefore tended to act in Elizabeth's favour during Mary's reign, trying to protect her from association with plots, improve her conditions and persuading Mary to recognise her as her successor. In his dispatch, Feria recounted how he visited Elizabeth just before Mary's death and of course reminded her of this support – particularly about the succession. According to him, she warmly acknowledged it. She would, however, have been well aware that any Imperial favour and any help from Paget which had been offered before she became queen had been motivated by their self interest.

After seeing Elizabeth, Feria called on Paget.

> I also visited Paget, who is suffering from a double quartan ague and yet is full of ambition and so deeply enmeshed in affairs as he used to be when younger and healthier. He received me well. Either he wanted me to believe he will play an important role in affairs or else he actually will do so.[1]

So right at the start of the reign, there was still the possibility that Paget might continue as a major player. The Venetian ambassador even thought he 'will be confirmed in his place or be made Lord Chancellor'.[2] But it was not to be. By the beginning of 1559, it had become clear he was out of favour. His deteriorating health did not help. Feria reported, 'I think Paget is dying as fast as he can. He was very bad before and the Queen seems not to have favoured him as he expected; indeed I do not think she will return him to office, and this no doubt has increased his malady.'[3]

Health was one reason for exclusion. Another was that Sir William Cecil may have feared him as a threat. There is no direct evidence for this, but it is certainly the case that Cecil was giving the role of Secretary, 'the kind of omnicompetence that it had enjoyed in the early days of Cromwell'.[4] In addition, Elizabeth, with a strong will of her own, was determined to reduce the size of her Privy Council from over thirty to twenty. She announced to those, like Paget, who were to be excluded that it was not 'for any disability in them, but for that I consider a multitude doth make rather disorder and confusion than good council'.[5] The final reason was of course Paget's close association with the previous regime and its religion. Feria even reported that he (Paget) had said that the Queen and her advisors 'considered him a Catholic'.[6] As he was evidently uncommitted in religion and had previously segued from one regime to the next without any problem, it is unlikely that this would have told decisively against him in itself. But, combined with the other reasons, it ensured that, while he had survived yet again without being totally cast aside, he was no longer the power he had once been.

He now had to assume the role of 'Elder Statesman', one who offered advice, sometimes asked for and sometimes proffered anyhow. But he was no longer at the centre of things. In the category of unsolicited advice is a message sent to Cecil and Sir Thomas Parry, Treasurer to the Queen's Household, in February 1559, in which, still smarting from the loss of Calais, he stressed the continuing perfidy of the French, 'and yet we believe their words still'. He urged, 'For God's sake move the Queen to put her sword in her hand.' What exactly he was wanting here is unclear. Elizabeth did, somewhat later, launch a minor, and very unsuccessful, attack on France at le Havre – aimed at forcing a return of Calais. In this letter, Paget mainly moaned, pessimistically and unhelpfully, about the dire situation. As before, his greatest fear was that the Habsburgs might gang up with the French against England.

> If the French invade us by sea or by Scotland, the King of Spain would also enter as our friend or foe. If we take part with neither, they will fasten their feet both of them here, and make a Piedmont of us. If we take part with the one, we ourselves shall be afterwards made a prey by the victor. God save us from the sword, for we have been plagued of late with famine and pestilence.[7]

Unwell and excluded, he was evidently not a happy man, as a further letter to Parry in April shows: 'If her Majesty think me not a man meet to continue in the place wherein I am, I would be a suitor to have writ of dotage, whereby I shall absent myself from all Parliaments, etc.'[8]

He had not lost all power: at any rate he was still perceived as having influence. Towards the end of 1559, England's representatives in Paris reported, 'It is said [at the French Court] that lately Lord Paget was two or three hours with her [Elizabeth]; and Secretary L'Aubespine said he was sorry for it, as Paget was a very wise man, and an enemy of the French nation.'

And, in January 1560, the French ambassador in England wrote that Paget was to be sent as ambassador to Madrid.[9] This was indeed considered and it was probably ill health that eventually prevented it happening. As well as illness, William and his family may have been suffering in other ways. There is a curious entry in a dispatch from the Spanish ambassador in February.

> ... everyone here does what best pleases him, and at the very gates of London robberies are committed in broad daylight. Only the day before yesterday one of Paget's servants took one of his master's daughters from the house and carried her to his own. They say he will marry her, and I hear that the affair was not done without the connivance of powerful people who bear ill will to Paget.[10]

It is difficult to know what to make of this story, which is not corroborated from any other sources. If true, it would obviously have been a major blow to the Paget family – though just how awful depends on the details of what really happened. But these ambassadors did love to send great quantities of gossip back to their masters – not all of it necessarily true. And Bishop Quadra, the Spanish envoy, particularly liked to pen pages and pages of speculation.

A problem William certainly had had as a result of loss of political power was maintaining his licence to import French wine. There is a 'Proposal Touching

Wine' in the Anglesey archives, undated and unsigned and with certain details left blank, but which indicates that he had obtained a lucrative licence under Philip and Mary. In exchange for paying certain monies to the royal coffers, he had the exclusive right to import wine into England. In addition, 'in the time of warre to bring in as well woad, salt, canvas and other commodities owt of Fraunce as wine, and to convey such commodities owt of England in to Fraunce.'

It has been estimated that this would have been worth between £4,000 and £8,000 a year: not surprisingly, it was considered a very good deal of which many at Court would have been envious. Paget did manage to get the Privy Council to renew the licence, but only for seven months and with an additional clause which would have been unsatisfactory from his point of view, because it stated, 'if it do appear that the gayne that shall come thereof to the sayde Lord Pagett [sic] shall amount to such great sommes as it is thought it wyll, her Hieghnes be consydered with suche parte thereof as shallbe thought fytt convenyent.'

Paget blamed the intrigues of hostile councillors with political pull for doing him down in this and other matters. In the draft of a letter, also undated and not addressed, he lists various reasons why people might have been against him, particularly citing his failure to advance them when he had power under Mary. But he concludes, 'Na, na, the matter is none of all these; my licence, my licence is the matter' and he hoped that, since it appeared his licence was not to be renewed, 'these displeasures and slanderous talkes should cease'.[11]

There are other indications that he was struggling to maintain his financial position after the loss of political power. An undated letter to Sir Thomas Parry 'begs him to obtain the stallment of his debts' to the Queen. When he heard that the incumbent Lord President of the Council in Wales was on his deathbed, he petitioned Cecil for the job. This involved hearing legal cases, enforcing religious laws and other duties with political power, and one imagines the salary and opportunities for patronage and earnings made it appealing. It is presumably the job referred to in the famous moment in the film about Thomas More, *A Man for All Seasons*, in which More accuses Sir Richard Rich of selling his soul 'for Wales': a scene that is typical of the film's ahistorical and sanctimonious, not to mention anti-Welsh, attitude. Anyhow, Paget failed to get the job: further evidence of his waning political influence. Through intense lobbying, he did succeed in keeping his pension from Philip II: in those quarters he was still appreciated.[12]

He was still consulted on some matters in England. As he had been centrally concerned with plans to reform government finance in the previous reign, he continued to be involved. He was instructed by the Privy Council to report on an enquiry set up under the late Queen 'for the understanding of the debts due to her Highnes'.[13] (One does somewhat wonder how this sat in relation to his own debts to her!) He wrote to Cecil and Parry in February 1559 suggesting a recoining, 'If the Queen amend the coin universally there shall grow thereby a great commodity to her and the realm.'[14] Two years later, in 1562, it was claimed that the decision *not* to reform the currency at that date was due to Paget's advice. Quadra wrote, 'The reason why the projected reforms in the coinage have not been effected is that Paget assured the Queen that it would cause disturbances in the country.'[15]

An anonymous journal held in the Yelverton manuscripts of the British Library is of the opinion that, 'The L. Paget was the occasion of the staye of the fall of the money by sending lettres to the quene with divers persuasions.'

This journal is interesting in other ways. Although its author is unknown, he is thought to have been a clerk of some kind, possibly at some time employed in Protector Somerset's household, and he obviously had it in for William Paget, probably regarding him as having betrayed his master and as being insufficiently Evangelical. He criticised his role in delaying currency reform, his influence on Scottish policy and, most of all his relationship to Elizabeth's favourite Robert Dudley (later Earl of Leicester) and his involvement in the question of her possible marriage to him. The journal is full of salacious but unverified gossip, some of which it claims originated with Paget. For example, there is the following entry on the subject of Dudley's relationship with his wife, Amy: 'P [almost certainly Paget] used to saye that when the Lorde Rob. went to his wief he wentt all in blacke, and howe he was commaunded to say that he did nothing with her, when he came to her, as seldome he did.'

The possibility of Dudley marrying Elizabeth became a hot topic after Amy 'fell' down the stairs and died, freeing him but also breeding widespread suspicion that she was pushed. Dudley was Elizabeth's Master of the Horse and Catherine de Medici, exuding snobbery, is alleged to have said, 'The Queen of England is to marry her horsemaster.' The author of the journal credits Paget with an unlikely role. He suggests that in 1561, Dudley and Paget were attempting 'the banishment of the gospell' and 'the restitution of the b. of Rome' if Paget 'should be a suitor to the queen that the L.R [Lord Robert] might marye the queen'.[16]

There is no other support for the idea that this was Paget's policy. Indeed, his general view on the royal marriage was the extremely wise one he expressed at the start of the reign that, 'there was no one she could marry outside the kingdom nor within it'. Which proved to be the case. An awful lot of candidates were considered in the first four years of Elizabeth's reign: as well as Dudley, there was Eric, the son of the king of Sweden, several Habsburgs, especially the Archduke Charles, and a French contender, the Duke of Anjou. William was peripherally involved in the negotiations – none of which got very far. Like Elizabeth, he was probably more interested in making favourable noises and stringing along the parties than in wanting any of them to succeed. Quadra reported in November 1559 that 'Paget came to me the other day and said that so far as he understood, the Queen was not entirely unfavourable [to marriage proposals], although she was still resolved not to marry until she had seen her future husband.' The Habsburg Archduke and Eric the Swede were mentioned in that dispatch. By the spring of 1561, Quadra was complaining that Paget was undermining plans being hatched to marry Dudley to Elizabeth to the advantage of the Habsburgs. This is directly contrary to the claim of the anonymous journal. Quadra wrote of 'the interference of Paget, who, knowing her [Elizabeth's] humour, has advised her to hold her hand until she can make a firm peace and alliance with France, when she could treat your Majesty more advantageously.'[17] This sounds like Paget, the advocate of playing off the French against the Habsburgs: a much more likely role than that of supporter of a Dudley marriage that would return England to Catholicism – a policy that was never going to succeed. As one historian of Elizabeth's reign puts it, 'Negotiations came and went, of infinite and baffling complexity … parties formed and dissolved around the various candidates.'[18] She remained the virgin queen. Actually, that is not so certain: but she never married.

Chapter 26

Retirement and Death

[Paget] submitted to Queen Elizabeth's Authority, out of Duty and Allegiance; being one of those moderate men that looked upon the Protestants primitive Foundations of Faith, Duty and Devotion, as safe: and on the Papists superstructures, as not damnable.

David Lloyd in *State-worthies*

There were ups and downs in William's health and his political involvement in the first four years of Elizabeth's reign – before he finally succumbed to the 'ague'. In 1559, reports from the Spanish ambassador, within a month of each other, had him first not leaving his house and being at death's door and next stating, 'Paget is better and has gone twice or thrice to the palace in a litter.'[1] Even as late as December 1562, Sir Thomas Challoner, English ambassador to Philip II's court in Madrid, considered him the man to write to in his attempt to get permission to return home. But from the beginning of 1561, Paget does seem to have been mainly in retirement in Staffordshire. The news sent to Sir Nicholas Throckmorton, Elizabeth's ambassador in Paris, in February of that year was that 'Lord Paget was lately at the Court, but now keeps the country altogether.' In May, a letter signed by the Queen was sent to him commanding him to officiate at the annual Garter Feast for Saint George's Day at Windsor Castle: but this was to be the last major public event in which he played a part.[2]

There is a mid-seventeenth-century book by one David Lloyd, catchily titled, *State-worthies, or, The statesmen and favourites of England since the reformation, their prudence and policies, successes and miscarriages, advancements and falls, during the reigns of King Henry VIII, King Edward VI, Queen Mary, Queen Elizabeth, King James, King Charles I*.

Lloyd is a big fan of William Paget and we shall return to some of his judgements in the Conclusion. His summing up of Paget's retirement is this:

When he had managed the Secrets and Negotiations of Henry the Eighth, with Dexterity and Faithfulness; the Lands of King Edward the Sixth, with Skill and Improvement; the Purses of Queen Mary & Queen

Elizabeth, with good Husbandry and Care; When he had lived enough of his Countries, to his Sovereigns, to his Friends, and the Publique Good; he retired to live to Himself first, and then to his GOD.[3]

One of the pleasures of country retirement he may have enjoyed, when health permitted, was hunting: another of our recovered royal letters from Queen Elizabeth gave him permission to hunt game in the royal forests.[4]

He will also have followed and taken pride in the European travels of his eldest son Henry. These are well documented in the State Papers, with Throckmorton reporting to Cecil from Paris in June 1559, 'On the 24th arrives Sir Henry Pagett [sic], who tarries here a month, and hence by Orleans into Italy.' This was a time of great confusion in France. The king, Henry II, died in July and was succeeded by his sickly 15-year-old son, who himself died in December 1560. He was succeeded by his 10-year-old brother, with Henry's widow, Catherine de Medici, acting as Regent. The chaos created by these events in the royal succession was exacerbated by religious conflict between Catholics and Huguenots. It is therefore not unexpected that Throckmorton's next dispatch to Cecil, in August 1559 reported that Henry Paget had left Paris, 'and gone to Lyons for his more safety, if the worst should fall'. Henry seemed nonetheless to have been enjoying his travels, writing to Throckmorton from Orleans in August with political information that he had heard from a good source, 'that the French mind to send a great man to England for the confirmation of the peace', but also indicating that he was entertaining himself, as shown by the tone of the following:

> I pray you tell my friend Robert Jones that if he have any more books to buy that I desire him to defer the buying of them till he come hither, whereas he shall find a bookbinder's daughter that keepeth the shop and selleth the books, who is the fairest maid without comparison in Orleans or Paris.

He was evidently still aiming to have fun when he reached Venice in the autumn, informing the Council of Ten there that he had 'come to this famous city for recreation [solazzo]' and requiring permission for himself and three servants to be allowed to bear arms. Whatever Henry got up to on his 'Grand Tour' was considered commendable, unlike the behaviour of Cecil's own son, Thomas, of whom his father complained to a neighbour, writing, 'Sir Henry Paget returned home with great commendation and fraughted with qualities: but I see in the end my son shall come home like a spending sot, meet to keep a tennis court.'

This was a bit unfair: although overshadowed by his father and by Robert, his half-brother, Thomas Cecil in fact turned out rather better than this prediction, becoming a reasonably successful political figure and soldier.[5]

While his son Henry was gaining commendation and having a good time on the Continent, William Paget's main focus in his retirement was to manage his land and properties and to plan the building of a grand country house in Staffordshire. In Henry VIII's day he had got his hands not only on the land and buildings of the bishopric of Lichfield – including the park of Beaudesert in Cannock Chase – but also on the Abbey at nearby Burton-on-Trent. At the start of the Dissolution of the Monasteries, this had been partly spared and temporarily re-founded as a worthy educational college. This was probably because the former abbot, William Benson, an Evangelical, was a good friend of Cranmer and Cromwell. However, after Cromwell's death, it went the way of other monasteries and in 1545 it was dissolved. Soon after that, the college and all its possessions – except for the parish church – was granted to Paget. From 1550, he had been actively involved in the detailed improvement of its woodlands, ordering, among other things, that no timber was to be felled without licence, and then only in designated coppices and between the beginning of March and the end of November. The existing manor house at Burton will have been the residence which he complained about as being too small and unsavoury, at the time when the family were to be banished to Staffordshire after his fall from grace and imprisonment. This house had nonetheless already been somewhat improved: for example, there is a record of alabaster from a gypsum deposit, probably on Paget land, being supplied for a new chimneypiece in 1546.

With time on his hands during his retirement, it was no surprise that William would get involved in a major building project. This, along with founding a successful dynasty, was often the preferred 'legacy' of powerful figures who moved in humanist, Renaissance circles. In this context, it is interesting to see a letter of this date from Ippolito d'Este, Cardinal de Ferrara, to Throckmorton. This was the man who spent his retirement – after having just failed to become Pope five times – creating the Villa d'Este at Tivoli and its astonishing water gardens. He was evidently a close friend of William, sending his affection towards the Crown of England, 'and especially to Paget, the English Ambassador in France in King Henry the Eighth's time. It is a great comfort to him that the Queen has vouchsafed to put him in the number of her dear friends.'[6] That was perhaps not quite true: but Paget was doing well enough to plan his own more modest project. Detailed plans and estimates for this have survived and a fascinating article on them has been published by the architectural historian, Nicholas Cooper. As he puts it,

[Paget] had by this time built up a considerable holding of land in Middlesex, Buckinghamshire and Staffordshire, had a title to pass on to his descendants and was in a position to found a territorial dynasty. What he lacked was a house worthy of his possessions, and with his precarious health he may also have sensed he lacked time.

There are three different sets of plans for this grand house, showing an evolution from what Cooper describes as a conservative and provincial design to 'one of the most progressive of its day'. He identifies the plans as early innovations in the move within English architecture from layouts that favoured traditional social hierarchies to the aesthetics of symmetry. The final drawings included a staircase to rise as a pair of dog-leg flights that he says were of a type and scale 'almost without English precedent' and, more prosaically, the 'modern' use of passages to provide independent access to rooms.

There is evidence of William's 'hands on' involvement in this project. At least one of the papers giving the costs and calculations for every trade employed is in his own handwriting. Some of the phraseology in the documents implies his detailed personal participation, as in '70 loads of wood being mine own' or 'to make me three floors of timber'. We know that he had previously shown interest in and knowledge of the architecture of military fortifications. Because of his friendships with European Renaissance figures such as Ippolito d'Este as well as his extensive travels in France and elsewhere on the Continent, he would have seen the best examples of 'modern' European architecture and he will also have spent a lot of time observing new royal places in England, particularly Henry VIII's magnificent and innovative Nonsuch which he probably saw being built. Sadly, his own stately home never materialised, because William's illness finally caught up with him. However, as Cooper puts it, 'It would be a pleasure to think of him towards the end of his life, after many years of the most stressful public service, trying to forget his many illnesses in discussions with his builder and calculation about the price of brickwork.' Although most of us do not necessarily find discussions with builders a relief from stress, this is rather a sweet thought, and I would like to think it was true.[7]

We do not know exactly what killed him. But I suspect it was malaria. More than once the incapacitating illness that came and went, afflicting him in his later years, was described as a 'quartan ague', in other words a fever that occurred every fourth day. This is typical of, though not exclusive to, malaria. It is known to have been rife in many parts of England and Continental Europe at this time, to a degree comparable to that in sub-Saharan Africa today. Shakespeare mentions it in eight of his plays. It has recently been proved that Charles V, who had similar symptoms to his friend William Paget, suffered from and probably died from it. In 2004, a medical team conducted clinical tests on a detached phalanx from one of the Emperor's fingers which revealed large quantities of malaria parasites.[8]

Whatever the cause, William Paget died on 10 June 1563 at West Drayton, aged 57 or 58: a good innings for the times. The house was hung with 258 yards of black cloth. The funeral was apparently impressive, with banners and shields and another 150 yards of black cloth involved. It took place in the local parish church, which was where he was buried. Despite his retirement, the death was considered worthy of report in Court and diplomatic circles. In Madrid, Philip II grieved when he heard the news. A grand monument to Paget was later erected in Lichfield Cathedral. Given his lifelong support of moderation in all things, particularly religion, it is entirely appropriate, if a shame, that this was smashed up by Puritan zealots during the Civil War a century later.[9]

Chapter 27

Conclusion

His Master-piece was an inward Observation of other Men, and an exact knowledge of Himself. His Address was with state, yet insinuating: His Discourse free, but weighed; his apprehension quick, but staid.

David Lloyd in *State-worthies*

If Paget has not always had a very good press, it is perhaps because he is that often-reviled figure – a moderate man in an age of strong passions. Such men's compromises are often seen as betrayals when they are alive, and as evidence of lack of principle after they are dead. Furthermore, Paget hitched his wagon to a series of stars, and then – to mix metaphors – when a star looked like falling, he adroitly changed horses. The ablest Tudor statesman between Thomas Cromwell and William Cecil, he was a survivor – a fact which seems itself to have been implicitly held against him when survival often depended not only on ability but also on ruthlessness and guile.

Nicholas Cooper in his article on Paget's Burton-on-Trent building project

How did this upstart from a yeoman's family manage to thrive and prosper at the highest level of government and society in a time of almost constant political upheaval? One answer is to look to his personal qualities. His intelligence, hard work and political acumen was evidently of great use to the four successive monarchs he served – despite the fact that their characters and agendas were so very different. As David Lloyd says, 'He was so able and trusty a Minister of State, that he was privy Councillor for four successive Princes.' He was also highly respected, and often held in real affection, by other great figures of the day, such as Somerset and Warwick in England, and Mary of Hungary, Charles V and Philip II abroad – as well as by their ministers and ambassadors. Apparently, the Emperor Charles V, who was no fool and the most powerful man in the world, 'in a rapture once cried, He deserved to BE a King, as well as to REPRESENT one: and one day as he came to Court, Yonder is the Man I can deny nothing to.'

In addition to administrative ability and skilful political instincts, William, like his mentor Thomas Cromwell, was seriously hard working. What these men seemed to have achieved in decision-making, networking with superiors and inferiors, satisfying the whims of their monarchs, administrative instructions, and letter writing, day after day, is quite phenomenal; exhausting just to read about. To quote Lloyd again, making comparison with the Classical world as was the habit of sixteenth- and seventeenth-century writers,

> Apollonius coming to Vespasian's gate betimes in the morning, and finding him up, said, Surely this man will be Emperor, he is up so early. This Statesman [Paget] must needs be eminent, who was up the earliest of all the English Agents in discovering Affairs, and latest in following those Discoveries.

Records of the times when dispatches were sent make it clear that early rising days full of constant meetings were followed by evenings spent on administrative work and letter writing – often stretching into the small hours.

As well as being considered one of the most efficient and hardworking general administrators, Paget had also established an unrivalled reputation as the foreign policy expert. This was based on an acquisition of languages and knowledge during his early travels. As Lloyd puts it, 'A general Learning furnished him for Travel, and Travel seasoned that Learning for Employment.' He was, he adds, Henry VIII's 'Table of Germany, France and Rome, so exact an account could he give of their Situation, Havens, Forts, Passages, Provision, Policies, Revenue and Strength.' His negotiating skills earned him the epitaph, 'Master of Practices'. His skill in dealing with foreign ambassadors was legendary. The author of the Preface to the *Calendar of State Papers, Spain*, is of the opinion that van de Delft, 'usually accepted Paget's version of the meaning of current events' and that 'Paget's handling of van de Delft is a masterpiece.'

An important element in his personality that partly explains his remarkable longevity at the top table of politics was his combination of modesty with achievement. We have seen how the egotistical and paranoid Henry VIII could rely on Paget without feeling threatened – so different to his attitude to Wolsey and Cromwell. Lloyd claims that Charles V also pointed to the contrast between 'Wolsey, whose great train promised much, as his Design did nothing', whereas 'Paget ... promised nothing, and did all.' Unlike not only Wolsey and Cromwell, but also Somerset and Warwick, he never aspired to regal or quasi-regal power and status. He never overplayed his hand. While disentangling the many names and titles of his contemporaries, I realised that it was perhaps significant that Paget never changed his. He was not unique in this. But his case contrasts with those who were endlessly becoming earl of this or marquess of that. An upstart was wise to be cautious in relation to the old aristocracy: Cromwell had not helped his situation by becoming Earl of Essex. Paget was evidently a thoughtful and cautious man, who had seen too many beheadings and who was happy to remain as an éminence grise, the power behind the throne. In the manoeuvrings of the factions at the end of Henry's reign, in the overthrow of Somerset and in Mary's triumph, there is general consensus, at the time and in subsequent histories, that Paget's role was central. Yet there is not a lot of direct proof. The case is persuasive but the evidence largely circumstantial. This might be partly because a lack of 'archival survival'. However, it may also be due to Paget's skill in leaving few traces. In every crisis apart from one he was on the winning side: but it might not have turned out that way. He must have been aware that it was wise to avoid too explicit a commitment to one side, just in case the other one won.[1]

Not only with regard to his own career, but also in his general attitude to government, he understood the limits of politics better than most of his contemporaries. One could point to many examples of this. When Henry died and the throne passed to a child of nine, there arose the real possibility of extreme political uncertainty, as had been the case in the previous minorities, of Richard II, Henry IV and Edward V, when great warlords and royal cousins had struggled for power – the stuff of Shakespeare's history plays. Rule by a council of equals, as Henry planned it, was likely to lead to a repetition of those unhappy times and the fix that Paget arranged with Hertford (Somerset) was a recognition of that political reality. Equally, when Somerset seemed to forget that politics was the 'art of the possible', Paget's repeated and varied advice was all aimed at trying to get him to be more realistic, to avoid 'the best becoming the enemy of the good'. Despite the religious differences and the built-in sexism of the times, Paget strongly supported the succession of both Mary and Elizabeth, knowing that they both had the strongest and most legitimate claims and that they were the most likely to be successful. His view on Elizabeth's marriage, that 'there was no one she could marry outside the Kingdom nor within it' was spot on; as was his assessment of the strengths, and particularly the weaknesses, of the English position in relationship to the European powers.

Allied to his modesty and political realism was his moderation in religious matters. It is worth considering specifically the subject of his religion. There is no conclusive evidence as to what his private beliefs were, if indeed he necessarily had any definite ones beyond a general Christianity. We have seen how he was considered to be broadly in the Evangelical camp under Henry and Edward. In 1544, hoping that the Protestant German princes would ally themselves with England, he added, in a letter to his friend Christopher Mont, 'you know my own affection [is] that way.' A pointer that is not as trivial as it appears is that throughout his life William sported a large beard, in common with most Evangelicals. Catholics tended to be clean-shaven or at least to have small, neat beards! Under Mary, most commentators, such as the Venetian ambassador, believed that Paget's power, although great, was ultimately limited 'by reason of his favouring Lutheran opinions'. Similarly, Charles V's ambassador Reynard wrote to the Emperor that 'Paget has been suspected of heresy because he ruled King Henry and influenced him in a heretical direction.'[2]

On the other hand, there is some contrary evidence suggesting that he inclined more to Catholicism. When discussing the likelihood of Paget becoming Lord Chancellor under Mary, the French ambassador reported that he was 'thought of as a serious Christian', to which statement, in an explanatory footnote, he added, 'He was however Catholic, and died in the bosom of the Church, in Elizabeth's reign.' This is the only hint as to his deathbed religion. The Spanish ambassador under Elizabeth reported that Paget had told him that many people considered him to be a Catholic – though he did not say he was one.[3] Anne Paget was definitely a committed Catholic. William's brother and two of his sons were also. But this is not by any means decisive proof, as many families were split in their religious commitments. It is also worth noting that, while religious beliefs were obviously very important, they by no means always trumped personal relationships. A clear example of that would be the friendship between Mary Tudor and Somerset's wife. Although Anne Somerset was if anything more Evangelical than her husband had been, Mary nonetheless released her from the Tower and resumed a close friendship with her when she became queen.

For Paget, as for others of his contemporaries who were not fanatically wedded to a particular position, it is impossible to disentangle his private beliefs from those determined by political expediency. He has certainly been accused of being a Nicodemite, one whose publicly held views differed from those held in private. Whether he changed his private religious views at some time between his imprisonment and the early days of Mary's reign, from a very moderate Protestantism to a very moderate Catholicism, or whether he was purely motivated by ambition, is an open question. Speaking to Renard, the Imperial ambassador, in April 1554, he claimed he had changed his mind, saying that he had been in error over Transubstantiation and now believed in 're-establishing' religion. However, he also stressed that religious change should never be made by 'blood and fire' as some, like Gardiner, favoured. And the phrase 're-establishing religion' could anyhow have meant returning to the very moderate 'high church' Protestantism of Henry VIII rather than returning England fully to Rome.[4]

Not only is it impossible to disentangle his private beliefs from cynical adjustments, it is likely that he saw no conflict between the two. If the overriding concern was to maintain political stability and avoid bloody civil conflict over religious beliefs, moderately adjusting one's religious position to that of the monarch, or of other prevailing powers in the realm, could be seen as a principled position even if it resulted in personal gain at the same time.

That personal and family gain was huge is not in doubt. William Paget died possessed of great wealth, with vast and profitable land and property holdings in Staffordshire, Middlesex, Buckinghamshire and London. These had been accumulated at a time of unprecedented opportunities for those close to the throne and in a position to enrich themselves from the Dissolution of the Monasteries. Henry VIII's 'new men', of whom Paget was a typical example, were able to establish themselves as the new elite by taking advantage of a radical change in English government. (In some ways not unlike the oligarchs that emerged in Russia with the break-up of the Soviet Union.) Henry's 'regime change' was not just a matter of destroying the power and grabbing the riches of the Church, it was also a more general assertion of royal authority in relation to the over-mighty subjects of the old nobility who had fought the Wars of the Roses. The clearest illustration of this is the important Act of Parliament passed in Cromwell's day which shook up the Order of Precedence for the most powerful men in the land. In a society where political power was expressed by public ceremony this was, in the words of Cromwell's biographer, 'a true Tudor Revolution in Government'. Under this Act, the great offices of State, such as the Lord Chancellor or Lord Privy Seal, often held by upstart 'new men' like Paget, outranked the old aristocracy. If peers, they would now sit in the House of Lords above any dukes apart from royal dukes. If a chief secretary was a baron, he was the top baron. 'This meant that service to the monarch outfaced any other form of dignity in the realm.' As another leading Tudor historian puts it, in relation to Henry VII, but which could apply also to his son, 'Henry chose men whose authority stemmed not from their lands or titles but from his choosing of them.'[5]

The increase in royal authority over the Church and the old aristocracy did not, however, mean that monarchs could rule without political support. This created a great opportunity for the new elite such as the Paget family. It has been pointed out that in order to consolidate their political base the Tudors needed to hand over the majority of ex-religious property. By Henry's death, two-thirds had been handed over and further grants under Edward and Mary brought the figure to three-quarters. Despite her Catholicism, Mary made little headway in returning Church property; though that might have changed had she lived longer. John Guy puts it succinctly in his book *Tudor England*: 'Reconciliation was as important as coercion in an age without a police force or standing army, when government remained a partnership between the magnates and the Crown.'[6]

Even if initially the creatures of royal authority, the 'new men', once established, wielded independent power from their regional bases, such as the South-west for the Russells or Staffordshire and Middlesex for the Pagets. In April 1551, under the Warwick regime – so not at the height of his power in Westminster – William Paget was nonetheless listed in the Acts of the Privy Council as one of the two 'Commissioners of Lieutenantships' in both Staffordshire and Middlesex.[7] His role in Mary's triumph was also partly based on his regional power base. And it is interesting to note that many of our family letters from the King and/or the Queen are to do with levying forces to quell disturbances.

* * *

To use the language of *1066 and All That*, were these 'new men' like Paget an unqualified 'bad thing'? The Marxist historian W. G. Hoskins, author of *The Age of Plunder*, appears in no doubt. The final sentence of his book states that Henry VIII was

> a disaster to his country, impoverishing its resources and stunting its growth for the sake of his futile wars, leaving it an empty treasury, and leaving its government in the hands of the most unprincipled gang of political adventurers and predators that England had seen for many centuries.

Yet in the same book he acknowledges that 'probably the great Plunder brought little change to the great mass of English people': the peasants went on tilling their fields and tending their stock and it was a matter of pure chance whether their new landlords were better or worse than their monastic or old aristocratic ones.[8]

A different question is how Paget's career and achievements stand in relation to the reality and myth of English 'nation-building', irrespective as to whether one considers that to be a good, bad, ugly, or possibly irrelevant, thing. The idea of England as a unitary state was really an anachronism before about 1530. An English national identity began to be forged by Henry VIII, by his break with Rome, by the force of his personality, by his assertion of royal authority and even by his wars. The Tudor period saw the growth of English hegemony in relation to the other parts of the British Isles. It is the period that saw that identity beginning to be synonymous with the coastline, the romance of an island nation; a process obviously enhanced by the loss of Calais, the last Continental possession, and which led in the direction of a global, rather than European orientation. Maintenance of the balance of power in Europe began to be a primary objective of foreign policy, and continued to be into the nineteenth or even twentieth century. William Paget took a leading role in establishing its pre-eminence.

In connection with this idea of independent English nation-building, it could be argued that Paget developed too close an association at certain times with the Habsburgs, particularly in Mary's reign after arranging the marriage to Philip. He was happy to receive a pension from the Habsburgs and over the course of his career he does seem to have developed a bit of an aversion to their rivals, the French. His support for Philip's war with France in 1557 was perhaps influenced too much by this and one can speculate that a combination of the shock of his imprisonment under the previous regime and the way in which his rivalry with Gardiner had taken on a life of its own may have made him just too keen to court royal favour at this moment. But these factors did not prevent him from being generally a strong advocate of 'balance of power' policies and from making sure that the Spanish influence that followed the marriage to Philip was severely limited. There is a story that, when Mary was thought to be pregnant, Philip sought an Act of Parliament to give him the Regency during the child's infancy while promising to surrender it when the child was of age. This unconfirmed account has it that it was Paget, fearing that it would be impossible to force Philip to keep his word, who prevented this from going through. Paget also advised very independently on the question of Elizabeth's possible marriage. And his close relationship with Charles V and Philip II was, after all, something that could, and did, cut both ways. His cosmopolitan attitude would never, of course, allow him to be seen as a hero in the more assertive 'mere English' circle of nationalism that runs from Elizabeth and the defeat of the Spanish Armada to Brexit.

In fiction, Secretary Paget is portrayed in C. J. Sansom's best seller, *Lamentation*, as Henry's ruthless fixer. He describes him as having 'hard eyes set in a slab face above a forked beard' – as depicted in some of his portraits. He is accused by the hero of the novel as waiting, in the last months of the reign, to see 'whether the Queen would fall and Bertano's mission [to restore Catholicism] succeed.'

I looked at his slab of a face and thought, you enjoy all this; you would side with radical or conservatives alike to keep your position. Another of those great men in the middle, bending with the wind.

Slightly more favourably, Paget is also shown having the following exchange with Henry:

The King sighed, 'You give me straight advice, Paget, you always have. Even though I may dislike to hear it.'
'Thank you, your majesty.'
Henry gave him a sharp look. 'And you know on which side your bread is buttered, eh? Always you act to further my will, never go down your own road, like Wolsey and Cromwell?'
Paget bowed deeply. 'I serve only to implement your majesty's chosen policies.'[9]

We can only speculate, as in fiction, about the real nature of the relationship between Paget and the monarchs he served. But it is reasonable to think that the giving of 'straight advice', though in a calculated fashion, was central to his success. There is clear evidence that he bombarded Protector Somerset with 'straight advice'. But the situation with Henry VIII and Mary and Philip was more complex, as Susan Brigden explains: 'Flattery posed the greatest danger to monarchy, for only honest counsel preserved it from descending towards tyranny. Yet at Court plain speaking was rare. Courts always had a dark reputation for intrigue and danger: the collective noun for courtiers was a "threat".'

She continues: 'To guide the king was the part of a loyal counsellor, but to challenge the royal will, or to seek to subvert or overrule it, was conspiracy and treason. This was the problem for those at court who opposed royal policy; they must work by devious means.'[10]

This is perhaps the reason why Paget, the 'Master of Practices', developed such a reputation for cunning. One of the most prominent of today's academic Tudor historians goes so far as to describe him as the 'patron saint of deviousness'.[11] William was also unable to prevent Henry and Mary from sometimes 'descending towards tyranny'. But he did have some success in cleverly steering the monarchs in slightly less extreme directions – for example with Henry's foreign and Mary's religious policies.

William the man of moderation and Paget the ruthless politico are not contradictory images, given the context of sixteenth-century England. The fact that he was not a religious fanatic does not mean that he was an advocate of toleration. He saw Somerset as far too lax, ignoring the Hobbesian necessity that 'Society in a realm doth consist and is maintained by means of religion and law'. Writing to Gardiner in 1547, he explained that he 'never loved extremes' because he always pursued 'that [which] should be thought meet for the quiet of the realm'.[12] Like the monarchs he served, he feared anarchy, rebellion and civil war and thought that law and order was the top priority of government. He was basically a conservative. The 'middle way', advocated by Paget and pursued by Tudor monarchs in their better moments, does not have a lot in common with modern liberal, democratic humanitarianism. But, at a stretch, it could perhaps be seen as a seed for the plant that later grew in that direction. And it was certainly different from what one historian has rightly called the 'spiritually sanctioned savagery' of Mary or the personal sadism of a Richard Rich torturing Anne Askew.[13]

Tudor England had all the necessary ingredients for chaos and civil war: fanatical views and massive divisions on religion, disputed questions of succession, disrespect for female and child monarchs, warlords with regional power bases, and factionalism within the ruling elite. Against this backdrop it is truly remarkable that the transitions of power from the tyranny of Henry VIII to the Protectorate of Somerset, from Somerset to Warwick during Edward's reign, to Mary on his death, and from her to Elizabeth, all occurred without significant bloodshed or disruption to the smooth working of government. The 'unprincipled politiques', men like Cecil, Petre, Paulet, and above all Paget, made this possible. Had the 'men of principle', the martyrs loved by Catholic and Protestant historians, figures such as Thomas More under Henry and Thomas Cranmer under Mary, been more successful, English history might so easily have moved in a disastrously different direction.

* * *

In a similar vein, Paget's influence on the foreign policy of the often warlike rulers he served – Henry in particular – was generally to promote peace. There is a telling letter, written in May 1546 in the midst of his year-long quest for peace, sent to his co-Secretary Petre while suffering from 'the cold by long sitting in the tent' negotiating with the French. He had gathered that Henry misliked him so often mentioning peace, and continued,

> No man living is so careful to avoid offending the King, not from fear but love, and as God is author of peace and Christ always praised peaceable men, he cannot but desire it; and ... he knows the continuance of war, the means to maintain it being at such an ebb, to be so dangerous that

he trembles to write it. Would gladly give his life for a peace to the King's satisfaction.[14]

The allegorical frescoes on the walls of the Palazzo Publico in Siena are the greatest expression, in a pictorial rather than verbal language, of the causes and effects of good and bad government. Many evils and virtues are represented, among the latter, the common good, wisdom, faith, prudence, magnanimity, fortitude and justice. But the central presiding figure is peace.

> She resolves the picture, offers it a centre, a place for the eye to rest. She is why this room, the Sala dei Nove, is also known as the Sala della Pace, 'Hall of Peace'. She is ... the organising principle both of the rest of the activities in the fresco, and by implication, the proposed system of government.[15]

These are the words of a modern writer who, as a refugee from Libya, should know a thing or two about the role of peace, or a lack of it, in good government. Subject to the constraints of his times and the whims of his rulers, all of William Paget's political efforts were centred on the quest for that sine qua non of good government, peace – at home and abroad.

To that idealistic and grandiose conclusion, one should perhaps add a cynical coda. This consummate survivor of the Tudor age may have promoted peace and good government but at the same time he managed do very nicely for himself and his family: my family.

Appendix

A Family Epilogue

> England will still be England, an everlasting animal, stretching into the future and the past like all living things having the power to change out of all recognition and yet remain the same.
>
> George Orwell in *The Complete Works of George Orwell: A Patriot After All*

William was survived by his wife Anne, by three sons, Henry, Thomas and Charles and by six daughters, Etheldreda, Eleanor, Grisold, Jane, Dorothy and Anne. His heir Henry was all set to be a prominent figure in Elizabethan society. His marriage to Catherine Knyvet at West Drayton in 1567 was evidently a major 'society wedding', with Sir Nicholas Throckmorton writing to the Earl of Leicester, 'I thynke you may doe my L. Paget a great pleasure to send him some venyson against hys great day wch shalbe solemnyzed at Drayton … Hys bidden gestes come from the Courte…'[1]

The couple had a daughter, Elizabeth. But soon after, Henry died and, as there was no direct male heir, it was thought at the time that the title passed immediately to his brother Thomas. In fact, it did not, because of a piece of retrospective legislation passed 100 years later by the House of Lords – according to which the barony could go to a female if there were no direct male heirs. So, although no one knew it at the time, baby Elizabeth was in fact Baroness Paget for the few months of her life. She died aged 1 – and Thomas did then inherit.

Elizabeth thus has a little niche in the legal textbooks concerned with the arcane issue of aristocratic inheritance. The law still stands. It is only a slight nod in the direction of equal rights for daughters, as it only applies to a minority of aristocratic families and only if there are no direct male heirs. Had Henry lived to have a male child, the boy would have inherited, even though Elizabeth was the firstborn. So the law had to do with keeping the inheritance in the main branch of the family, which necessitated the rare possibility of a female inheriting, rather than being concerned with gender equality. Although primogeniture became absolute (i.e. not gender-based) for the British royal family in 2013 before the gender of Prince William's firstborn was known, it remains male-based for the aristocracy, despite many attempts to change it by those correctly campaigning for daughters' rights. The fact that it has not been changed may be partly due to entrenched sexism. But there are also thorny issues to do with whether legislation should be retrospective and, if so, to what degree. Normally, legislation should not be: but the campaigners for daughters' rights are understandably concerned with fairness for eldest daughters already born. Above all, the lack of change is because, although it is a genuine feminist issue and an outrageous anachronism in an age of equal rights, it only affects a very small number of generally very privileged people.

Returning to the sixteenth century, Thomas became 3rd Baron Paget – although the fourth holder of the barony if we count baby Elizabeth, as we should. As his mother, Anne, was still living at the West Drayton house, he set about building his own grand country house in Staffordshire. Rather than using his father's plans for a house at Burton-on-Trent, he decided to reshape what had been the Bishop of Lichfield's palace at Beaudesert, in Cannock Chase, to his own design. Although built around the old hall of the bishop's place and with various additions and changes at a later date, the Beaudesert House that survived until the twentieth century was a typical example of Elizabethan country house architecture of the 1570s. Sadly it was destroyed in the 1920s and 1930s and now exists only as a rather romantic ruin. But many paintings and photographs of it show that it must have been a magnificent building in its heyday.

Anne, who lived on until 1587, will have been satisfied to see all her six daughters well married and in some cases well remarried: Etheldreda to Sir Christopher Allen, Eleanor first to Jerome Palmer and then to Sir Rowland Clarke, Grisold first to Sir Thomas Rivett and then to Sir William Waldergrave, Jane to Sir Thomas Kitson, Dorothy to Sir Thomas Willoughby and Anne to Sir Henry Lee. The Pagets appeared to be well bedded into the English 'establishment'. However, their position in the generation that followed William was actually very precarious because of the devotion of some of them to the old religion. Anne's Catholicism became clear after the death of her husband. She apparently kept a priest in the West Drayton household, ostensibly serving as a steward, and there were reports from government spies that she gave money for the relief of priests held in prison and that priests on the run were sheltered at her house. William Byrd, the 'father of English Music', who was a staunch Catholic, was accused in 1581 of hanging around the 'Padgettes house Draighton'.

Anne's Catholicism was one thing but more threatening to Queen Elizabeth's Protestant state was the active support for Catholic conspiracies by Thomas and his younger brother Charles. Charles seems to have been the leader in this. In exile in France, he was associated with Thomas Morgan, an agent of Mary, Queen of Scots, and was part of the plotting against Elizabeth. Thomas Paget was initially accused by the Bishop of Coventry and Lichfield of various crimes of papistry, such as forcing the parishioners of Burton-on-Trent, at Communion, 'to use little singing cakes, after the old popish fashion' and, after the failed Throckmorton Plot of 1583, he joined his brother in Paris.[2] The Paget estates were confiscated. Lady Lee, living with her mother, wrote of the sad change in family fortunes, 'now we live alone and almost ther is none that either dareth come to us or loke apon us'. The brothers in Paris continued to be involved in conspiracies including the 1586 Babington Plot to assassinate Elizabeth which resulted in the execution of Mary, Queen of Scots, and they were attained of treason by an Act of Parliament. The manor at West Drayton was granted to Sir Christopher Hatton for life. He was a favourite of the Queen and one of the judges who found Mary, Queen of Scots guilty of treason. Old Lady Anne Paget was, however, allowed to stay in residence until her death in 1587: perhaps this arrangement was possible because Hatton, although fiercely loyal to Elizabeth, was considered to be a Roman Catholic in all but name.[3]

In this tangled world that intermingled the niceties of religion with State and family loyalties and interests, Charles Paget's position was particularly ambiguous. While plotting against Elizabeth, he appears to have also been a double agent working for her spymaster, Sir Francis Walsingham, attempting to 'play both sides against the middle'. In September 1582 he wrote to Walsingham,

> In answer to her Majesty's command for my return to England, assist me that she may yield me her favour and liberty of conscience in religion … If this cannot be done, then solicit for her my enjoying my small living on this side of the sea, whereby I may be kept from necessity, which otherwise will force me to seek relief of some foreign prince.

He wrote to Cecil, suing for pardon from the Queen and offering intelligence about what the Jesuits were up to. On the other hand, at the time when the triumph of the Spanish Armada looked likely, he bragged to a friend, 'When the day of invasion happens, the proudest Councillor or Minister in England will be glad of the favour of a Catholic gentleman.'

He and his brother Thomas actually entered the service of Philip II for a while, no doubt aided by the Spanish monarch's favourable memories of the much more worthy service of their father. In fact, Charles seems to have inherited all of the devious characteristics of his father without any of the balancing statesman-like ones. An admittedly biased Catholic source excoriates his character: 'from the first hour his years permitted him to converse with men, he has been tampering in broils and practices, betwixt friend and friend, man and wife, and, as his credit and craft increase, betwixt prince and prince.'[4]

Luckily for the future fortunes of the Paget family, he ended up emulating his father in one crucial respect, by finally choosing the winning side. After the death of Mary, Queen of Scots and the failure of the Armada, the Catholic exiles split into two groups, the Spanish party favouring the claims of the Spanish Infanta to the English Crown, and the Scottish party supporting the right of James VI of Scotland, son of Mary, Queen of Scots. Charles gave up his Spanish employment, returned to Paris and became the acknowledged head of the Scottish faction. In the first years of the next reign, the government of James (VI of Scotland, I of England) seems to have fully restored the position of the Pagets, reversing the act of attainder and returning most of their estates. This was partly because of Charles's backing for James but also because, while his father and uncle had been conspiring abroad, Thomas's son William – who became the 4th Baron Paget when his father died in 1590 – had been proving himself back home as a loyal Protestant supporter of Elizabeth. He was, for example, part of the successful attack on Cadiz led by the Earl of Essex in 1596. He also married well. The *Calendar of State Papers* for October 1602 reads, 'young [William] Paget has married Knollys's daughter [Lettice, Letty], and heir to Mr Controller's brother.'[5] The Knollys, who descended from relatives of Anne Boleyn, were an interesting and influential bunch. Letty's many uncles were all courtiers. The Comptroller of the Royal Household (an office previously held by Lord William Paget), Sir William Knollys, was known as 'Party beard' because his beard had three colours, white at the root, yellow in the middle and black at the end. He is believed to be the inspiration for Shakespeare's Malvolio in *Twelfth Night*. Another uncle, Sir Francis Knollys, was a pirate with Sir Francis Drake in the Caribbean in his youth and then lived to be the oldest MP, 'the ancientest Parliament man in England'. Letty's aunt Letty (same name, Lettice Knollys) incurred the Queen's displeasure when she married Elizabeth's favourite, Robert Dudley, Earl of Leicester. Things did not get any better for her when her next husband and her eldest son, the 2nd Earl of Essex, were both executed in 1601 for conspiring against the Queen.

But her niece, young Letty, and her husband William, the 1st Lord William Paget's grandson, seem to have done pretty well after the return of the family estates, iron and coal mining under their Staffordshire land greatly enhancing their wealth. Less profitable in the end, but rather fascinating, was a close involvement with Bermuda. Although first discovered much earlier, Bermuda's colonisation began inadvertently in 1609, when a ship travelling to Virginia, where a colony had been established two years earlier, was wrecked on its shores. There is another Shakespeare connection here, as the account of that shipwreck is thought to be one of the sources of *The Tempest*. Over the next ten years, the island was settled, divided into eight administrative areas named after the principal 'Adventurers' (investors) in the company that financed the venture. One of those was 'young' William Paget and the central parish of Bermuda is still called Paget and displays our coat of arms as its crest. The next William Paget, the 5th Baron, fought for the King in the Civil War, had his estates sequestered by the Commonwealth and then had them restored again after the Restoration.

* * *

In the next 400 years, the Pagets included an array of eclectic and eccentric characters, several of whom were prominent in the public life of Britain.

The first Lord William's great-great-grandson, yet another William and the 6th Baron (1637–1713) was a distinguished diplomatist under William and Mary and Queen Anne. Echoing the achievements of the founder of the family, he made a major contribution to the peace of Europe. Sent as ambassador-extraordinary to Istanbul, he was instrumental in negotiating the Treaty of Karlowitz between the Turks and their Christian enemies. The treaty established peace for many years between the Ottoman Empire and the Habsburgs, Russia, Poland and Venice. Based on the principle of 'uti possidetis' ('as you possess'), it represented an advance in a concept of international law confirming the then-current territorial holdings of each of the powers. Significantly, it marked the first time in the Ottoman Empire's history that it ceased to be a law unto itself, acknowledged the territorial integrity of its opponents by accepting well-defined borders, and began to work with reciprocal diplomatic arrangements. Just as the 1st Baron Paget had been a favourite of the Emperor Charles V, the 6th was apparently much liked by the Sultan, who persuaded William III to keep him at his court and who showered him with presents when he eventually left Istanbul. There are still some Turkish shamshir swords at Plas Newydd. Twelve magnificent Turkish horses were one of the Sultan's presents, and these Paget astutely presented as his gift to the new monarch back home, Queen Anne.

The next three generations of Pagets were relatively undistinguished but retained their positions in the British establishment by acting a courtiers to the King Georges. The 7th Baron was created Earl of Uxbridge by George I

– Uxbridge being very close to the family base at West Drayton. His son was Gentleman of the Bedchamber to George II and was an amateur poet in the style of Pope, writing, 'during the intervals of bad Weather, in Hunting-seasons'. His son, the 8th Baron, died unmarried and intestate. So a distant cousin, Caroline Paget, who had married Sir Nicholas Bayly, owner of Plas Newydd and of land on Anglesey, was the link that now passed the barony on to their son Henry and established the Welsh connection. Henry not only united the Welsh inheritance of his family with the Pagets but also received another fortune when a rich West Country landowner without heirs put him in his will – for reasons unknown. He now owned about 100,000 acres. This was the moment when the Industrial Revolution was just beginning to transform Britain and the agricultural value of his lands was greatly added to by the iron, lead, copper and coal beneath. For the icing on the cake, in 1784, the Earldom of Uxbridge, which had died out when the 8th Baron died, was revived for him by George III.[6]

We now come to the life of the 1st Marquess of Anglesey. Henry William was the eldest son of this Henry Bayly-Paget, who had become Earl of Uxbridge by the second creation. On the outbreak of the Napoleonic Wars, Henry William became a very successful soldier, rising rapidly through the ranks to command the British cavalry during the Peninsular Wars against the French in Spain and Portugal. After fathering eight children with his first wife, he scandalously ran off with the wife of the Duke of Wellington's brother. She was the love of his life and he produced another ten children with her. Not surprisingly, this did not endear him to Wellington and his military career was hindered. However, in 1815, the War Office and the Prince Regent – who was effectively the monarch after George III had gone mad – insisted that Uxbridge, as he had then become, command the cavalry and act as second in command to Wellington in the Waterloo campaign. By then the scandal was six years old and Wellington's reluctance to have him was probably more to do with his cautious and methodical approach to war, which contrasted with Uxbridge's more instinctive, even romantic, idea of how to use cavalry in battle. Wellington wanted someone sound and solid, believing that 'cavalry should always be kept well in hand ... men and horses not be used up in wild and useless charges.' Whereas Uxbridge was known as a wild imaginative cavalry genius who thought his role was to 'inspire his men as early as possible with the most perfect confidence in his personal gallantry. Let him lead, they are sure to follow, and I believe hardly anything will stop them.'

Probably the most famous remark about Waterloo was Wellington's that the result, which arguably determined the fate of Europe, was incredibly close – that it might have gone either way. In his words, the battle was 'a damned nice thing – the nearest run thing you ever saw in your life'. In essence, it was a question as to whether the troops under Wellington defending the ridge at Waterloo could hold out against the generally superior quality troops of Napoleon long enough for the Prussian army to arrive on the battlefield. In the event, they did and then the overwhelming numerical superiority of the allies decided the battle. But there were several moments during the day when the French nearly broke through and, at one of these, possibly the most important, Uxbridge's role and attitude was critical. In the early afternoon, the French forces under d'Erlon were smashing through the lines and threatening an allied defeat. Without any hesitation, Uxbridge ordered the British heavy cavalry into the gap and routed the French. It was an uncontrolled charge, the inevitable result of his impulsive way of operating, including leading from the front, and therefore mistakenly went too far and for too long into the French lines, causing unnecessary casualties. But his decisive action – the timing of his instantaneous response at the moment of crisis – was vital. One of the participants put it that 'had the charge been delayed for two or three minutes, I feel satisfied it would probably have failed, for the leading Frenchmen had already gained the crest of the position when the attack was ordered.' To quote from a couple of recent books about Waterloo, Andrew Roberts writes that 'if d'Erlon had been capable of consolidating his position at the crest of the ridge he could have turned Wellington's flank.' And Bernard Cornwell says, 'the great attack on Wellington's centre-left had come so close to success, but was now routed.'[7]

Uxbridge's other claim to fame at Waterloo was his wounding. One of the last cannon shots of the battle hit his leg. The story goes that he said to the Duke, as they sat on horses next to each other, 'By God, sir, I've lost my leg,' to which Wellington tersely replied, 'By God, sir, so you have,' before immediately resuming his observation of Napoleon's retreat through his telescope. The story is probably apocryphal but has been taken to indicate that Wellington was heartless and/or still resentful that Uxbridge had run off with his brother's wife; or is used as a supreme example of the cool professionalism of the British officer class, an exhibition of the 'stiff upper lip' by both Wellington and Uxbridge. The stories about the subsequent amputation continue in the same vein. When told he was to lose his leg, he smiled and replied, 'I have had a pretty long run. I have been a beau these 47 years and it would not be fair to cut the young men out any longer.' His behaviour during the actual amputation, done by a saw without any anaesthetic, was reported to be incredibly cool and brave. I like to think this is the case, though apparently pain can be blanked out in a proportion of patients who undergo severe trauma. Anyway, he was feted as a hero, fitted with an innovative articulated wooden leg, and promoted to Marquess of Anglesey and to the Order of the Garter – in the latter respect following in the footsteps of his ancestor Lord William Paget. He lived on another thirty-nine years, heavily involved in the politics of the day, particularly with issues to do with Ireland, where he twice served as Lord Lieutenant and was a progressive in favour of Catholic emancipation. He lived magnificently and extravagantly, at Plas Newydd in Anglesey, at Beaudesert in Staffordshire, at Uxbridge House at 42 Savile Row/7 Burlington Gardens in London and on his yacht *Pearl*. He was an enthusiastic yachtsman, sailing regularly, on the Menai Straits between Anglesey and the mainland, off Cowes in the Isle of Wight and on one occasion in 1839 taking the *Pearl* to visit Tsar Nicholas I in St Petersburg. It was he who donated to the Royal Yacht Squadron the 'Auld Mug', which is also known as the 'America's Cup' after the first round the Isle of Wight race in 1851 was won by the yacht *America*. This, the oldest international competition held in any sport, still continues as a hugely important event in the sailing world, though sometimes under the name of its varying sponsors – Louis Vuitton and Prada in recent years.[8]

* * *

Three of the 1st Marquess's younger sons achieved minor prominence, as soldier, sailor and courtier. Lord George Paget, following in his father's cavalry tradition, was in charge of the Light Dragoons in the Crimean War and became famous for being Cardigan's second in command during the Charge of the Light Brigade – and for smoking his cigar during it, as mentioned in my Introduction. Lord Clarence joined the Royal Navy and took part in the battle of Navarino at which the allied forces of Britain, France and Russia, fighting for Greek independence, decisively defeated the Ottoman Empire. He went on to become a vice admiral and to command the Mediterranean Fleet in the 1860s. Lord Alfred stayed at home and was Chief Equerry to Queen Victoria. The eldest son of the 1st Marquess, one of a run of three Henrys during Victoria's reign (2nd, 3rd and 4th Marquesses), was also briefly a courtier but was mainly a devoted sportsman: shooting, coursing, racing and founding the Worthing Cricket Club in Sussex in 1855. I could not find a single interesting thing to say about the 3rd Marquess and the best I could do for the 4th was to note that he acted as if in character for a Henry James or Edith Warton novel, or a *Downton Abbey* TV series, by taking as his third wife an American heiress. She was Mary 'Minna' Livingston King, daughter of John Pendleton King, who could feature in any story as the evil patriarch, since he was a lawyer, president of the Georgia Railroad and Banking Company, the owner of sixty-nine slaves and a US Senator for Georgia.

Henry, 4th Marquess, also fathered, by his second wife Blanche, Henry Cyril Paget, who was to become the famous, or infamous, 5th, 'dancing', Marquess. Much has been written about him since he became a cult figure. The Fin de Siècle world in which he featured, the world of Oscar Wilde and Proust, mixed great freedom of artistic, personal and sexual expression for a small elite alongside a horrified, and usually hypocritical, condemnation of the same by a wider and more powerful group who saw it as immoral and decadent. The judgemental view predominated, both in British society as a whole and in my family, until things began to change, first with the sexual liberation of the 1960s and more recently the LGBTQ movement. When I grew up in the 1950s, the 5th Marquess was regarded as the crazy 'black sheep' of the family who had squandered his inheritance. We knew him as 'Mad Ux', a bit of a giggle: eccentricity or insanity being safer grounds than 'dubious' sexuality.

Unfortunately, as a result of embarrassment about him, it is probable that most of his letters were deliberately destroyed, meaning that much of the information that survives comes from rumours or often sensational press reports. The bare bones of his story are this. His mother died when he was two. The details of his early life are uncertain: it may or may not have been in a theatrical environment in Paris. He was brought to Plas Newydd aged 8 and was then later sent away to Eton. His father died and he inherited when he was 23, becoming extremely rich. He married a cousin, but the marriage was annulled three years later on the grounds of non-consummation. His passion was the theatre and jewellery. Creating a theatre at Plas Newydd, he wrote and starred in his own plays, alongside famous professional actors, who were very well paid, and took his company on a British and European tour. He liked to cross-dress and his most famous act was the 'Butterfly Dance', performed in transparent white silk and based on the act of an American dancer, Loie Fuller. Although he has now been adopted as a gay icon, his actual sexuality is uncertain. The acknowledged expert on his life, Viv Gardner, thinks he was 'a classic narcissist: the only person he could love and make love to was himself'.

His extravagance was legendary: he blew his massive inheritance on fancy dress, theatrical projects and, above all, jewels. After five or six years, he is said to have got through the equivalent of about £400 million in today's money: he was declared bankrupt and there was a huge sale of his possessions to pay off his debtors. Prominent among these was Morris Wartski, who was transformed from a travelling merchant selling watches door to door to Welsh farmers to running a vastly successful international jewellery business partly due to the Marquess's patronage. I like to think that a sizeable chunk of the wealth Lord William Paget had acquired from his service to the Tudor monarchs and from the Dissolution of the Monasteries ended up in the hands of an enterprising Polish Jew who was a refugee from the antisemitic pogroms of Russia.

Henry Cyril died shortly after his bankruptcy, of tuberculosis, in a hotel in Monte Carlo. There are many 'over the top' stories about him. On honeymoon in Paris, his wife pointed out a jewel she liked in a shop window, he bought (take your pick) all the other jewels in the shop window, all the jewels in the shop, the above plus the shop. He never touched his wife but he liked her to lie naked on the bed covered in jewels. At Plas Newydd, he had burning brasiers tended to all over the grounds, so he could warm up instantly if necessary. On one occasion, when he was passing close to one such and felt a bit too hot, he took off the expensive fur coat he was wearing and threw it on the fire. He converted his car exhaust to spray perfume. Really? One suspects that, although as one commentator has said, 'flamboyant' is not a strong enough word to describe him, there might be a bit of exaggeration. A rather lovely musical based on his life, called *How to Win Against History*, was recently written and performed by Seiriol Davies.

Not surprisingly he died without issue and a cousin, Charles, my grandfather, became the 6th Marquess. Despite the ravages of the 5th Marquess, the 6th was not exactly penniless. He had to abandon Beaudesert, but, as well as Plas Newydd, he had a lovely Norman Shaw London house in Queensgate – now part of Imperial College, a gorgeous villa at Opio in Provence and a couple of yachts. The guest book at Plas Newydd reveals an endless social whirl of house parties in the 1920s and 1930s, with the cream of society lured by the glamourous and 'fast' Paget sisters, my aunts Caroline, Liz, Rose and Kitty. Charles commissioned the fashionable and talented artist, Rex Whistler, to paint a beautiful mural in the dining room – which is the top attraction for the public visiting Plas Newydd today.

Death duties and changing social patterns did for the high aristocratic lifestyle by the time my father inherited in 1947. Both my parents had a serious sense of civic duty and a work ethic that Lord William Paget would have recognised. After serving as head of the National Federation of Women's Institutes, my mother was on endless government or quasi-governmental committees to do with nuclear power, pollution, broadcasting and the arts. In the lists of the 'good and great' kept by the Civil Service in the latter half of the twentieth century, she ticked a lot of boxes: as a woman, as Welsh and as an aristocrat – a unique combo. She was also very good at the job – particularly at asking the 'naïve' questions that went to the heart of the matter, the questions the 'experts' avoided. My father was an early and passionate campaigner for conservation and saving the natural environment: also renowned for his wicked sense of humour and for not giving a damn what narrow-minded people thought of him.

* * *

My personal connection to the 'founder' of my family may have magnified the usual biographer's bias in favour of their subject. But my initial ignorance of Tudor history could have had some benefit – in that the professional historian can be so immersed in their subject as to take for granted things that need explanation to the contemporary reader. I noticed a phrase in a review of the classic history of Imperial Spain by J. H. Elliot, saying that the author brings 'the political, social, religious and intellectual movement of his chosen period as close to the modern reader as the ethics and limits of well-tempered scholarship permit'.[9] That has been my aim; although I may have pushed those well-tempered limits on occasion.

Looking back at my family history, from the very lucky position of having access to extensive records about it, I have been able to see something of the degree of continuity and change in society as a whole. Building on the foundations laid by William, the Paget family over the years accumulated all sorts of property, now mostly gone. Viewing these as they are today, you can trace several historic trends. The property at West Drayton is criss-crossed by the M4 and M25 motorways and the next-door fields of Heathrow are now the airport. If a third runway is built there, it will run right alongside the still extant Harmondsworth Great Barn that William owned. The ruins of Beaudesert House in Staffordshire are surrounded by campsites visited by children from the inner cities on 'outward bound' courses. Plas Newydd is a popular site of the National Trust, enjoyed by thousands, whose first sight when they enter the 'Gothick Hall' is three portraits of Lord William Paget. Paget parish in Bermuda has mercifully seen the end of slavery and colonialism. Uxbridge House, at 42 Savile Row, which was the 1st Marquess of Anglesey's London house, became a bank in 1855. I was once entertained to lunch there in the 1980s in the days when there were still people at the Royal Bank of Scotland who had some interest in the building where they worked. In 2005, it became the first European mega-store of the US fashion house, Abercrombie & Fitch. That did not last long – as 'in store' shopping has contracted – and they 'downsized' to the smaller number 3 Savile Row opposite, itself famous for having been the Beatles' Apple Corps headquarters and the site of their last ever concert on its roof. Number 4a Calais Road, Burton-on-Trent, in a street named after England's last Continental possession lost on Lord William's watch and the final family-owned property in Staffordshire from his days, was sold in 2021. In a Britain that rightly celebrates multiculturalism, it was bought by a family of Pakistani origin, with all the other bidders being of Asian descent.

To examine in detail the actions and motives of people who lived several hundred years ago, even if from the same place and blood as yourself, is to visit a distant land, where wonder at how much has changed alternates with surprise at how much has stayed the same.

Notes

The more readable popular histories tend to ignore footnotes, while the 'heavy' academic ones often attempt to 'footnote' every sentence, resulting in hundreds per chapter. While the latter appears very impressive, I have found that when you actually look up the references, you quite often find they are inaccurate, the wrong page number or whatever. This is not surprising as the business of getting hundreds right must be mind-numbingly taxing and boring.

I have compromised, not footnoting everything and keeping the total to about 300, largely to cover direct quotes, while also including some other main references.

Foreword
1. Andrew Johnston. PhD thesis. *William Paget and Late Henrician Polity, 1543–47*. University of St Andrews, 2004, p. viii.
2. G. R. Elton. *The Tudor Revolution in Government: Administrative Changes in the Reign of Henry VIII* (H VIII hereafter) (Cambridge, 1955), p. 5. Quoted in Johnston PhD thesis.

Introduction
1. David Starkey. *The Reign of Henry VIII* (Vintage paperback ed., 1985), Introduction.
2. Natalie Mears. 'Courts, Courtiers, and Culture in Tudor England', *The Historical Journal*, Cambridge University Press, Sep 2003, vol. 46, no. 3, p. 715.
3. Susan Brigden. *New Worlds, Lost Worlds: The Rule of the Tudors 1485–1603* (Penguin paperback ed., 2001), p. 51.
4. Geoffrey Parker. *Emperor: A New Life of Charles V* (Yale University Press, 2019), p. 523.
5. Margaret Scard. *Tudor Survivor: The Life and Times of William Paulet* (History Press paperback ed., 2012), p. 215.

Chapter 1
1. John Guy. *Tudor England* (Oxford University Press paperback ed., 1990), p. 32. Most of the statistics in this section from that book, 'The Condition of England', pp. 30–52.

2. Diarmaid MacCulloch. *Thomas Cromwell, A Life* (Penguin paperback ed., 2019), p. 9.
3. *Letters and Papers of Henry VIII*, vol. 20, part 2, 788 (hereafter cited as e.g., L&P, H VIII, 20(2), 788), Stephen Gardiner 13 Nov 1545. Gardiner compares the parts played by himself, Paget and Lord Chancellor Wriothesley, in running English foreign policy, with the parts the three played in a play when they were at Cambridge.
4. James P. Carley. 'John Leland in Paris: The Evidence of his Poetry', *Studies in Philology*, University of North Carolina, vol. LXXXIII, winter 1986, no. 1, pp. 32–33.
5. L&P, H VIII, 4(2), 4440.
6. Samuel Rhea Gammon. *Statesman and Schemer: William, First Lord Paget, Tudor Minister* (David and Charles, 1973) p. 21 (hereafter cited as Gammon).
7. L&P, H VIII, 5, 363 and 427; Gammon, p. 25.

Chapter 2
1. Public Records Office (hereafter PRO), State Papers (hereafter SP) 1 / 82 / ff 201-2, as quoted in Gammon, p. 27.
2. L&P, H VIII, 7, 21.
3. L&P, H VIII, 6, 89.
4. L&P, H VIII, 7, 220.
5. See footnote 4 of Chapter 1.
6. PRO SP1, 199, f 176 & 209.
7. S. A. J. McVeigh. *Drayton of the Pagets* (private publication). Copy in National Trust collection, Plas Newydd.
8. Gammon, p. 34.
9. British Museum (hereafter BM), Vespasian FXIII, 157b, 37 Paget (hereafter P) to Wriothesley.
10. Gammon, pp. 31 and 32.
11. For the Anne of Cleves story, see Retha M. Warnicke. *The Marrying of Anne of Cleves* (Cambridge University Press, 2000); Sarah-Beth Watkins, *Anne of Cleves* (Chronos Books, 2018); and Alison Weir. *The Six Wives of Henry VIII* (Vintage, 1991), Chapter 13.
12. MacCulloch. *Cromwell*, p. 106.
13. Andrew H. Harrison. 'The Books of Thomas, Lord Paget', *Transactions of the Cambridge Bibliographical Society*, 6, 1972–1976, pp. 226–242. Quoted in Johnston PhD thesis.
14. William Macray (ed.). 'The Remonstrance of Anne of Cleves', *Archaeologia* 47 (1883), 259, 265; SP H VIII, 652; Warnicke, pp. 247, 248, 255; Watkins, p. 141.

Chapter 3
1. Geoffrey Gibbons. *The Political Career of Thomas Wriothesley, First Earl of Southampton, 1505–1550* (Edwin Mellen Press, 2001) p. 58.

2. G. R. Elton. *Reform and Reformation, England 1509–1558* (Edward Arnold, 1977, paperback ed.), p. 296.
3. L&P, H VIII, 20(2), 1031.
4. L&P, H VIII, 16, 932.
5. Ibid., 1197.
6. Ibid., 1253.
7. *Calendar of State Papers, Spain* (hereafter CSPS), 6 (i), 199.

Chapter 4
1. L&P, H VIII, 16, 1276.
2. Ibid., 1335, 1440, 1448.
3. Ibid., 1334.
4. BM, Cotton Ms, Caligula, E, iv, p. 115; Weir. *The Six Wives of Henry VIII*, p. 475–476.
5. L&P, H VIII, 17, 485 & 494.
6. L&P, H VIII, 16, 1253.
7. L&P, H VIII, 17, 838.
8. Ibid., 479.
9. Ibid., 838.
10. L&P, H VIII, 18(1), 92.
11. Ibid., 62, 71, 106.
12. Ibid., 217.
13. Ibid., 106.
14. BM, Egerton Ms 2214.
15. L&P, H VIII, 18(1), 250.
16. Gammon, p. 53.

Chapter 5
1. Simon Thurley. *Houses of Power: The Places that Shaped the Tudor World* (Black Swan, 2019), p. 177.
2. Tracey Borman. *Henry VIII and the Men Who Made Him* (Hodder & Stoughton, 2018), p. 384.
3. MacCulloch, *Cromwell*, p. 275.
4. Peter Marshall. *Heretics and Believers* (Yale, 2018), p. 295.
5. CSPS, 9, van der Delft to the Emperor, 12 Feb 1547.
6. Based on Johnston PhD, pp. 106–110 and the documents to which he refers, mainly in PRO, SP 1/225.
7. G. Elton. *The Tudor Constitution: Documents and Commentary* (Cambridge, 2nd ed., 1982), p. 102.
8. Gibbons. *Wriothesley*, etc., p. 113.
9. Acts of the Privy Council (hereafter APC), vol. 17, 1558–70, pp. 393–394. Available British History Online (BHO).
10. Issues explained in Coleman and Starkey (eds.). *Revolution Reassesed* (Clarendon Press, 1986).

11. Diarmaid MacCulloch. *Thomas Cranmer* (Yale, 2016), p. 329.
12. L&P, H VIII, 20(2), 38.
13. L&P, H VIII, 20(1), 1022, 1218.
14. L&P, H VIII, 19(1), 803.
15. Ibid., 188, 230; 20(1) 1032, 1121, 1222, 1284; 20(2), 225, 412, 427, 496; 21 (1), 121.

Chapter 6
1. Alison Weir. *Henry VIII, King and Court* (Vintage, 2008), p. 464.
2. Ibid.
3. E. G. Emmison. *Tudor Secretary: Sir William Petre at Court and Home* (Longmans, 1961).
4. Johnston PhD thesis, p. 204 and, in general, pp. 174–207.
5. Parker. *Emperor*, p. 511.
6. L&P, H VIII, 20 (1), 1145.
7. L&P, H VIII, 20(2), 9, 153.
8. Ibid., 212, 453, 746, 752; Gibbons. *Wriothesley* etc., pp. 146–154.

Chapter 7
1. Parker. *Emperor*, pp. 382–386.
2. L&P H VIII, 19(1), 572, 767, 1013; 19(2), 220, 308, 643, 658; 20(1), 213, 590, 634, 794, 846 (31); 20(2), 111, 217, 991, 1004; 21(1), 1310; 21(2), 638, 673.
3. L&P, H VIII, 20(2), 217; 21(1), 106, 291, 1374.
4. L&P, H VIII, 20(1), 257.
5. Parker. *Emperor*, p. x.
6. Ibid., p.131.
7. L&P H VIII, 17, 263.
8. L&P, H VIII, 19(2), Preface.
9. L&P, H VIII, 19(1), 520, 525, 527.
10. Ibid., 566.
11. Ibid., 619, 625, 626.
12. Ibid., 648, 666, 682, 703.
13. L&P, H VIII, 21(1), 691.
14. L&P, H VIII, 19(1), 676.
15. Ibid., 716.

Chapter 8
1. L&P, H VIII, 19(1), 940, 946.
2. L&P, H VIII, 19(2), 223.
3. Ibid., 175, 424.
4. Ibid., 216, 235, 250.
5. Ibid., 374, 391–392, 403 & 4, 456.
6. Ibid., 470.
7. Ibid., 582, 747.

8. Ibid., 784; 20(1), 30, 36, 41, 43, 76.
9. L&P, H VIII, 20(1), 257, 281, 302, 305.
10. Ibid., 372; PRO SP1 / 199.
11. L&P, H VIII, 20(1), 544.
12. Ibid., 485, 496.

Chapter 9
1. L&P, H VIII, 20(1), 772.
2. L&P, H VIII, 20 (2), 2.
3. Peter Marsden. *1545, Who Sank The Mary Rose* (Seaforth Publishing, an imprint of Pen & Sword Books, 2019).
4. L&P, H VIII, 20(2), 455.
5. Ibid., 818, 827, 828.
6. Ibid., 732, 788, 836, 1001; 21(1), 23.
7. L&P, H VIII, 21(1), 488.
8. Ibid., 633.
9. Ibid., 691.
10. Ibid., 763, 771.
11. Ibid., 784, 806, 816.
12. Ibid., 840, 841.
13. Ibid., 838.
14. Ibid., 862, 866, 877, 903, 943, 974, 1007, 1014, 1015, 1024.
15. Odet de Selve. *Correspondance Politique*. Felix Alcan, ed. (Paris, 1888), available online, Internet Archive. De Selve to Connetable, 29 Aug 1547.
16. L&P, H VIII, 21(1), 1122, 1133, 1160.
17. L&P, H VIII, 21(2), Preface; 21(2), 13, 23, 27–32, 128, 134, 149, 157, 159, 191.
18. 'A Consultacon In August 1546'. Northampton Records Office, Fitzwilliam of Milton Correspondence, The Paget Letter Book. Quoted in full as Appendix 3 of Johnston, PhD thesis.
19. L&P, H VIII, 20(1), 372.

Chapter 10
1. L&P, H VIII, 21(1), 1138; Gibbons, *Wriothesley* etc., pp. 171–177.
2. L&P, H VIII, 21(1), 1181.
3. Foxe, J. *Acts and Monuments of the English Martyrs*, ed. S. R. Cattley and G. Townsend (London, 1837–41). Vol. 5, pp. 553–561.
4. Starkey. *The Reign of Henry VIII*, p. 131.
5. L&P H VIII, 21(1), 1398.
6. Ibid., 1463.
7. MacCulloch. *Cranmer*, p. 356.
8. Selve. *Corr. Politique*, p. 51; Glyn Redworth. *In Defence of the Catholic Church* (Blackwell, 1990), p. 239.
9. Northampton Record Society, Fitzwilliam, Paget Letter Book, 31; APC, vol. 2, paperback ed., p. 15.

10. Redworth, pp. 231–247; James Arthur Muller, ed. *The Letters of Stephen Gardiner* (Cambridge University Press, 1933), 2013 paperback ed., pp. 247–249; L&P, H VIII, 21(2), 493.

Chapter 11
1. L&P, H VIII, 21(2), Preface p. viii.
2. L&P, H VIII, 21(2), 548, 552.
3. Ibid., 533, 546.
4. Ibid., 554, 696.
5. Ibid., 555.
6. Ibid., 697; the Spanish Chronicle of H VIII, ed. Martin Hume 1889, Available online, Google Books, pp. 143–147.
7. Starkey. *The Reign of Henry VIII*, p. 136.

Chapter 12
1. The Third Act of Succession, 1544. Available online Luminarium: Encycliopia Project, sourced from G. B. Adams and H. M. Stephens eds., *Select Documents of English Constitutional History* (Macmillan, 1914), pp. 264–267.
2. L&P, HVIII, 21(2), 634; Transcription of the will, Suzannah Lipscomb. *The King Is Dead* (Apollo, 2018), Appendix I, pp. 165–192.
3. CSPS, 8, 371.
4. APC, vol. 2, pp. 10–16; Fox. *Book of Martyrs* (New York, 1846, 4th ed.), Available online on Internet Archive 2010, pp. 298–300.
5. L&P, H VIII, 21(2), 770.
6. APC, vol. 2, p. 15.
7. L&P, H VIII, 21(2), 713, 743.

Chapter 13
1. John Strype. *Memorials Ecclesiastical* (Clarendon Press, 1822), vol. 12, Part 1, p. 17. Available online, Internet Archive.
2. Strype. vol. 2, Part 1, pp. 429–437, a modernised text. Full details of the letter, Barrett L. Beer and Sybil M. Jack. *The Letters of William Paget, 1547–63* (hereafter Beer & Jack), p. 54.
3. *The Chronicles and Political Papers of King Edward VI*, ed. W. K. Jordan (1966), p. 4.
4. P. F. Tytler. *England Under the Reigns of Edward VI*, etc., vol. 1, p. 15. Available online via Haithi Trust Digital Library.
5. APC, vol. 2, pp. 10–16.
6. Richard Hutchinson. *The Last Days of Henry VIII* (Phoenix, 2005), p. 235; Starkey, *Henry VIII: Personality and Politics*, p. 142; APC, vol. 2, pp. 10–16.

Chapter 14
1. The source for the majority of this chapter is the privately published Drayton of the Pagets, by S. A. J. Mcveigh (copy in the National Trust Collection at

Plas Newydd). His information is largely from a May 1556 Inventory of the West Drayton house contained in Middlesex Records Office Acc 446 / H2.
2. F. G. Emmison. *Tudor Secretary* (Longmans, 1961), p. 38.
3. L&P H VIII, 20(2), 962.
4. Thomas Tusser. *Five Hundred Points of Good Husbandry*, ed. William Mavor, 1580. The author's Epistle, footnote 1. Chicago Scholarship Online, and other online sources.

Chapter 15
1. P. F. Tytler. *England Under the Reigns of Edward VI and Mary* (1839). Available online, University of Michigan, pp. 21–22.
2. Gammon, p. 136.
3. APC, vol. 2, pp 33–35.
4. CSPS, vol. 9, van der Delft to the Emperor, 16 Jun 1547.
5. APC, vol. 2, pp. 26–31.
6. David Crowther. *Early Tudor Court, The History of England, Great History Podcasts from the Shed* (2017); CSPS, vol. 10, Scheyfve to the Emperor, 18 Oct 1551.
7. J. A. Muller. *The Letters of Stephen Gardiner*, pp. 268–272; Tytler, pp. 24–26.
8. CSPS, vol. 9, van der Delft to the Emperor, 23 Oct 1547.
9. Redworth. *In Defence of the Catholic Church*, Chapter 11.
10. Tytler, pp. 26–29.
11. Tytler, p. 17; L&P, vol. 19 (1) 293.
12. Tytler, pp. 27–29; Beer & Jack, p. 11.
13. Gammon, p. 138.
14. CSPS, vol. 9.
15. Gammon, pp. 138–139.
16. History of Parliament online, Paget entry by A. D. K. Hawkyard.
17. CSPS, vol. 9, van der Delft to Queen Dowager 4 May 1547, van der Delft to Emperor 2 Sep, Emperor to van der Delft 18 Sep, Emperor to Paget 18 Oct 1547.

Chapter 16
1. CSPS, vol. 9, 2 April 1547, van der Delft to Emperor.
2. Ibid. Preface by Royall Tyler.
3. Ibid.
4. *Correspondence politique de Odet de Selve* (Paris, 1888), de Selve to Connetable 21 April 1547; CSPS, vol. 9, van der Delft to Queen Dowager 23 Oct 1547.
5. Letter 14 July 1547 to WP signed with stamp, Edward at head and at foot by Duke of Somerset. Reproduced and part 'translated' in Sotheby's catalogue July 2019, 'English Literature, History, Children's Books and Illustrations'.
6. CSPS, vol. 9, 23 Oct 1547, van der Delft to Queen D.
7. De Selve to the (French) King 8 & 9 Sep 1547.
8. CSPS, vol. 9, van der Delft to Emperor 21 Aug 1548.

9. Ibid. Secretary Jehan Dubois to Loys Scors (Louis de Schore, President of the Flemish Council of State), 4 Oct 1548; same to same 15 Oct 1548.
10. Ibid., Preface.
11. Ibid., van der Delft to Emperor, 8 Feb 1549.
12. Samuel Haynes. *A Collection of State Papers, relating to affairs in the Reigns of H VIII, King Edward VI, Queen Mary and Queen Elizabeth from the year 1542 to 1570* (London, William Bowywer, 1840) Available online Books on Google Play, pp. 82–87.

Chapter 17
1. Beer & Jack, pp. 14–15. P to Somerset 2 Feb 1548.
2. Ibid., pp. 17–18. P to Somerset Jul 1548.
3. P to Somerset, 25 Dec 1548. Modernised text by Beer in Huntington Library Quarterly, xxxiv (May 1971), pp. 277–283.
4. Beer & Jack, pp. 19–20.
5. Beer. *Sir William Paget and the Protectorate, 1547–49*. Ohio Academy of History Newsletter, Nov 1971.
6. Beer & Jack, pp. 22–27.
7. Ibid., pp. 28–29.
8. Ibid., pp. 29–32.
9. Ibid., pp. 33–74; CSPS, vol. 9, van der Delft to Emperor, 13 Jun 1549.
10. P to Somerset 7 Jul 1549, modernised text in Strype, ii (ii), pp. 429–437.
11. Ibid.
12. John Guy. *Tudor England* (OUP, 1990), p. 201.
13. Document in McVeigh, *Drayton of the Pagets*, see footnote 1 of Chapter 14.
14. Gammon, p. 159. Quoting Inner Temple, Petyt MS, 538, xlvi, pp. 451 & 456–457.

Chapter 18
1. CSPS, vol. 9, van der Delft to Emperor, 13 Aug 1549.
2. APC, vol. 2, pp. 114–119.
3. W. K. Jordan. *Edward VI: The Young King* (Belknap Press of Harvard, Cambridge, Mass 1968), p. 510. And, in general on the 'coup', pp. 494–523.
4. Beer & Jack, Duchess of Somerset to P, 8 Oct 1549.
5. Ibid., pp 79–83; APC, vol. 2, pp. 114–119; BHO, *Calendar of State Papers*, Domestic, 1547–80, vol. 9, Oct 1549, 22, 26, 35, 37, 42; Tytler, vol. 1, pp. 235–252; CSPS, vol. 9, van der Delft to Emperor, 8 & 14 Oct 1549.
6. CSPS, vol. 9, van der Delft to Emperor, 17 Oct 1549.

Chapter 19
1. Gammon, p. 170. Quoting from Council letter, BM, Cotton MS, Caligula E, iv, p. 204b.
2. Beer & Jack, p. 98, P to Warwick, 15 Mar 1550.
3. CSPS, vol. 10, van der Delft to Emperor, 22 Apr 1550.

4. Ibid., 31 Jan 1550.
5. Ibid., 22 Apr 1550.
6. CSPS, vol. 11, Scheyfve to Bishop of Arras, 10 Apr 1553.
7. W. K. Jordan. *Edward VI: The Threshold of Power* (Harvard University Press, 1970), p. 451. Quoting BM, Egerton MS, 2603, pp. 33–34. Annotated 'Advice to the King's Council' & 'The Remembrance given to my master by my Lord Paget'.
8. CSPS, vol. 10, Scheyfve to Queen Dowager, 4 Nov 1550.
9. Jordan, *Threshold*, p. 51 and quoting BM, Cotton MSS, titus, B, ii, 28, pp. 57 & 8, 22 Jan 1551.
10. CSPS, vol, 10, Scheyfve to Emperor, 1 Sep 1550.
11. Foxe's *Book of Martyrs*, vol. 8, p. 232. Available online, WaHpad.com.
12. CSPS, vol. 10, Scheyfve to Emperor, 10 Oct 1551.

Chapter 20

1. Ibid., 26 Oct 1551.
2. Jordan. *Threshold*, pp. 87–88.
3. For conditions in the Tower, see Derek Wilson. *The Tower of London* (Alison & Busby, London, 1978), p. 101 and in general; Scard. *Tudor King in All But Name* (History Press), pp. 379–380.
4. APC, vol. 3, pp. 401–402, 407, 426, 503.
5. Ibid., pp. 414–415, 442.
6. CSPS, vol. 10, Scheyfve's Reports, 12 Feb & 6 Mar 1552.
7. Scard. *Tudor King*, p. 384.
8. Gammon, pp. 181–182.
9. CSPS, vol. 10, Scheyfve, 18 Jun 1552 and footnote 2.
10. Jordan. *Threshold*, p. 115.
11. Strype. *Ecclesiastical Memorials* (Clarenden Press, 1822), vol. II, Pt II. p. 45. Available online at Internet Archive.
12. APC, vol. 3, pp. 176–177; Beer & Jack, p. 103, P's offer to the King.
13. CSPS, vol. 10, Scheyfve to Arras, 20 Nov 1552.
14. Beer & Jack, p. 139, Anne Paget to the Council 1552. No exact date.
15. Gammon, p. 275.

Chapter 21

1. Jordan. *Threshold*, p. 498.
2. Gammon, p. 185.
3. Jordan. *Threshold*, pp. 526–527.
4. APC, vol. 4, p. 293, 16 Jul 1553.
5. Anna Whitelock. *Mary Tudor, England's First Queen* (Bloomsbury, 2009) paperback ed. 2010, p. 173. Refers to C.V. Malfatti. *The Accession, Coronation and Marriage of Mary Tudor as Related in Four Manuscripts of the Escorial* (Barcelona, 1956).
6. CSPS, vol. 11, Advice for an Imperial ambassador, 20 Jul 1553.

7. Ibid.
8. CSPS, vol. 11, ambassadors to Emperor, 22 Jul 1553.
9. Ibid., 27 Jul 1553.
10. Letter from 'Marye the Queen' to P and Arundel, 27 Jul 1553. Reproduced and part 'translated' in Sotheby's Catalogue 12 Jul 2016 of Sale of English Literature, History, Children's Books and Illustrations.
11. CSPS, vol. 11, Ambassadors in England to Emperor, 2 Aug 1553.
12. Ibid., 16 Aug 1553.
13. Ibid., 27 Aug 1553.

Chapter 22
1. CSPS, vol. 11, Simon Renard to Arras, 7 Aug 1553.
2. Ibid. Emperor to Prince Philip, 30 Jul 1553.
3. Ibid. Arras to Renard, 14 Aug 1553.
4. Ibid. Renard to Emperor, 5 Oct 1553.
5. Ibid. Emperor to Renard, to Mary, and to P. All three, 10 Oct 1553.
6. Ibid. Renard to Emperor, 12 Oct 1553.
7. Ibid. Renard to Emperor, 15 Oct 1553.
8. Ibid. Renard to Emperor, 28 Oct 1553.
9. Ibid. Renard to Emperor, 31 Oct & 21 Nov 1553.
10. Ibid. Renard to Emperor, 4 Nov 1553.
11. Ibid. Renard to Emperor, 28 & 29 Nov 1553.
12. Ibid. Queen Dowager to Renard, 19 Nov 1553, Renard to Queen Dowager, 29 Nov 1553, Mary to Emperor, 1 Dec 1553.
13. Ibid. Renard to Emperor, 20 & 28 Nov, 12, 17, 20 & 29 Dec 1553; CSPS, vol. 12, Treaty of Marriage, 1 Dec 1554; Gammon, pp. 199–200.

Chapter 23
1. Whitelock. *Mary Tudor*, pp. 210 & 214. Quoting J. G. Nichols (ed.), 'The Chronicles of Queen Jane and Queen Mary', *Camden Society* 48 (London, 1850), p. 34. And J. Proctor, 'The historie of Wyatt's rebellion' in A. F. Pollard (ed.), *Tudor Tracts* (London, 1903) p. 230.
2. CSPS, vol. 12, ambassadors in England to Emperor, 29 Jan 1554.
3. Mary to P, 28 Jan 1554. Reproduced and part 'translated' in Sotheby's Catalogue of Sale 1–9 Jul 2019 of English Literature, History etc., p. 11; Foxe. *Acts and Monuments*, 10, pp. 1418–1419.
4. CSPS, vol. 12, Renard to Emperor, 22 Mar & 3 Apr 1554.
5. Ibid. Count d'Egmont and Renard to Emperor, 8 Mar 1554; Renard to Emperor, 14 Mar 1554; List of names to be gifted gold chains, 15 Mar 1554.
6. Ibid. P to Renard 19 Apr 1554; M de Courriers and Renard to Emperor, 22–25 May 1554.
7. Ibid. Renard to Emperor, 13 May 1554.
8. *Calendar of State Papers*, Venice. Report of Soranzo to the Senate, 18 Aug 1554.
9. CSPS, vol. 12, ambassadors in England to Emperor, 14 Jun 1554; Arras to Emperor, 19 Jue 1554; Renard to Emperor, 20 Jun 1554; Notes for Prince

Philip, June 1554; Renard to Emperor, 28 Jun & 9 Jul 1554; Don Juan de Figuera to Emperor 26 July 1554; Whitelock. *Mary Tudor*, pp. 230–234.
10. CSPS, vol. 13, Queen Dowager to Arras, 14 Aug 1554; Ruy Gomez to Francisco de Eraso, 23 Aug 1554.
11. Ibid. Emperor to de Eraso, 20 Oct 1554.
12. Ibid. Mary to Emperor, 5 Nov 1554; An account of the negotiations at Brussels of Lord Paget and the other English envoys, 14 Nov 1554.
13. Queen Mary & Philip of Spain to P, 29 Jan 1555. Reproduced and part 'translated' in Sotheby's Catalogue for 12 Jul 2016 Sale of English Literature, History, etc., p. 13.
14. CSPS, vol. 13, An account of the negotiation at Brussels of Lord Paget and other English envoys, 14 Nov 1554.
15. Ibid. Renard to Emperor, 10 Feb & 27 Mar 1555.
16. Whitelock. Mary Tudor, pp. 262–263.

Chapter 24

1. CSP Venice, vol. 6. Giovanni Michiel, ambassador to England to the Doge & Senate (D&S hereafter), 9, 23 & 27 May 1555; Federico Badoer, ambassador to the Emperor, to D&S, 21 & 23 May 1555; Giaccmo Soranzo, ambassador to France, to the D&S, 23 May 1555.
2. CSPS, vol. 13, 199 & 211.
3. CSP Venice, vol. 6, Badoer to D&S, 8 Jun 1555.
4. Ibid. Badoer to D&S, 24 Nov 1555; Michiel to D&S, 25 Nov 1555; Badoer to D&S, 8 Apr 1556.
5. Ibid. Badoer to D&S, 8 Apr 1556.
6. CSPS, vol. 13, 264.
7. CSP Venice, vol. 6, Badoer to D&S, 460.
8. Ibid. Badoer to D&S, 26 April & 12 May 1556; Michiel to D&S 19 May 1556.
9. Ibid. Michiel to D&S, 25 Aug 1556.
10. Ibid. Michiel to D&S, 627.
11. Ibid. Michiel to D&S, 723.
12. CSPS, vol. 13, 289.
13. Ibid. Don Bernardina de Mendoza to the Duke of Savoy, 28 Apr 1557.
14. Beer & Jack, pp. 121–122. P to Thirlby, 28 Aug 1557.
15. CSPS, vol. 13, 324.
16. Ibid., 406.
17. Ibid., 413.
18. Ibid., 425.

Chapter 25

1. 'The Count of Feria's dispatch to Philip of 14 Nevemeber 1558', ed. M.J. Rodriquez Salgado and Simon Adams, *Camden Misceliany*, 28 (1984). Published online by Cambridge University Press, Dec 2009.
2. CSP Venice, vol. 7, Schifaneya to Gabriel e Calzont Charcellor of the Duke of Mantua at Brussels, 17 Dec 1558.

3. Simancas, *Calendar of State Papers*, Spain, vol. 1, 1558–67 (Simancas hereafter), Count de Feria to the King (Philip), 14 Dec 1558.
4. David Loades. Elizabeth I (Hambleden & London 2003), p. 127.
5. L. S. Marcus, J. Mueller & M. B. Rose (eds.). *Elizabeth I, Collected Works* (Chicago & London, 2000) p. 52.
6. Simancas, vol. 1, Feria to King, 18 Apr 1559.
7. Cecil Papers, 568, P to Cecil, 20 Feb 1559.
8. Ibid. P to Parry, 23 Apr 1559.
9. *Calendar of State Papers*, Foreign, vol. 2, 413 & 524.
10. Simancas, vol. 1, 86.
11. Beer & Jack, pp. 130–132.
12. Ibid., p. 134; *Calendar of State Papers*, Domestic 1547–80, P to Cecil March 1559 and P to Parry, undated 1560.
13. APC, vol. 7, pp. 58–70, 18 Dec 1558.
14. Cecil Papers, 567.
15. Simancas, vol. 1, Quadra to the King, Feb 1562.
16. The Journal of Matters of State, BL Additional MS 48023: All Things Robert Dudley website entry by Christine Hartweg, Aug 16 2018, 'Did William Paget Talk About Elizabeth and Robert Dudley?'
17. Simancas, vol. 1, 74 & 123.
18. Loades, Elizabeth I, p. 145.

Chapter 26
1. Simancas, vol. 1, de Feria to King, 19 Mar & 11 April 1559.
2. CSP Foreign, vol. 5, Challoner to P, 20 Dec 1562; CSP Foreign, vol. 1, Robert Jones to Throckmorton, 26 Feb 1561; Elizabeth to P, 1 May 1561, reproduced and part 'translated' in Sotheby's Catalogue, English Literature, History, etc., 1–9 July 2019, p. 15.
3. David Lloyd. *State-worthies*, etc., vol. 1, Observations on the Life of Sir William Paget, pp. 109–112. Original in Bavarian State Library. Digitalised & available online at Google Books.
4. Letter signed by Queen Elizabeth to Paget, 19 Jul 1559. Displayed at Plas Newydd, National Trust.
5. CSP Foreign, vol. 1, Throckmorton to Cecil, 28 Jun & 1 Aug 1559; CSP Foreign, vol. 3, Henry Paget to Throckmorton, 7 Aug 1560; CSP Venice, vol. 7, 106–108; CSP Foreign, vol. 4, Cecil to Sir Thomas Windebank, 4 Nov 1561.
6. CSP Foreign, vol. 4, Ferrara to Throckmorton, 20 Dec 1561.
7. Nicholas Cooper. *A Building Project for William Lord Paget at Burton on Trent*. Online Cambridge University Press, 7 Aug 2013.
8. Parker, *Emperor*, pp. 488–489.
9. McVeigh, *West Drayton*, etc., p. 19; CSP Foreign, vol. 6, Challoner to Sir John Mason, 14 Aug 1563; Gammon, pp. 249–50.

Chapter 27
1. David Lloyd, *State-worthies* etc., vol. 1, pp. 109–112 CSPS, vol. 9, vii–lxi.
2. L&P, vol. 19, part 2, 596; CSP Venice, vol. 6, 450; CSPS, vol. 12, Renard to emperor, 12 Dec 1554.
3. Ambassades de Messieurs de Noailles en Angleterre, by abbé de Vertot (Leyde, Paris 1763), vol. 5, pp. 194–195, 10 Nov 1555. Available online Internet Archive; CSPS, vol. 12, Renard to Emperor, 22 Mar 1554.
4. CSPS, vol. 12, Renard to Emperor, 3 Apr 1554.
5. MacCulloch. *Cromwell*, p. 502; Brigden. *New Worlds*, etc., p. 35.
6. John Guy. *Tudor England*, p. 7.
7. APC, 1550–51, pp. 251–276, 14 Apr 1551. Available online British History Online.
8. Hoskins, *Age of Plunder* (Longman, 1976), p. 148 & 233.
9. C. J. Sanson. *Lamentation* (Pan, 2015), pp. 660–678.
10. Brigden. *New Worlds*, etc., p. 110.
11. MacCullock, *Thomas Cranmer*, p. 409.
12. P to Somerset, 7 July 1549. Beer & Jack, p. 54 & Strype, ii (ii) pp. 429–437; P to Gardiner, 2 March 1547, Beer & Jack, p. 11 & Tytler, i, pp. 24–26.
13. Starkey, Elizabeth (Vintage, 2001), p. 324.
14. L&P, vol. 21, Part 1, 771.
15. Hisham Matar, *A Month in Siena* (Penguin, 2020), p. 37.

Appendix: A Family Epilogue
1. McVeigh, *West Drayton* etc., p. 20. Quoting Throckmorton to Leicester, 9 May 1567, PRO SP 12/42/60.
2. *Dictionary of National Biography* (DNB) entry on Thomas Paget by Peter Holmes.
3. McVeigh, p. 21.
4. DNB entry on Charles Paget by Peter Holmes.
5. CSP Domestic, Elizabeth, 15 Oct 1602.
6. *Marquess of Anglesey: One Leg* (Leo Cooper, 1996 ed.). Footnotes on Early and Later Pagets, pp. 344–348.
7. Andrew Roberts, *Waterloo, Napoleon's Last Gamble* (Harper Perennial, 2006), p. 66; Bernard Cornwell. *Waterloo* (Collins, 2014), p. 201.
8. *Anglesey: One Leg*, Chapters 8 & following.
9. *Daily Telegraph* review of J. H. Elliott. *Imperial Spain 1469–1716*. Quoted on cover of Penguin edition, 2002.

Sources and Bibliography

Thousands of academic and popular books have been written on Tudor political history: it is a very well-trodden corner of the past. But, despite pages and pages of 'scholarly apparatus' (footnotes, bibliographies, etc.), the books are often unclear as to where exactly they get their information from. I do not think the historians deliberately 'keep it all hid', but perhaps they fail to be crystal clear either because they think their readers know it all already or, subconsciously, in order to maintain the exclusivity of the experts.

A huge number of letters and documents from this period, relating to kings and queens, nobles, politicians, civil servants, ambassadors, etc., have been preserved. The originals are housed in a wide variety of libraries and collections all over the place, and they are not organised in a particularly logical or user-friendly way. In addition, although mainly written in what are essentially the same languages as the modern ones (English, French, Spanish, etc.), these documents are very difficult to decipher because of archaic and inconsistent usages and spellings, and particularly because of the variety and difficulty of the handwriting. I have had a go with one or two of the original letters I have in my possession: without great success. Unless you are a trained expert, it takes many hours to 'translate' one letter, and you would be unlikely to conquer all the meanings. Even for the experts, it must be very time consuming.

However, what has made possible those thousands of Tudor history books (including this one) is the dedicated and laborious work that has been done over the years by historians who have 'translated' and organised the documents. Preeminent is the massive *Letters and Papers, Foreign and Domestic, of the Reign of Henry VIII*: a collection of thirty-seven volumes, the life's work of three historians, J. S. Brewer, James Gardiner and R. H. Brodie, done over a period of seventy years, from 1862 to 1932. This essential source is now available free online. Also available at British History Online (BHO), and partly free, are other similar 'translated' and organised collections: the Domestic and Foreign Papers of Edward VI, Mary and Elizabeth; the Acts of the Privy Council, private collections such as the Cecil Papers, and reports from the Imperial, Spanish and Venetian ambassadors, which 'translate' the originals which are held at Simancas in Spain and the Correr Museum in Venice. A large number

Sources and Bibliography

of other original sources from the period are now available free online, provided by the excellent Internet Archive, by Google Books and by innumerable, mainly American, universities and institutions. A collection of Paget's post-Henry VIII letters, edited by B. Beer and S. Jack, and a couple of other groups of letters, those of Bishop Gardiner and the French ambassador, have also been published in book form, enabling further access to primary sources.

I reckon this book has been based roughly 50 per cent on the above primary sources and 50 per cent on secondary sources. But it has to be stressed that the primary sources are not truly primary – i.e. the actual documents: but are from these collections of organised 'translations'. However, I do assume that the creators of these collections can be trusted to have largely got it right. Along with all other modern historians of the Tudor period, I am immensely grateful to them. Our work is dependent on theirs.

As for the secondary sources, I include here only a very short bibliography of the main books I have actually used: rather than following the usual practice of creating a very long list of books, often copied from other books, in order for the author to appear well-read and scholarly.

Ackroyd, Peter, *Tudors: The History of England Vol. II* (London, 2012)
Adams, Simon, *Leicester and the Court* (Manchester, 2002)
Archer, Ian W., *Religion, Politics, and Society in Sixteenth Century England* (Cambridge, 2003)
Borman, Tracy, *Henry VIII and The Men Who Made Him* (London, 2018)
Brigden, Susan, *New Worlds, Lost Worlds: The Rule of the Tudors* (London, 2000)
Beer, B. L., *Northumberland: The Political Career of John Dudley* (Kent, Ohio, 1973)
Beer, B. L., *Rebellion and Riot: Popular Disorder in England during the Reign of Edward VI* (Kent, Ohio 1982)
Chadwick, Owen, *The Reformation* (London, 1964)
Cleland, E. and Eaker, A., *The Tudors: Art and Majesty in Renaissance England* (Metropolitan Museum, New Haven and London, 2022)
Coleman, Christopher and Starkey, David, *Revolution Reassessed* (Oxford, 1986)
Elliott, J. H., *Imperial Spain 1460–1716* (London, 1963, 2002)
Elton, G. R., *England Under the Tudors* (London, 1955)
Elton, G. R., *Reform and Revolution* (London, 1977)
Emmison, F. G., *Tudor Secretary: Sir William Petre at Court and Home* (London 1961)
Erickson, Carolly, *Bloody Mary* (London, 1995)
Foxe, John, *Acts and Monuments*, ed. G. Townsend (8 vols, London, 1843–49)
Gammon, Samuel R., *Statesman and Schemer* (Newton Abbot, 1973)
Garrett, C. H., *Marian Exiles* (Cambridge, 2011)
Gibbons, Geoffrey, *The Political Career of Thomas Wriothesley, First Earl of Southhampton* (Lewiston, Queenston, Lampeter, 2001)
Guy, John, *Tudor England* (Oxford, 1988)
Harris, Barbara J., *English Aristocratic Women 1450–1550* (Oxford, 2002)
Hibbert, Christopher, *The Virgin Queen* (London, 1990)

Hoskins, W. G., *The Age of Plunder 1500–1547* (New York, 1976)
Hutchinson, Robert, *The Last Days of Henry VIII* (London, 2005)
Ives, E. W., *Anne Boleyn* (London, 1986)
Jack, Sybil M., *Trade and Industry in Tudor and Stuart England* (London, 1977)
Jordan, W. K., *Edward VI: The Young King* (Cambridge, Mass, 1968)
Jordan, W. K., *Edward VI: The Threshold of Power* (Cambridge, Mass, 1970)
Lipscomb, Suzannah, *The King Is Dead* (London, 2015)
Loades, David, *Elizabeth I* (Hambledon & London, 2003)
Loades, David, *Mary Tudor* (Stroud, 2012)
MacCulloch, Diarmaid, *Thomas Cromwell* (London, 2018)
MacCulloch, Diarmaid, *Thomas Cranmer* (New Haven and London, 2016)
MacCulloch, Diarmaid, *The Boy King, Edward VI and the Protestant Reformation* (Berkeley & Los Angeles, 1999)
Marshall, Peter, *Heretics and Believers* (New Haven and London, 2017)
Marsden, Peter, *1545: Who Sank the Mary Rose?* (Seaforth Publishing, an imprint of Pen & Sword Books, Barnsley, 2019)
Matar, Hisham, *A Month in Siena* (London, 2019)
Muller, J. A., *The Letters of Stephen Gardiner* (Cambridge, 1933)
Parker, Geoffrey, *Emperor: A New Life of Charles V* (New Haven and London, 2019)
Parker, Geoffrey, *The Grand Strategy of Philip II* (New Haven and London, 1998)
Quinn, D. B., *England and the Discovery of America* (London, 1973)
Redworth, Glyn, *In Defence of the Catholic Church: The Life of Stephen Gardiner* (Oxford, 1990)
Sansom, C. J., *Lamentation* (London, 2014)
Scard, Margaret, *Tudor Survivor: The Life and Times of William Paulet* (Stroud, 2011)
Scard, Margaret, *Tudor King In All But Name: The Life of Edward Seymour* (Cheltenham, 2016 & 2020)
Scarisbrick, J. J., *The Reformation and the English People* (Oxford, 1984)
Scarisbrick, J. J., *Henry VIII* (New Haven and London, 1997)
Starkey, David, *The Reign of Henry VIII* (London, 2002)
Starkey, David, *Elizabeth* (London, 2000)
Thurley, Simon, *Houses of Power: The Places that Shaped the Tudor World* (London, 2017)
Warnicke, Retha M., *The Marriage of Anne of Cleves* (Cambridge, 2000)
Watkins, Sarah-Beth, *Anne of Cleves* (Winchester & Washington, 2018)
Weir, Alison, *Henry VIII, King and Court* (London, 2001)
Weir, Alison, *The Six Wives of Henry VIII* (London, 1991)
Whitelock, Anna, *Mary Tudor* (London, 2009)
Wilson, Derek, *The Tower of London* (London, 1998)
Woodward, G. W. O., *The Dissolution of the Monasteries* (London, 1966 & 1969)

And Wikipedia! Sometimes maybe a bit dodgy, but mostly accurate and incredibly useful. While some authors are snobby about it, I bet most use it extensively. I certainly did.

Acknowledgements

Thanks to my first cousin, Louisa Lane Fox, who gave me invaluable early encouragement, made excellent editorial suggestions and helped with research. She also rightly got me to explore Anne Paget's role in William's success, more than I otherwise might have done.

To another first cousin, Octavian von Hofmannsthal, who gave me vital motivation later in the process, pushing me to find a publisher, and, through him, to Leanda de Lisle, who suggested I approach Pen & Sword. To Sarah-Beth Watkins for being my commissioning editor there and to Cecily Blench for excellent copy-editing. To Margaret Willson for giving me the confidence to complete a book and get it published.

To David Starkey, whom I met at the Bangor University History Festival, where he was the star lecturing on Henry VIII while I was giving a talk on the 1st Marquess of Anglesey at Waterloo. An admirer of 'the founder' of my family, he inspired me to find out more about him and gave me some early pointers, such as to Paget's wise view on Elizabeth's marriage, that 'there was no one she could marry outside the kingdom nor within it', or to read the massively informative 'Prefaces' to each section of the Letters and Papers of Henry VIII.

To Charles Howard, Nick Emley, Amelia Singleton, Raoul Coombes and Hugh and Harriet Geddes for reading the text, making helpful suggestions, and spotting inaccuracies or stylistic lapses.

To Rob Keir and my wife, Susie De Paolis, for the same, but with the addition of extensive copy-editing.

I am of course grateful to Susie for much more than that, as to all our extended family of children and grandchildren: Ben, Clara, Saskia, Francesca, Elise, Uma, Shiloh, Lucille, Enzo, Dash and Ludo.

Index

Allen, Christopher 93, 198
Anne Boleyn 9, 11, 14, 22, 58, 62, 80, 141, 159, 200
Anne of Cleves 16–20, 41, 156
Antwerp 5, 15, 44, 47, 53, 54, 57, 61, 97, 99, 159, 175
Arras, Bishop of 56, 154, 167
Ascham, Roger 42
Askew, Anne 71, 195

Badoer, Federico 171
Bellay, Jean du 28, 29, 55–58
Bertano, Gurone 73, 193
Blagge, George 71
Bletchingly 18
Boulogne 31, 35, 37, 39, 55–57, 59, 61–67, 113, 115–116, 121–123, 133
Bourchier, James 36
Brandon, Charles, Duke of Suffolk 38, 39, 55, 61, 109
Brooke, George, Lord Cobham 23, 36, 37, 57, 101
Browne, Anthony 89, 110
Butts, William 42

Cabot, Sebastian 133–136
Calais 9, 25, 27, 28, 31, 36–37, 48–49, 55, 56, 57, 61, 63, 65, 101, 114, 117, 132, 172, 174–175, 177, 193
Canon Row 35, 110
Carew, Peter 162
Cecil, William, Lord Burghley 129, 138, 143, 148, 177, 179, 180, 183, 187, 195, 199
Chaloner, Thomas 98
Chamberlain, Thomas 41, 47, 97, 146
Chapuys, Eustace 12, 15, 24, 28, 34, 50, 52
Charles V 8, 9, 12, 15, 16, 17, 22, 23, 26, 28, 39, 43, 46, 51, 57, 62, 63, 70, 110, 113, 116, 119, 133, 134, 137, 145, 149, 153, 160, 185, 187, 188, 193, 201
Cheke, John 138, 152
Clerk, William 83–84
Colet, John 5, 13
Courtenay, Edward, Earl of Devon 153, 155–158, 160–161, 170

Cox, Richard 42–43, 146
Cranmer, Thomas 20, 25, 33, 34, 38, 42, 70, 73, 82, 127–130, 143, 152, 168, 184, 195
Cromwell, Thomas 3, 5, 7, 11–22, 32–35, 37, 41, 48, 65, 69, 70, 75, 77, 143, 145–146, 171, 184, 188, 189, 191

Dacre, Lord 3
Denny, Anthony 5, 42, 70, 74, 82–84, 90–91, 110
Dereham, Francis 26
Don Luis of Portugal 122–123, 155
Douglas, Margaret 54
Dover 46, 48, 63, 65, 109
Dudley, Guildford 148, 152, 163
Dudley, John, Duke of Northumberland 38, 39, 50, 63–65, 70, 73–75, 79, 82, 90, 107, 109–110, 116, 118, 121, 124, 126–127, 129–133, 136–140, 143, 148, 187, 188, 192, 195
Dudley, Robert, Earl of Leicester 110, 180–181, 200

Edward VI 3, 8, 16, 18, 32, 39, 64, 66, 81, 88, 93, 108, 114, 137, 148, 151, 153
Elizabeth I 3, 42, 57, 58, 80–81, 88, 110, 114, 117, 118, 129, 158–159, 163, 164, 167, 172, 175, 176–183, 189, 193, 195, 200
Ely Place 127
Exeter House (Paget House) 110

Feria, Count de 175–177
Fitzalan, Henry, Earl of Arundel 73, 127, 132, 150–153, 157, 159, 163, 166, 168, 172
Framlingham Castle 149, 151
Francis I 9, 16, 19, 22, 23, 25–29, 36, 46, 49, 50, 55–56, 58, 67, 70, 73, 114

Gardiner, Stephen, Bishop of Winchester 6–10, 18, 20, 33, 62, 63, 67, 70–74, 79, 82–83, 105–108, 137–138, 145, 153, 157–160, 163–170, 190, 193, 195
Gates, John 76, 83
Gomez de Silva, Ruy 166, 172
Gresham, Thomas 175

Grey, Henry, Duke of Suffolk 138, 149, 151–152, 162–163

Hampton Court Palace 21, 34, 55, 93, 115, 127–128, 130
Harmondsworth 13, 96, 98, 207
Harvel, Edmund 47
Hastings, Edward 150
Heneage, Thomas 74
Henry II 114, 183
Henry VII 69, 191
Henry VIII 3–6, 9, 11–14, 17–18, 21–22, 25, 33, 40–43, 49, 55, 67, 69, 80–85, 90–91, 93, 97, 106, 109, 117, 120, 126, 138, 148, 150–151, 156, 159, 168, 184, 188, 191–195
Herbert, William 74, 82, 90–91, 124, 127, 129, 138
Hever Castle 18
Hoby, Philip 128–131
Holland, Elizabeth 75–76
Howard, Henry, Earl of Surrey 3, 75–78, 98
Howard, Thomas, Duke of Norfolk 18, 20, 39, 62, 70–72, 75–78, 90, 153
Howard of Effingham, William 23–25, 167, 175

Ingatestone Hall, Essex 96

James V 51
James VI 81, 200
Jane Seymour 15–17, 80, 106

Katherine Howard 18, 20, 24, 25–26, 78
Katherine of Aragon 9, 15, 27, 41
Katherine Parr 18, 54, 58, 70–72, 78, 80–81, 117–118, 126
Kenninghall 75, 76, 149

Lady Jane Grey 81, 107, 147–152, 163
Leland, John 6
Lichfield Cathedral 186
Lily, William 5, 6

Marguerite de Navarre 58, 59
Marillac, Charles de 24, 27, 29, 30, 31
Mary I 42, 80–81, 107, 112, 113, 117–118, 122–123, 129, 137, 141, 147, 148–161, 163–168, 170–176, 179, 189–195
Mary of Guise 114
Mary of Hungary 50–51, 54, 145, 187
Mary Rose 61
Mary, Queen of Scots 32, 63, 81, 114, 115, 154, 158, 172, 176, 199–200
Mason, John 37, 41, 133, 143, 166
Maxstoke Castle 14
Melanchthon 12

Mont, Christopher 41, 57, 190
Montmorency, Constable of France 141
More, Thomas 5, 10, 34, 141, 179, 195
Muhlberg, Battle of 113

Noailles, Antoine de 170
Northumberland Place 13, 15

Orleans University 10

Paget, Anne (daughter) 197
Paget, Anne (nee Preston) 48, 59, 60, 95, 97, 101, 109, 124, 144, 146, 150, 166, 190, 197–199
Paget, Charles 197, 199, 200
Paget, Dorothy 93, 197, 198
Paget, Etheldreda 93, 197, 198
Paget, Eleanor 197, 198
Paget, Grisold 197, 198
Paget, Henry 42, 183, 197
Paget, Jane 197, 198
Paget, Robert 124
Paget, Thomas 18, 100, 197–199
Paget, William
 appointed ambassador to Francis I's court 25
 appointed secretary to Queen Jane 15
 birth 3
 Boulogne 55
 children 18, 43, 93, 100, 197–200
 Clerk of the Council 21
 Clerk to Parliament 21
 Chancellor of the Duchy of Lancaster 111
 Comptroller of the Royal Household 95
 death 186
 Duke of Prussia 11
 education 5–6, 8, 18
 elected to parliament 7
 father 4
 first letter 11
 Germany 10
 health 30, 48, 62, 63, 65, 132, 172–173, 177, 182
 high steward of Cambridge University 110
 house arrest 140
 household 93–101
 imprisonment 140–141
 knighted 32
 marriage 12
 Order of the Garter 106, 143
 personal qualities 187–190
 Principal Secretary of State 46
 retirement 182–185
 wife, Anne 48, 59, 60, 95, 97, 101, 109, 124, 144, 146, 150, 166, 190, 197–199
Paget, William (son) 197, 200–201

Palmer, Thomas 119
Paris 6, 8, 46, 47, 64, 133, 178, 182, 183, 199, 200, 205, 206
Parry, Thomas 177–180
Petre, William 33, 38, 41, 49, 53, 59, 60, 63–65, 68, 96, 122, 127–128, 143, 146, 153, 157, 163, 195
Philbert, Emmanuel, Prince of Piedmont & Duke of Savoy 155, 163, 167
Philip II 27, 153–160, 162, 164, 166–167, 170–176, 179, 186, 187, 193–194, 199
Pilgrimage of Grace 16
Pinkie, Battle of 114–115
plague 7, 55, 60, 116
Plas Newydd 4, 6, 8, 95, 145, 201, 204–207
Pole, Reginald 16, 158, 161, 167
Portsmouth 39, 61, 109
Preston Patrick Hall, Cumbria 12

Quadra, Alvaro de la 178, 180, 181

Renard, Simon 152, 154–161, 163–166, 168, 190
Rich, Richard 71, 73, 107, 122, 123, 127, 165, 179, 195
Richmond 18, 130
Robsart, Amy 180
Rochester, Robert 161, 164
Russell, John 18, 71, 121, 124–125, 127, 129

Sadler, Ralph 15, 20, 32, 70, 143, 147
Scheyfve, Jean 135, 137, 139, 140, 142, 144, 149
Selve, Odet de 67, 111, 114–115
Seymour, Edward, Duke of Somerset 39, 44, 50, 63, 64, 66, 82–93, 98, 99, 105–107,109–112, 114–124, 126–132, 136–143, 145–146, 180, 187–9, 194–195
Seymour, Thomas, 1st Baron Seymour of Sudeley 83, 90, 107, 117, 118
Silva, Ruy Gomez de 166, 172
Smith, Thomas 127–131
Solway Moss 29

Somerset (Seymour), Anne 109, 122, 128, 146, 190
Soranzo, Giacomo 165
Southampton 61, 106, 160, 166
Southwell, Richard 76, 83, 132, 161
St Paul's School 5, 13
sweating sickness 7, 60

Thirlby, Thomas, Bishop of Westminster 82
Throckmorton, Nicholas 149, 182–183, 184, 197, 199
Titchfield 16
Tower of London 78, 118, 128, 130, 131, 132, 140, 141–142, 144, 146, 149, 150, 151, 153, 159, 163, 164, 166, 190
Treaty of Camp 65–66
Trinity Hall, Cambridge 5, 6
Tusser, Thomas 100–101

Van der Delft, Francis 35, 73, 82, 106, 108, 110–114, 117, 126, 130, 132, 134–135, 188
Vane, Ralph 140
Vaughan, Stephen 41, 44, 46–8, 53, 57, 71

Warner, Edmund 77, 98
Wendy, Thomas 42, 72, 83
West Drayton 13, 14, 18, 32, 35, 40, 54, 55, 93–101, 111, 112, 117, 138, 146, 150, 175, 186, 197–199, 202, 207
Willoughby, Thomas 93, 198
Winchester 10, 61, 74, 138, 166
Windsor 34, 97, 128–130, 182
Wingfield, Anthony 130
Wolsey, Thomas 3, 4, 6, 7, 9, 10, 21, 22, 35, 37, 41, 65, 69, 70, 77, 143, 145, 188, 194
Wotton, Nicholas 39, 57, 121
Wriothesley, Thomas 5–7, 14, 16, 20, 23, 32, 33, 36, 37, 42, 44, 45, 70–73, 82, 85, 89, 90, 106–108, 121, 127, 132
Wyatt, Thomas 18, 162–163

Yetsweirt, Nicasius 36, 41